RESPONSIBLE INVESTMENT IN TIMES OF TURMOIL

Issues in Business Ethics

VOLUME 31

For further volumes:
http://www.springer.com/series/6077

Responsible Investment in Times of Turmoil

edited by

WIM VANDEKERCKHOVE

University of Greenwich Business School, UK

JOS LEYS

Ghent University, Belgium

KRISTIAN ALM

BI School of Management, Oslo, Norway

BERT SCHOLTENS

University of Groningen, The Netherlands

SILVANA SIGNORI

University of Bergamo, Italy

and

HENRY SCHÄFER

University of Stuttgart, Germany

 Springer

Editors
Prof. Wim Vandekerckhove
Dept. of Human Resources and
Organizational Behaviour
University of Greenwich Business School
Park Row
London SE10 9LS
UK
wim.vandekerckhove@gmail.com

Kristian Alm
BI Norwegian School of Management
Nydalsveien 37
0442 Oslo
Norway
kristian.alm@bi.no

Silvana Signori
Dept. of Business Administration
University of Bergamo
Via dei Caniana 2
24127 Bergamo
Italy
silvana.signori@unibg.it

Jos Leys
Center for Ethics and Value Inquiry
Ghent University
Blandijnberg 2
9000 Ghent
Belgium
djleys@skynet.be

Bert Scholtens
University of Groningen
Fac. Economics & Business
Nettelbosje 2
9747 AE Groningen
Netherlands
L.J.R.Scholtens@rug.nl

Prof. Dr. Henry Schäfer
Universität Stuttgart
Betriebswirtschaftliches Institut Abt. III:
Allgemeine BWL und Finanzwirtschaft
Keplerstraße 17
70174 Stuttgart
Germany
h.schaefer@bwi.uni-stuttgart.de

ISSN 0925-6733
ISBN 978-90-481-9318-9   e-ISBN 978-90-481-9319-6
DOI 10.1007/978-90-481-9319-6
Springer Dordrecht Heidelberg London New York

Library of Congress Control Number: 2011923541

Printed on acid-free paper

Springer is part of Springer Science+Business Media (www.springer.com)

Foreword

During a weekend in mid-April 2010, a volcano eruption in Iceland brought European air traffic to a near total halt. Similarly, the collapse of Lehman Brothers in September 2008 released a toxic cloud provoking a global economic crisis from which we still have to recover. Partly in response to this latter phenomenon, the contributing authors and editors present us with this volume dedicated to the theory and practice of responsible investment which I now have the honour to introduce.

I do not like the term 'responsible investment' for the same reasons I disapprove of expressions such as 'responsible business' or 'social enterprise'. It is not because I find them simply wrong or self-contradictory, but because they irritatingly belabour the obvious. At least, something that seems to me should be obvious. For how else are we to understand business and investment, if not as responsible human acts? The alternative of conceiving them as the execution of purely technical procedures – either by humans or by machines – on the basis of expert, codifiable knowledge, at this point, plainly has ceased to hold ground.

In the spirit of 'not letting a crisis go to waste', we should welcome this opportunity offered us by the authors to seriously consider the purpose and significance of investment and finance. The task of establishing the causes of the current global economic malaise belongs to historians. Nonetheless, many have already ventured to indicate the disproportionate weight of the financial sector in the overall economic activity as one of the possible culprits. Inadvertently or not, we have allowed the tail to be wagging the dog. We have somehow forgotten that the purpose of finance ought to be to provide resources for productive investments. Instead, we have been misled by some captains of industry to believe that there is essentially no difference between investment and gambling, between financial institutions and casinos. Except that they always win whilst we are doomed to pick up all the broken pieces. And I am not only referring to the profits Goldman Sachs made on synthetic collateralized debt obligations (CDOs), such as the Abacus 2007-AC1.

There may still be some wisdom in Aristotle's insistence on the perversity of accumulating resources, especially financial ones, for their own sake. There ought to be a limit, based on what we want those resources for. Whatever that may be, perhaps it should be something more substantive than the mere thrill of 'keeping score'. Aristotle's answer, of course, depended on those resources' contribution to *eudaimonia,* the good life, which among other things, is necessarily a life shared with other fellow human beings.

I wish, therefore, to congratulate the editors for having put together such a fine and cohesive collection of scholarly studies. That they have been able to do so under the aegis of EBEN (European Business Ethics Network) as one of our 'special interest groups' provides me with special pride and satisfaction. For this book clearly signifies a step in the right direction of clearing up the dust and fog that unfortunately envelops much of today's investment theories and practices.

President   Alejo José G. Sison
European Business Ethics Network
University of Navarre
Pamplona, Spain
April 2010

Introduction

So far, responsible investment seems to be a success story. Year after year, 'responsible' assets under management (AUM) grow, its market share increases, and new asset classes are included (such as responsible bonds, 'green' real estate investments and venture capital). Responsible investment draws the attention of policy makers, for example the Pension Disclosure Regulation 2000 in the UK which had following in many other countries, or the debate in Belgium on making responsible investment a protected label. Last but not least, we saw the rise of an influential institution dedicated to responsible investment, namely the UNPRI (United Nations Principles for Responsible Investment). Even the financial crisis that started in 2008 has not brought an end to the growing popularity of responsible investment. On the contrary, many investors and politicians require financial institutions to behave 'really' responsibly.

Responsible investment has emerged from its somewhat obscure crack in the wall, evolving from a marginal activism into a vehicle to which many cling with aspirations for a better world and a more sustainable society. Many factors have contributed to this, including the increased importance of the financial sector, a series of business scandals, concern about global environmental and social problems, and a changed discourse to make sense of it all – from 'ethical investment' to 'socially responsible investment' and more recently 'responsible investment'. Whatever turned responsible investment into what it is today and into what might happen tomorrow, most market participants will agree that it has to be taken seriously.

That is exactly what this book aims to do. We did not feel the need to bring together papers for yet another volume campaigning responsible investment. Instead it seemed to us that there was a lack of publications pointing out inconsistencies, difficulties, and silences within and surrounding the responsible investment phenomena. For us, taking responsible investment seriously implies moving beyond the urge of defending it, to the stage where one can analyze its assumptions and critically examine its claims without tearing it to pieces. Without such endeavours responsible investment risks to outgrow its ethical foundations and to lose its credibility. Hence this book immerses responsible investment in more than one type of turmoil.

Many chapters offer a view on how the field of responsible investment might or must evolve through and beyond the current financial turmoil. Some authors (like Del Bosco and Misani, and Syse) assume the crisis will result in more responsible investments. Others (like Cadman, Sandberg, and Waddell) put responsible investment through a more philosophical turmoil and are more critical of it. In the context of this book, what they suggest is that the field of responsible investment itself is heading for a crisis, either because the epistemological assumptions are problematic (how do we build knowledge? how do we screen?) or because the claims it makes are not feasible (can we change the world?).

Although each chapter addresses particular issues, we would like to draw your attention to an implicit discussion at play throughout this book before we give a consecutive introduction to the chapters in this book. It does not take an expert in responsible investment to know that what is meant with 'responsible investment' (or its corollary terminology) tends to differ from speaker to speaker as well as over time. This book does not have the ambition to close that sense-making exercise. Where the authors of the chapters preferred to speak of 'socially responsible investment' we have left that unedited. Some authors (Aßländer and Schenkel, and Sievänen) even implicitly suggest 'responsible investment' carries an additional meaning, namely that responsible investment also implies a rethinking of internal governance and risk management systems, rather than simply looking for particular governance characteristics in investee corporations. Emphasizing governance criteria favours a procedural ethic, where what is important is more how things get decided than what gets decided. Hence we can understand the growing weight governance issues get within responsible investment as an attempt to come to grips with a plurality of substantial ethics – green, Catholic, Muslim, pacifist, etc. At the same time, the need to put more weight on governance criteria signals the upswing of cultural and religious particulars.

The chapters in this book will take you from a macro 'International Relations' perspective in the first chapters, over the middle chapters situated at a meso level and dealing with financial intermediation and with explicitly ethical claims, to a micro 'reflections from a practitioner' perspective in the final chapters.

Steve Waddell's contribution opens this book. His chapter takes issue with the global financial system and how responsible investment actors can address it. Waddell shows that there is little connection between responsible investment actors on the one hand and global financial system actors on the other hand. While the first are strategically positioned around the UN, the latter (Bank for International Settlements, Financial Stability Board, International Association of Insurance Supervisors, IMF, World Bank, International Organization of Securities Commissions) do not strategically connect to the UN. The point Waddell wants to make is that if it is the 'responsible investment' community that is going to change the global financial system, it is talking in the wrong places.

The impact of responsible investment on a global level is also implied in the concept of 'universal ownership', which is the hallmark of the UN. *Neil Eccles* points out the very significant contribution of the UNPRI activities on the responsible investment community, such as a practitioners and an academic network, the production of text and of discourse through conferences, webinars and research digests. Eccles points out that the mainstreaming of responsible invest-ment was only possible because what it meant and stood for and did, somehow got altered. Others have described this adaption as a professionalization of information gathering services with regard to non-financial or ESG criteria. Eccles brings out the underlying paradigm of 'universal ownership', namely that of the 'rational man'. Interestingly, we find precisely the same thought pattern in the mainstream eco-nomic theories that were being questioned as the financial crisis unfolded. Eccles' reframing of universal ownership in terms of 'a tragedy of the commons' – if there is a business case for responsible investment the implication is that responsible invest-ment can only exist because irresponsible investors bear the costs – leads him to a philosophical critique of ideas and strategies proposed by UNPRI. Such a critique is possible while at the same time acknowledging the contribution of that which is the subject of critique. We also believe such critique is necessary as a means to improve theoretical concepts and practical tools.

Tim Cadman takes issue with the range of governance criteria used in respon-sible investment practice. He argues for an improved and expanded understanding of 'governance' concept and standards. His analysis shows the development of a broad and confusing spectre of governance initiatives and issues. In this ideologi-cal plurality investors have to find support from the consultancy industry in order to implement the most relevant standards, but among multiple alternatives, which one should they choose? According to Cadman the confusion reflects a fundamental lack of common standards. He is thereby in line with Aßländer and Schenkel their criticism of the tendency among RI funds to chose private exclusion criteria which reflects personal opinions rather than standards of common interest. Cadman aspires to develop a universal set of principles, criteria and indicators of governance quality. In this sense, he is quite optimistic that good governance is possible and that it can solve the problem of too much variety.

The next four chapters consider issues of financial intermediation mechanisms. There is no responsible investment without financial intermediation but the spe-cific intermediation mechanism used has its own implications for how responsible investment finds its expression. *Peter-Jan Engelen and Marc van Essen* look at how the stock market intermediates between corporate behaviour and investments. They offer a meta-analysis of stock price fluctuations following an event that dam-ages the reputation of a corporation, such as product recalls, news about product unsafety, fraud, environmental violations, insider trading, and financial misrepresen-tations. For some types of misbehaviour, stock market interactions do seem to reflect investor distrust. However, for misbehaviour with less identifiable 'victims' such as environmental violations, stock prices remain unaffected. This leads Engelen and van Essen to conclude that the stock market as a financial intermediary for respon-sible investment has potential for certain types of misbehaviour, but certainly does not work for 'victimless crimes' by corporations. The reason for this is that these latter have no impact on the business operations, hence investors are not worried about a lower return. This then suggests there is an important role for government regulation towards business behaviour rather than investment practices.

Olaf Weber, Marco Mansfeld and Eric Schirrmann look at the performance of responsible investment funds during the financial crisis. While the quest for the business case has been attempted many times before, and that quest is being critiqued in this book by Eccles, Weber et al. draw important lessons. They find that while the responsible investment funds do outperform the MSCI World Index, the particular ESG screens do not succeed in avoiding the influence of general financial market tendencies. Weber et al. tell us that regardless of the screens our funds have, if they are going to take part in the global financial market, they will ride the waves of that market. In this sense, Weber et al. offer the meso-version of Steve Waddell's macro-story in Chapter 1.

Riikka Sievänen looks at how the crisis has made pension fund managers think differently about responsible investment. She provides two important findings. First, it seems those who were engaged with responsible investment before the crisis became more convinced that their choice was the right one. However, the crisis did not make the others turn to responsible investment. Some even postpone the implementation of a responsible investment policy because of the crisis. This finding is important because it shows that we cannot simply assume the financial crisis will give responsible investment a landslide victory. Her second important finding is that the crisis has led pension fund managers to evaluate and reflect upon governance and risk management of the pension fund. They use the word 'responsible' for that. Hence, the impact of the crisis might very well be that responsible investment not only designates governance practice in investee corporations, but also gets bearing on the governance practices of the investment fund itself.

While previous chapters are concerned with secondary markets, *Barbara Del Bosco and Nicola Misani* discuss financial intermediation in the primary market. Undoubtedly, private equity has gained attention in the aftermath of the financial crisis. Del Bosco and Misani sketch out a new asset class: Responsible Private Equity (RPE). They identify the characteristics of RPE and how these could satisfy certain responsible investors where these were let down by stock market investment. The chapter offers a way out of Sandberg's fatalistic picture of what real impact we can achieve through responsible investment.

The next three chapters in this book tackle the explicitly ethical claims prevalent in responsible investment. Ethical concerns and intuitions can only be put to work by translating them in screening criteria and/or asset management techniques (exclusion, best-in-class, engagement).. The question these three chapters deal with is whether these translations of our ethical concerns are adequate. This is what Eccles in his chapter tackled in a more general way. Or, as *Michael Aβländer and Markus Schenkel* put it in common sense language: 'is it really ethical?' They distinguish market-led funds from deliberative funds. In the first, ESG criteria are chosen on the basis of market demand. For example, if we know a lot of people want to invest in green technology we can make an investment fund that uses green criteria. In contrast, in deliberative funds ESG criteria are derived from and justified by what those running the funds believe to be moral. Aβländer and Schenkel focus on a Catholic fund within a Catholic bank. They expect that a particular religious morality would make a difference in criteria used as well as in the strictness of their application, but are rather disappointed in what they find. The Catholic fund does not seem to differ much from market-led funds. However, Aβländer and Schenkel argue that if responsible investment is to have a future, its practices will have to become stricter and less heterogeneous.

Reza Jaufeerally also focuses on responsible investment based on a particular religious morality, namely Islam. Islamic finance enjoys a growing popularity, also in the West and not only among Muslims. According to Jaufeerally, part of this popularity is because Shari'ah prohibits from dealing in CDOs – one of the decisive elements in the financial crisis. Whilst many regard Islamic finance as 'the Muslim version of Western responsible investment', Jaufeerally makes clear this is not as straightforward as it may seem. Although there is significant conceptual overlap, Jaufeerally argues that certain governance mechanisms in Islamic finance, for example the composition and functioning of Shari'ah boards, would need to change in order to level the transparency and functionality of Western responsible investment vehicles. These will need to evolve regardless of Western standards, simply due to the scale Islamic finance is growing into.

Hence, where Aβländer and Schenkel see a future for responsible investment only when it is built on particular morality that succeeds in clearly distinguishing itself, Jaufeerally seems to suggest that particular moralities have a future as underpinners of responsible investment only when they succeed in adapting to demand-size.

A different set of questions pertains not to particularizing moralities but to universal morality, which considers not convictions or metaphysical sources but procedural or governance issues. Cadman's chapter entails an attempt to steer away from this particularism by developing a universalist governance model. This suggests good governance and appropriate standards might ease these particulars and offer an overriding or universal ground.

Where Weber et al. give us an account of what ESG does to your finances, *Joakim Sandberg* does the opposite. Sandberg is skeptical regarding the potential of responsible investment when it comes to actually having an impact. He discusses what interaction on the stock market can do for your ESG concerns. Sandberg argues that if we are out to make a change, as individual investors we cannot make much of a difference by refraining from investing in certain kinds of companies.

We also include three chapters consisting of reflections from practitioners on the current state and possible futures of responsible investment. They write not from an academic point of view but from their day-to-day experiences and difficulties within responsible investment practices. *Johan A. Klaassen* worries about how sustainability has been narrowed down to meaning environmental sustainability. Because this has excluded social justice issues from falling under the 'sustainability' umbrella, responsible investment discourse tends to be less concerned with social justice issues. Klaassen explains that whereas the two sets of issues are intertwined, both issues can and must be addressed when engaging as an active responsible investor with corporations. The examples he gives from his practice show that this is not always easy nor well understood by beneficiaries of investment funds.

Carlos Joly sees the financial crisis as well as the ecological crisis as one and the same systemic crisis. He wonders where responsible investment has been within that system, and what role it could play now. Joly was co-chair of the expert group that drafted the UNPRI of which the aim was to channel savings in the direction of sustainable development. However, Joly now believes this has not been sufficiently achieved. Hence he raises the idea that the UNPRI self-regulatory approach needs to be complemented by government regulations and sanctions. In line with Engelen and van Essen, he is in favour of legislation that would further the greening of the economy. In line with Del Bosco and Misani, he suggests responsible investors ought to realise there are also non-listed investment objects.

Finally, *Henrik Syse* reflects on being part of setting up and managing the 'Norwegian Government Pension Fund- Global' (NGPF). Syse worked from 2005 to 2007 for Norges Bank Investment Management (NBIM), for most of this time as their Head of Corporate Governance. NBIM is part of the Norwegian Central Bank, and it functions as the manager of one of the world's largest sovereign wealth funds, the 'Norwegian Government Pension Fund – Global' (NGPF). From setting up and managing NGPF Syse draws lessons about what responsible investment could hope for and what it must endeavour. Syse argues in a pragmatist vein that a typology of investors with a pure financial interest versus investors with purely ESG concerns, is far too simplistic. Most of mainstream investors agree ethical factors play a role – albeit an instrumental one – and most of responsible investment fund managers have a financial incentive. In his chapter, Syse simply tears down the supposedly contrasting categories of responsible and mainstream investment, with pension funds and similar public funds (such as the NGPF) that have a large base of end owners and a long time horizon illustrating his arguments. Instead, Syse defends a down-to-earth approach to integrating ESG concerns in investment strategies.

We conclude this book with a chapter that formulates further questions and issues on the path this book set out on. Many of these came up during our editorial meetings when we were discussing draft versions of the chapters you find in this book. Along with the authors of these chapters, we hope this critical but earnest work can inspire others to make responsible investment more sound in its assumptions, methods, claims, and results. Of course, this book is but a beginning, but great oaks grow from little acorns.

London, UK	Wim Vandekerckhove
Ghent, Belgium	Jos Leys
Oslo, Norway	Kristian Alm
Groningen, The Netherlands	Bert Scholtens
Bergamo, Italy	Silvana Signori
Stuttgart, Germany	Henry Schäfer

Contents

Contributors

Michael S. Aßländer University of Kassel, Kassel, Germany, michael.asslaender@gmx.de

Kristian Alm BI Norwegian School of Management, Oslo, Norway, kristian.alm@bi.no

Tim Cadman Faculty of Business, School of Accounting, Economic and Finance, University of Southern Queensland, Toowoomba, QLD, Australia, tim.cadman@usq.edu.au

Barbara Del Bosco Entrepreneurial Lab, Centre for Research on Entrepreneurship, University of Bergamo, Bergamo, Italy, barbara.del-bosco@unibg.it

Neil Eccles University of South Africa, Pretoria, South Africa, Ecclens@unisa.ac.za

Peter-Jan Engelen Utrecht University, Utrecht, The Netherlands, P.J.Engelen@uu.nl

Reza Zain Jaufeerally Centre for Economics & Ethics, Catholic University of Leuven, Brussel, Belgium, rjaufeerally@gmail.com

Carlos Joly Ecole Superieur de Commerce, Toulouse, France; BI Norwegian School of Management, Oslo, Norway, carlos.joly@gmail.com

Johann A. Klaassen First Affirmative Investment Committee, Colorado Springs, CO, USA, johann@firstaffirmative.com

Jos Leys Center for Ethics and Value Inquiry, Ghent University, Ghent, Belgium, djleys@skynet.be

Marco Mansfeld Care Group AG, Zurich, Switzerland, m.mansfeld@caregroup.ch

Nicola Misani Università Bocconi, Milan, Italy, nicola.misani@unibocconi.it

Joakim Sandberg University of Gothenburg, Gothenburg, Sweden,
joakim.sandberg@filosofi.gu.se

Henry Schäfer Betriebswirtschaftliches Institut, University of Stuttgart, Stuttgart,
Germany, h.schaefer@bwi.uni-stuttgart.de

Markus Schenkel University of Kassel, Kassel, Germany,
Markus.Schenkel@uni-kassel.de

Eric Schirrmann Care Group AG, Zurich, Switzerland,
e.schirrmann@caregroup.ch

Bert Scholtens Faculty of Economics & Business, University of Groningen,
Groningen, The Netherlands, L.J.R.Scholtens@rug.nl

Riikka Sievänen Department of Economics and Management, University
of Helsinki, Helsinki, Finland, riikka.sievanen@helsinki.fi

Silvana Signori Dept. of Business Administration, University of Bergamo,
Bergamo, Italy, silvana.signori@unibg.it

Henrik Syse Peace Research Institute Oslo (PRIO), Oslo, Norway,
HENRIK@prio.no

Wim Vandekerckhove Dept. of Human Resources and Organizational
Behaviour, University of Greenwich Business School, London, UK,
wim.vandekerckhove@gmail.com

Marc van Essen Rotterdam School of Management, Erasmus University,
Rotterdam, The Netherlands, marc.vanessen@yahoo.com

Steve Waddell NetworkingAction, Boston, MA, USA,
swaddell@networkingaction.net

Olaf Weber School of Environment, Enterprise and Development, University
of Waterloo, Waterloo, ON, Canada, oweber@uwaterloo.ca

List of Figures

List of Tables

About the Editors

Kristian Alm is Associate Professor of Ethics at BI Norwegian School of Management, Oslo (Institute for Strategy and Logistics, Centre for Ethics and Leadership). He holds a Master in Theology and a PhD in Ethics from the University of Oslo. He has held a number of scholarships and was editor and secretary to the Norwegian Government Commission on Human Values (1998–2001). He publishes on the intersection between philosophy, theology and ethics, with special emphasis on the development of the ethical management of the Norwegian Government Pension Fund Global. He is also the coordinator of the SRI Interest Group within EBEN.

Jos Leys holds a Master in Philosophy and an MBA (Finance). He served 20 years in the financial services industry and was senior researcher for the *Dexia Chair in Ethics and Finance* at the Catholic University of Leuven (hiva). He is currently researcher at the Center for Ethics & Value Inquiry of Ghent University, Belgium. He published on Aristotle, Socially Responsible Investment and on the ethics for practitioners of finance.

Henry Schäfer holds the Chair of Finance at the University of Stuttgart. His main focus in research is on the valuation of assets, in particular regarding real options and non-financial parameters. Other research fields are project finance, behavioral corporate finance and the valuation of real estate projects. Particular relevance is given to research regarding 'Sustainability and Finance'. Professor Schäfer is one of the leading German research capacities in SRI and CSR. He has also published several text books in finance and is consulting several major well-known global firms.

Bert Scholtens is Professor with the Department of Economics, Econometrics and Finance of the University of Groningen in the Netherlands and holds a chair in Energy and Sustainability. His research is directed at international finance and banking, and environmental and sustainable finance and economics. He teaches about a wide range of economic topics and coaches both Bachelor and Master students in completing their thesis. He also supervises several PhD-students. He has published in international academic journals like the Journal of Banking and Finance, Ecological Economics, Corporate Governance: An International

Review, Sustainable Development, The Energy Journal, World Development, Land Economics, Natural Resources Forum, Journal of Business Ethics.

Silvana Signori is Assistant Professor with tenure at the University of Bergamo – Department of Business Administration. She holds a PhD in Business Administration and Strategies with a dissertation on 'Ethical Investors'. Her main areas of research are ethical investments, business ethics and corporate social responsibility, non-profit organization accounting and accountability. She is one of the founder members of the Italian chapter of EBEN, of which she is currently executive secretary.

Wim Vandekerckhove is Senior Lecturer at the University of Greenwich Business School, London. His research interests include whistleblowing, global ethics, and socially responsible investment. Together with Kristian Alm he started the SRI Interest Group within EBEN.

About the Authors

Michael Aßländer studied Management, Philosophy, Sociology, Psychology, Political Economy and Russian language in Bamberg (D), Vienna (A), Bochum (D) and Moscow (RUS). He holds a MBA in Business Administration (1988), a Master in Philosophy (1990), a PhD in Philosophy (1998) and a PhD in Social Sciences (2005). From 1997 to 1999 he worked as an Assistant at the Chair of Philosophy at the University of Bamberg. From 1999 to 2005 he was Senior Assistant at the Chair of Social Sciences at the International Graduate School of Zittau. Since 2005 he holds the Plansecur Endowed Chair for Business, Ethics and Economics at the University of Kassel. He is member of the board of the German and the Austrian Business Ethics Network and member of the Executive Committee of the European Business Ethics Network.

Tim Cadman BA (Hons) MA (Cantab) PhD (UTas) is the Sustainable Business Fellow of the Faculty of Business in the School of Accounting, Economic and Finance at the University of Southern Queensland. He is a research fellow of the Earth Systems Governance network and a member of the Australian Centre for Sustainable Business and Development and the UN Principles for Responsible Investment Academic Network. He specialises in the study of sustainable development, particularly market-based systems including climate change management, timber certification and labeling and responsible investment. He spent 20 years working in the non-governmental sector and as an environmental consultant before undertaking his PhD in 2004. He published his first book *Quality and legitimacy of global governance: case lessons from forestry*, with Palgrave Macmillan in 2010.

Barbara Del Bosco is Assistant Professor of Management at University of Bergamo and she is research fellow at the Entrepreneurial Lab, Centre for Research on Entrepreneurship of the same University. She received her PhD in Business Administration from the University of Pavia. Her research concentrates on Corporate Social Responsibility, Entrepreneurship, Social Entrepreneurship and the financing of sustainable ventures.

Neil Eccles is the Acting Head of the Institute for Corporate Citizenship at the University of South Africa (Unisa). In addition to this academic management role, he also manages a research chair: the Noah Chair in Responsible Investment. Before joining Unisa he spent 6 years in the consulting industry in both a mainstream business consulting company as well as a specialist Corporate Social Responsibility consulting firm. He has a PhD in Ecology of all things. He has published in the field of Ecology but more recently his interest has shifted to the disciplines of Corporate Citizenship and Socially Responsible Investment. He is married to Funeka and together they have beautiful daughter called Vuyani.

Peter-Jan Engelen is an Associate Professor of Finance at Utrecht University, the Netherlands. He holds a PhD in Economics, an MSc in Finance and Tax Management, and an MSc in Economics. He was also reading Law, obtaining an LLB and LLM. Some recent research topics include real options, law and finance, IPOs, insider trading, reputational penalties, securities regulation, and the ethics of financial markets. In 2002 he was awarded with the prestigious *European Joseph de la Vega Prize*, and in 2006 he was awarded as *Best Researcher in Economics* at Utrecht University. He has published in several journals including the *Journal of Banking and Finance, Research Policy, the Journal of Business Finance and Accounting*, the *Review of Law and Economics*, the *European Journal of Law and Economics and* the *Journal of Business Ethics*.

Reza Zain Jaufeerally is a Researcher in Islamic and Ethical Finance at the Centre for Economics & Ethics (Catholic University of Leuven). A Barrister by training (Middle Temple), he holds a triple LLM (International Business, Intellectual Property and ICT law specialisations) from the Catholic University of Leuven. His research focuses on the synergies between Islamic Finance, Ethical Finance, and Socially Responsible Investment.

Carlos Joly is an investor and investment manager with over 20 years experience integrating environmental and social criteria in portfolio management. He is Chair of the Scientific Advisory Committee of Natixis Asset Management and designed the Natixis Impact Funds – Climate Change. He is Visiting Professor of Finance and Sustainable Development at the Ecole Superieur de Commerce, Toulouse and at the Norwegian School of Management. He is a co-founder and was on the board of the UNEP Finance Initiative and was Chair of its Asset Management Working Group for over 10 years. He Co-Chaired the Expert Group that drafted the UN Principles of Responsible Investment. He served on the Commission dÍnvestissement Socialement Responsable of Paris Europlace-Euronext. He has advised the Fonds de Reserve de France on SRI manager selection. Carlos was Senior Vice President of Storebrand Investments, founded Storebrand Principle Funds and Storebrand Scudder Environmental Value Fund. He also founded and was Managing Director of Vesta Funds/Skandia Funds in Norway. In the eighties, he worked at Citibank as a Vice President in New York, London, and Buenos Aires. Carlos has lectured at Oxford, Cambridge, Yale, Kellogg Business School, Haute Ecole de Commerce, Universite de Paris-Dauphine, and the Chartered Financial Analyst Institute. In 1996 he received the Environmental Leadership Award awarded by Tomorrow Magazine. He has an A.M. in Philosophy from Harvard University. Born in Buenos Aires.

Johann A. Klaassen is Vice President of Managed Account Programs and a member of the First Affirmative Investment Committee. He earned a BA in liberal arts (the Great Books Program) from St. John's College in Santa Fe, New Mexico, and a PhD in Ethics and Social Philosophy from Washington University in St. Louis. Having joined First Affirmative in 2001, he is responsible for developing asset allocation strategies and investment policy statements, and serves as the primary administrator for the First Affirmative's managed accounts. Previously, he taught in the Philosophy departments of various universities, including teaching courses in Ethics and Critical Thinking. His scholarly articles have appeared in such journals as *Philosophy and Literature, Journal of Social Philosophy*, and *Journal of Value Inquiry*; he has presented papers to international conferences in Helsinki, Las Vegas, and Washington, DC, among others.

Marco Mansfeld is Head of Sustainability Research at Care Group AG. He holds a Master Degree in Environmental Sciences from the Swiss Federal Institute of Technology Zurich. His field of expertise is the sustainability analysis of companies and primarily sustainability funds and the categorisation of sustainability funds on a global basis.

Nicola Misani is an Assistant Professor of Management at Università Bocconi, Milan (Italy). His current research revolves around Corporate Governance, the strategic implications of Corporate Social Responsibility, and the financing of sustainable ventures. His academic work has appeared on national and international refereed journals, including the *Journal of Business Ethics, Business Strategy and the Environment, and Business Ethics: A European Review*.

Joakim Sandberg is Research Fellow in Practical Philosophy at University of Gothenburg, Sweden. He is currently also Honorary Research Fellow in Global Ethics at University of Birmingham, UK, and Associate Researcher at the Centre for European Research on Microfinance at Université Libre de Bruxelles, Belgium. Joakim has published extensively on the ethics of finance in general and responsible investment in particular; most notably his book *The Ethics of Investing: Making Money or Making a Difference?* (2008). His main academic interests are Moral Philosophy and Applied Ethics, especially Business Ethics.

Markus Schenkel studied Sociology, Political Science and Business Management in Freiburg and Madrid. Since finishing his studies in 2005 he is employed as a research assistant at the Plansecur endowed chair for Business, Ethics and Economics at the University of Kassel.

Eric Schirrmann is CEO of Care Group AG. He holds a Master degree in Economics from the University of St. Gallen, Switzerland (lic.oec.HSG). His strong experience in analysis, portfolio management and advisory skills was built with different financial houses.

Riikka Sievänen is a PhD student at the University of Helsinki, Department of Economics and Management. Her research focuses on how pension funds in Europe determine their stance towards responsible investment. Before starting her doctoral research, Riikka worked in a financial research company and in a multinational company's marketing department.

Henrik Syse is a philosopher with an MA degree from Boston College and a PhD degree from the University of Oslo. He was Head of Corporate Governance for Norges Bank Investment Management (NBIM) 2005–2007. He has written and lectured on various topics within moral philosophy, including the ethics of warfare, the ethics of business, and religious ethics. He is currently a Senior Researcher at the Peace Research Institute Oslo (PRIO).

Marc van Essen is a PhD student at the Rotterdam School of Management, Erasmus University. He holds an MSc degree in Economics and law from Utrecht University. His research interests include shareholder activism, comparative corporate governance, reputational penalties and meta-analytic research methods.

Steve Waddell responds to the twenty-first century's enormous global challenges and its unsurpassed opportunities, which require new ways of acting and organizing. Through *NetworkingAction* he responds to these opportunities with consulting, education, research, and personal leadership. Steve focuses upon business-government-civil society collaborations to produce innovation, enhance impact, and build new capacity. This may be local, national and/or global; the issue arenas are varied. Steve Waddell has done this for more than 20 years.

Olaf Weber (PhD) holds the Export Development Canada Chair in Environmental Finance at the School of Environment, Enterprise and Development, University of Waterloo, Canada. Furthermore he is managing partner at the GOE, Zurich, Switzerland. Olaf Weber holds a master degree in Organizational Psychology. His fields of expertise are the relation between sustainable performance and business success and the integration of sustainability issues in banking and finance.

Chapter 1
Global Finance and the Role of Responsible Investors

Steve Waddell

Introduction

The advent of the biggest global financial meltdown since the field of socially responsible investment (SRI) was established raises important questions about SRI's role in global financial system rule-setting. This chapter explores questions about SRI's role and its potential role. It also asks: Can responsible investors realize their goals by simply acting within the current global financial system rules, or do they have to change the system? Are there qualities of the current system that are antithetical to the very values of responsible investors that will limit SRIs' ability to achieve their goals? Is it even possible for SRIs to influence the 'global finance system'?

While recognizing that there are numerous and diverse 'goals' and 'values' that SRIs (SRIs) articulate, this chapter aims to help SRIs answer these questions by:

(1) describing the global finance system from a strategic change perspective;
(2) describing SRIs' role in that system in the 2008–2009 crisis;
(3) explaining why influencing the global finance system (i) might be the most direct way to influence SRIs' goals, and (ii) without doing so SRIs will not be able to reach their goals; and
(4) suggesting possible actions for those who conclude that they want to influence the global finance system.

A Strategic 'The Global Finance System' (GFS) Definition

Of course there are many organizations that, collectively, make up the 'global finance system'. However, all systems possess strategic leverage points; moreover, some ways of looking at systems are better than others. Describing the GFS to

S. Waddell (✉)
NetworkingAction, Boston, MA, USA
e-mail: swaddell@networkingaction.net

W. Vandekerckhove et al. (eds.), *Responsible Investment in Times of Turmoil*,
Issues in Business Ethics 31, DOI 10.1007/978-90-481-9319-6_1,
© Springer Science+Business Media B.V. 2011

provide strategic change guidance in ways that make the GFS relatively easily understood was a core goal of the first phase of the Global Finance Initiative. The GFI began in January 2008 – before the 2008–2009 crisis hit – as an investigation into strategies for integrating social-environmental concerns into the global finance system. As an 'action learning' project, it undertook its investigation through actions that began developing the necessary strategy. This includes mapping, interviews, stakeholder meetings and formation of a stakeholder stewardship team.[1]

GFI approached its work with a very broad understanding of what comprises the global finance system, but looks at it from two different boundary definitions. To identify strategic leverage points, it is described from the perspective of the global public (government-controlled) institutions that define global rules for finance. To guide a change strategy the GFS is described from the perspective of distinct stakeholder groups that control or are affected by it. This is, of course, distinct from the concept of the GFS as a set of global public institutions.

One of the most powerful forces behind large system change comes with emphasizing 'contradictions' between how a system claims to work as the basis of its legitimacy, and the way it actually works. In the physical sciences this gave rise to the term 'paradigm shift' (Kuhn 1962); adapted in the social sciences and paired with the concept of erosion of legitimacy, emphasizing contradictions is behind the concept of 'revolutions' and 'punctuated equilibrium' (Gersick 1991).

GFI decided to focus upon the parts of the GFS that claim to direct that system in the broad public interest, and to be accountable to the public. Therefore, by the global finance public policy system, GFI means the people and institutions that are working with a global public (government) mandate to address issues of finance broadly – banking, investment, and insurance services and products. The following organizations are key to this system:

(1) **Bank for International Settlements (BIS):** This is arguably the most important and least recognized of all the organizations. It is the organization of central bankers, such as the Federal Reserve of the US and the Bank of England. Central bankers are appointed by governments for set terms to establish monetary policy – most often associated with setting interest rates. Usually they are also associated with regulation of banks. The BIS Board of Governors (Central Bankers) meets every 2 months.

BIS's name reflects its anachronistic founding in 1930, as an institution to manage reparation payments imposed on Germany by the Treaty of Versailles following the First World War. Today BIS provides a critical forum for information exchange, social network development, research, workshops and seminars, and a range of banking services for central banks.

(2) **Financial Stability Board (FSB):** This is *the* key coordinating organization for the global finance system. It brings together representatives from the other

---

[1] For more information go to: http://www.scalingimpact.net/projects/global-finance-initiative

organizations listed here, to align activities and address key issues. For example, it was tasked with developing responses to the early 2008 global finance problems. Important to note is that it is formerly structured as part of BIS.

The FSB has grown out of two crises. It was established in 1999 by the G7 as the Financial Stability Forum out of the Asian crisis to promote cooperation among the various national and international supervisory bodies and international financial institutions so as to promote stability in the international financial system. As a product of the most recent crisis, in April 2009 it was renamed the Financial Stability Board with expanded G20 membership, and its role was enhanced to address vulnerabilities and to develop and implement strong regulatory, supervisory and other policies in the interest of financial stability.

(3) **G7 to G20:** These are gatherings of specific sets of countries. The G7 includes the largest western economies and Japan; the G20 includes those countries and a broader set such as China, Brazil and India. The G7 was the traditional summit gathering place for global finance decisions, led by finance ministers and their deputies and with annual gatherings that included Presidents and Prime Ministers. Anyone wishing to interact with these groupings is stymied by their opaque, virtual nature – they do not have permanent secretariats or even web-sites.

(4) **International Association of Insurance Supervisors (IAIS):** This brings together all the heads of the insurance regulatory bodies, and is based at the BIS.

(5) **International Monetary Fund (IMF):** Arguably the second most important institution, the IMF is mandated to support exchange rate stability. It does this most notably through loans to countries with often controversial 'conditions' that influence countries' public and fiscal policy.

(6) **International Organization of Securities Commissions (IOSCO):** This brings together all the heads of the security exchange commissions (SEC as it is known in the US) that regulate stock exchanges.

(7) **Organization for Economic Development and Cooperation (OECD):** As part of its broader mandate to coordinate information and data between its 30 member countries with the general goal of economic growth and financial stability, OECD plays host to meetings between central bankers and ministers of finance.

(8) **World Bank (WB):** With a board made up of Ministers of Finance (US: Treasury) or their appointees (central bankers), the World Bank's focus is upon poverty reduction. Its role in global finance is one of lender/donor to poor countries.

(9) **US Government:** Of course this is not a global entity like the others. However, the US Federal Reserve, Treasury and the dollar play such a pre-eminent role, that any description of the global finance system would be incomplete without referring to it.

There are four noteworthy points associated with this list of nine institutions. One is the absence of the United Nations and its affiliated organizations. The UN

Conference on Trade and Development (UNCTAD), for instance, only plays a supporting role by providing technical guidance to finance and trade ministries and relevant accounting bodies. Although the World Bank and IMF are technically Bretton Woods institutions that grew out of the UN, they are independent of it and the UN has never succeeded in its numerous attempts to have a meaningful role in the GFS.

The UN has tried to assert leadership in some parts of the global finance system, arguing that it has the greatest legitimacy to act given its global membership. One major effort was a series of international conferences on 'financing for development' that began in Monterrey, Mexico in 2002. The final of these conferences in June 2009 tried to expand its scope to include the on-going financial crisis. However, it was widely ignored by the G8 and engaged no significant world leaders.

In response to the 2008 finance crisis the President of the General Assembly established the 'Commission of Experts of the President of the General Assembly on Reforms of the International Monetary and Financial System' – usually referred to as 'the Stiglitz Commission' after its high-profile, Nobel Prize-winning Chair. Of all the processes growing out of the 2008–2009 crisis, its membership was perhaps the most global and its process of crisis review the most public. However, it has also been side-lined as a UN product (Saiz 2009).

A second noteworthy point is the reminder that this list excludes private sector ones. This includes rating agencies, the International Accounting Standards Board (IASB) that aims to standardize financial reporting, the Geneva Association that brings together the 80 largest insurance companies, and the Washington-based Institute of International Finance (IIF) which bills itself as 'the world's only global financial institution. . .(including) most of the world's largest commercial banks and investment banks, as well as a growing number of insurance companies and investment management firms.' (IIF 2010) Some commentators argue that some of these organizations' powers should be public, rather than private.

The third noteworthy point is to emphasize that this list of nine organizations is not a list of equals and that their relationships are complex. In terms of power, some refer to meetings of public financial powers of the United States as 'G1' (Held 2009). Also, many over-estimate the weight of expanded representation in the 'G20' – its meetings on finance give votes to international institutions on the list that are essentially controlled by the 'G7'. BIS itself is controlled by the 'G10' group of developed country central banks.

Figures 1.1 and 1.2 aim to further describe the complexities of the relationships and emphasize the importance of the BIS and FSB. The latter and several other critical parts of the GFS are either housed at, or directly controlled by, the BIS. Part of BIS is the Committee on Payment and Settlement Systems (CPSS), which sets standards with respect to payment, clearing, settlement and related arrangements – the bank analogue to the Global Postal Union.

The FSB includes virtually all the major parts of the GFS, with the notable formal absence of some private sector actors. Also important to recognize is the repetitive representation on the FSB of BIS by institutions it houses or controls.

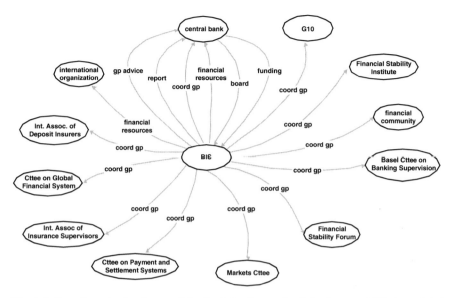

Fig. 1.1 Inter-Organizational map of the Bank for International Settlements (BIS) (gp=global policy; coord=coordinates)

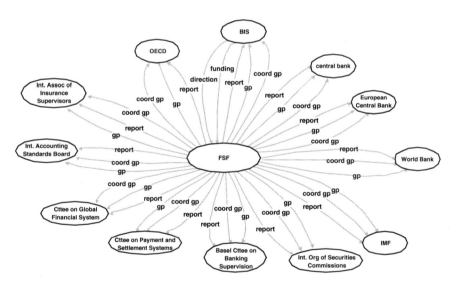

Fig. 1.2 Inter-Organizational map of the financial stability forum

The final noteworthy point is that the GFS has not grown out of a 'grand design,' but in an ad hoc manner. BIS was founded in 1930 with the original focus of reparation payments from Germany. The grandest design-like era followed World War II with the founding of the WB, IMF and shortly after that the pre-cursor to OECD. The G7 first met in 1976 as the G6, IOSCO in 1983, IAIS was founded in 1994, FSF in 1999. The 'system' is confused by often overlapping and sometimes competing institutions such as with setting financial standards. Moreover, it is arguably historically an anachronism, given the domination of a small group of countries that are not currently the most important ones financially or in terms of population.

Another way to look at the GFS is by answering 'What are the major GFS stakeholders, defined by groups of interests, roles and powers that influence or are influenced by the global financial system?'[2] This question is producing new approaches to global governance where stakeholders in an issue create a network to manage the issue. These are referred to as global public policy networks (Reinicke 1998, Reinicke and Deng 2000) or Global Action Networks (GANs) (Waddell 2003, Waddell and Khagram 2007).

From this stakeholder perspective, the Global Finance Initiative found useful to distinguish between the 'traditional insiders' who write the rules of the global finance system, and the 'outsider innovators' who are pressing for change. The major stakeholder groups that make up the first category are:

(1) **The G7 Governments and Regulators:** From a roles perspective these could be placed in two groups, since governments have a broad responsibility for national welfare and regulators have a more narrow responsibility for financial institutions. However, the latter are appointed by the former and in fact there is rarely significant disagreement or division – concerns of Ministers for Environment, for example, never trump Ministers of Finance representations in the GFS.

(2) **The Global Financial Services Industry**: In January 2008 when the GFI commenced its work, people almost universally objected to the suggestion that it is appropriate to refer to the 'global financial services industry'. Based upon history, products and risk profiles, most claimed that separating banking, investment services and insurance is critical. However, within 9 months the value and pretense of these divisions was eliminated in terms of broad policy as the term 'global financial crisis' came into daily use.

The GFS traditionally is controlled by these two groups. Divisions between even these two groups have eroded with the increasingly common hiring by the first of people from the second. Collectively they include a large group of academics, experts and consultants, and they all derive substantial power by promoting the complexity and mystique of finance and the danger of significant changes. Their power is reinforced by division among the following outside innovators who are pressing for change:

(3) **Responsible Investors, Asset Owners and Managers:** This stakeholder group might be expected to be one of the most powerful of the stakeholder groups. However, it is very poorly organized. Whereas the financial services industry

---

[2]This is a broader definition of stakeholder than that of Freeman (1984) 'those groups without whose support the organization would cease to exist', but well within common usage. Mitchell et al. 1997.

is extremely well organized on national to global levels, there are only weak counterparts for asset owners. Asset owners are a widely varied group: many of the most wealthy associate with the insiders, the insiders have created rules that make organizing of asset owners difficult, there is great deference to the 'expertise' of the insiders, and there are often 'intermediaries' (insiders) who claim to represent asset owners' interests.

In the United States, the Council for Institutional Investors represents a group of asset owners. As well, there are some national organizations of social investors and managers who have a much more active say in the direction of their assets. However, their power is modest next to the financial services industry.

Perhaps most important is the emergence over the past 5 years of more global networks. This includes an emerging social investor network, the Principles for Responsible Investment, the UNEP-Finance Initiative, the Network for Sustainable Financial Markets, the Carbon Disclosure Project, and the Global Reporting Initiative's finance project. Moreover, insurance companies are perhaps the leaders in integrating climate change concerns into investment, and large endowments are pioneers in social impact. In addition there are Sovereign Wealth Funds that incorporate principles beyond simple financial ones. Many trillions of dollars of investment are involved.

(4) **Progressive Academics:** To date only traditional economists and financial academics have been brought into the official debate about the future of the financial system. However, there is a large number of critics from these fields and others such as sociology and political science who have financial system expertise to contribute. The particular strengths of this group are with theory-building, analysis and policy development.

(5) **Civil Society Organizations:** This includes those traditionally working on the World Bank/IMF, consumer groups, environmentalists, human rights activists, labor unions, religious groups, and the broad universe represented by CIVICUS.[3] The particularly important contribution of this group is its power to press for a broader public and participative debate to bring in the innovators and ensure decisions are not left to the traditionalists.

(6) **Beyond G7 Governments:** A large part of the world is not represented within the G7. Although the 'G20' is promoted as the new framework, the actual participants in that group include representatives from the Europe Union, the European Central Bank and the seven global public policy institutions. This means that the power of the traditional global brokers (insiders) is still overwhelming. Moreover, the G20 still leaves 172 nations unrepresented.

(7) **Real Economy Business:** Traditionally the finance industry was in service of the rest of the economy; today the situation is largely reversed. Non-financial

---

[3]CIVICUS: World Alliance for Citizen Participation, is an international alliance of members and partners which constitute an influential network of organizations at the local, national, regional and international levels, and span the spectrum of civil society.

businesses are bearing the brunt of high finance costs and increasingly common financial crisis that depress business, require expensive bailouts, depress share prices and complicate borrowing. Critical voices of non-financial business can be found in trade associations and networks for social responsibility.

SRIs Current Role in the Global Financial System

The GFI also investigated the relationship of these stakeholder groups with the GFS institutions with a web crawl methodology. This approach takes advantage of the internet's structure around sites that have unique URL addresses. Most sites have (hyper) links to other sites that, when clicked on, take you to other sites or pages. These are inserted because they have more detailed information with regards to a topic (including, of course, ads), because the host wants to connect people to allies or colleagues, or because they may be foes on an issue. These connections between unique URLs provide the basis for mapping relationships by 'doing a web crawl'. A software program[4] draws relationships between organizations' web links, to describe the virtual network of the organization.

Although web presence is not uniform around the world, certainly for issues like global finance major players will have a web presence. The methodology is useful for identifying organizations in a specific issue arena and to make general comments about its structure; it is not appropriate for more surgical analysis.

Crawls produces maps that graphically represent issue arenas (such as socially responsible investment) as links between web-sites. The maps are of *outlinks* only – a node appears based upon how many links are sent to it from other sites. The size of the dots is related to the number of links, and relative location is determined by the number of links. In this case, crawls were done beginning with 23 'seed' web addresses with three categories of organizations: (1) SRI firms (e.g.: Calvert, Hermes), (2) associations (e.g.: Social Investment Forum, Association for Sustainable and Responsible Investment in Asia, EuroSIF), and (3) multi-stakeholder networks working on SRI (e.g.: Principles for Responsible Investment, Global Reporting Initiative).

Figure 1.3 is a map of the immediate networks of the 23 sites, referred to as the 'social network' – sites that link directly to the seed addresses.

This crawl and map suggests several important points.

(1) The crawl produces a list that can be considered to roughly approximate the totality of the major web sites concerned with SRI (and a good organizing tool). A total of 144 were identified (Diagram 3 has only 100 to simply visually). As

---

[4]This project generated web crawler maps by the Issue Crawler (issuecrawler.net) from the Govcom.org Foundation, Amsterdam, directed by Prof. Richard Rogers, Chair in New Media & Digital Culture, University of Amsterdam.

Fig. 1.3 SRIs' social network

well as the three categories mentioned above, there are also an expanded group
of civil society organizations interested in SRI (e.g.: Greenpeace, Pew), more
traditional financial institutions (e.g.: UBS, Morgan Stanley) and governmental
agencies (e.g.: United Nations, Environmental Protection Agency). Missing due
to the methodology are academic/research institutions (which tend to have individual rather than institutional connections), and smaller organizations (without
or with very simple websites), and ones not connected because of language
issues.

(2) GFS institutions are not connected to the SRI organizations on the map, nor
is one present in the list of 144 sites. There are no links from the eight key
institutions (the G7 does not have a website) identified earlier to the SRI
organizations.

(3) There are two types of important central connectors for the SRI organizations.
One is the SRI associations and multi-stakeholder organizations (predictable
from the original seeds), and includes the Social Investment Forum (socialin-
vest.org: 17 links from the network shown and 77 links from the total crawled
population which includes out- and in-links), GRI (16 and 389 links), and

CERES (15 and 175 links). The other center is the UN, where the UNEP has 11 and 817 links, and the UN itself with 10 and 951 links.
(4) Worthwhile to note is the suggested importance of 'environmental' as compared to other issues at least in terms of organizational presence and connections: the UNEP, Carbon Disclosure Project and CERES are all key issue nodes that do not have strong counterparts with other issues.
(5) Nevertheless, the network is quite decentralized and evenly dispersed. In many crawls there would be much more dominant nodes, and much clearer groupings that would suggest connecting unassociated parts is an important task.

Another crawl was done with the same 23 sites, but this time with 'three iterations' which means it maps connections to the connections of those found in Fig. 1.3. This is sometimes referred to as 'the establishment' – it describes the large institutional environment that is the broad reference environment for the 23 SRI organizations. This is shown in Fig. 1.4. Again, for visual simplicity only 100

Fig. 1.4 SRIs' Establishment Network: Stars are UN lead organizations; squares are GFS institutions

nodes are shown, but the crawl identified 280 organizations. The squares are GFS organizations, with the Federal Reserve treated as a proxy for the US; there is no G7 site.

This suggests that:

(1) Of the GFS organizations (squares), the SRIs are oriented towards the World Bank (24 links from the diagram nodes, 551 from the crawled population), the IMF (11 and 153), and the OECD (8 and 297). Although the BIS and FSB are key GFS entities, they do not appear even on the expanded list of the 280 organizations. Moreover, the location of the GFS organizations – on the lower left periphery – suggests that they do not even have a central role in this network.

(2) The UN organizations (the stars) are much more important: this includes the UN (28 links from the diagram nodes, 2267 from the crawled population), UNDP (21 and 1166), and UNEP (26 and 3421) provides the most significant organizing focus, along with their associated institutions – of the top six nodes rated by in-links, five are UN-associated organizations and the sixth is the World Bank.

(3) The map shows all these inter-governmental organizations clustered lower left; the rest of the network is quite dispersed. The GRI is the largest of these other nodes (13 and 868 links). This suggests quite a weak and unfocused institutional environment in general.

Similar maps were developed for NGOs working on finance issues; this includes Bank Watch, New Rules for Global Finance, and others involved in the global finance arena. These maps and the two for SRI organizations suggest the same major orientation towards the United Nations. That is to say, SRIs and NGOs treat the UN as the most important actor globally. There is undoubtedly a number of reasons for this, including a sense of the UN being more 'legitimate' than other intergovernmental organizations, it being more globally inclusive, and it being more connected to the issues of interest to SRIs. However, this all emphasizes that the SRIs are not paying attention to, and do not consider particularly important to them, the key GFS organizations.

This contrasts with web crawls run for investment services firms. Similarly, 23 such firms were identified from the Board of Directors of the Securities Industry and Financial Markets Association (SIFMA) which is the global association for investment services firms. There are three particularly outstanding points that arise:

(1) The firms are notably much more poorly linked – the social network produces only 19 nodes in contrast to the 144 for the same number of SRIs. This is undoubtedly a product of their competitive nature, but nevertheless the comparatively cooperative nature of the SRIs is important to emphasize.

(2) The GFS institutions are much more powerful reference organizations for the traditional investment services industry – BIS and the World Bank are among the 19 nodes in the social network, and they together with the IMF and the Federal Reserve are the top four nodes by inlink in the establishment networks.

The UN does not even show among the 240 organizations identified in the establishment networks.
(3) The multi-stakeholder organizations that appear so prominently in the SRI world – GRI, UNPSRI, UNEPFI – do not even show in the investment services one.

All this suggests that the SRIs think of the world like NGOs, rather than like financial institutions. The SRIs are indeed 'outsiders' of the GFS – in fact they appear to ignore its existence.

Further, this all suggests that the SRIs had essentially no role in the 2008–2009 turmoil since these maps were generated in July 2009. These maps are artifacts of the SRI world; it would be hard to conceive that SRI could have suddenly developed social ties and orientations to the GFS organizations without having some imprint on their virtual worlds.

SRI Goals, Trends and Global Finance

The question of whether or not SRIs *should* become engaged in shaping the GFS is one of goals, strategy and resources. Some might frame their goals from a very personal perspective and be content if they know that their personal wealth is invested in a socially responsible manner. However, even for these investors a powerful argument can be made that their ability to invest in such a manner is heavily determined by the rules that governments set for financial investment. Furthermore, Louche and Lydenberg suggest that this group of SRIs is today quite small:

(The) shift from pure moral concerns towards more societal preoccupations starting in the 1970s in the United States and in the 1980s in Europe. Its purpose was not only to align investors' personal values with their portfolio but also to provide a vehicle for action and change. (Louche and Lydenberg 2006: 7)

This suggests that most SRIs think of their responsible investments simply as one strategy to realize a broader change goal – albeit one that for most remains connected to concerns about rates of return.

Of course the emphasis and focus of change will vary with SRI. However, in general a consensus is emerging with the focal concept of 'ESG'. The Principles for Responsible Investment (PSRI) are endorsed by institutional investors who represent $18 trillion in assets. The Principles begin with the statement:

As institutional investors, we have a duty to act in the best long-term interests of our beneficiaries. In this fiduciary role, we believe that environmental, social, and corporate governance (ESG) issues can affect the performance of investment portfolios (to varying degrees across companies, sectors, regions, asset classes and through time). We also recognise that applying these Principles may better align investors with broader objectives of society. (Available at; www.unpri.org/principles Accessed July 20, 2009)

Certainly the 'G' of ESG refers to 'corporate governance', and fewer would argue it relates to broader political governance issues. Nevertheless, SRIs are increasingly turning to public policy forums such as reviews of laws regarding corporate governance (as with the United Kingdom review that shifted issues for reporting and fiduciary consideration), and the public offices overseeing finance (such as the Security Exchange Commission in the United States). The PSRI, reflecting the ongoing dance around the heart of the issue, include as 'possible actions' to 'support regulatory or policy developments that enable implementation of the Principles.' (PRI 2009) As Lydenberg and Sinclair more forthrightly declare:

> At the heart . . . lies the question of whether mainstreaming means that responsible investing will become a niche market within a fundamentally unchanged mainstream or, whether it means that the mainstream as a whole will adopt the basic tenets of responsible investing. (Lydenberg and Sinclair 2009: 48)

The authors point to the necessity to change 'the rules of the game' to realize what they hold out to be the inspiring potential to:

> . . .drive fundamental changes into the current markets, which today create as many social and environmental challenges as they address. (Lydenberg and Sinclair 2009: 54)

For those interested in fundamental change, integration into public policy would be a victory.[5] And for this latter group, given the categorical globalization of finance over the past two decades, ignoring the global finance system means both ignoring a fundamental set of actors and perhaps the most effective strategy to realize their objectives.

For SRIs interested in 'mainstreaming' and 'driv(ing) fundamental changes into the current market', the GFS might seem simply too abstract, amorphous, of questionable influence, impervious or beyond the comfort zone of action. There are several reasons to argue that all of these claims should be challenged.

(1) The work of the GFI gives concrete definition to the global financial system from a systemic change strategic perspective.
(2) Virtually everyone agrees that the 'global' quality of finance has increased, will continue to increase, and is beyond the scope of control of isolated traditional national-level strategies. Clearly, the trend is for further strengthening the GFS as a standard-setter and rule-maker as evidenced by the increasing role of the G20 and speculation about the fall of the dollar as the reserve currency in favor of a basket of currencies.

---

[5]There is an interesting parallel with the niche-market versus deep change with the way the health care debate played out in Canada and the United States in the 1960s. The Canadian union movement was a strong proponent of a public health care system, arguing that 'what we have (health care – provided in our contracts) for ourselves, we want for all.' In the US the unions took the niche market position that people would join unions in order to get health care, and therefore opposed public health care. Today, the Canadian health care costs are far lower and outcomes far superior, and the union movement represents a far larger percentage of the work force.

(3) The GFS is a *network,* and anyone familiar with diseases will immediately start describing control strategies by understanding how disease is spread through network connections. Similarly, if the key nodes of the GFS can be infected by SRI values, this is surely one of the most influential ways to get them adopted widely.

(4) The GFS is described here from the perspective of accountable, public institutions. These are more influenced by arguments about public interests – arguments aligned with the values of SRIs. So there are good public policy reasons for the GFS to attend to SRI concerns, beyond those that exist for other investors.

(5) SRIs have adopted certain strategies with which they are quite comfortable for realizing their goals. However, there are good reasons to believe whether those strategies on their own will ever be successful, if the core global institutions do not reflect SRIs' goals.

Perhaps the most powerful argument for SRI involvement with the shaping of the GFS is simply because they have a critical piece of the puzzle about how to avoid turmoil such as the 2008–2009 crisis (and many before!). They are the innovators and inventers of market-based processes that can indeed lead to a more *sustainable* finance system. However, this requires moving behind concerns about environmental and social sustainability as narrowly defined, and to make the connection with the questions about sustainability of the global financial system itself.

An SRI Strategy to Influence the Global Finance System

Of course the scale of challenge is huge, and it will require new strategies and alliances. The climate change challenge may be larger in scale, but the challenge to reform the global finance system will likely be much more difficult. To address both requires changes by powerful interests. However, climate change is associated with an external reality validated by physical science; the finance system is associated with diverging ethical, political and economic beliefs. Nevertheless, the latter is the heart of the challenge for the SRI community that is searching for fundamental change.

Hopes that the crisis of 2008–2009 would produce significant change quickly evaporated over the first 6 months of 2009. There was no meaningful public debate about real change, as the insiders focused entirely upon avoiding total short-term collapse. Crisis is an important but insufficient ingredient for realizing real change. At least two other ingredients are necessary: a vision about how things can be different, and power to realize it.

The GFI convened outsider stakeholders pressing for change in order to define a strategy to realize the type of fundamental change that they were working for. Many commentators had ideas; perhaps the most insight ones were produced by the Stiglitz-led *Commission of Experts of the President of the UN General Assembly on Reforms of the International Monetary and Financial System* (Stiglitz 2009). But scratch a little beneath the surface, and all quickly appeared rather shallow. There was no compelling, comprehensive and inspiring vision of how things can be different.

But there was also no power to realize a vision, should it even exist. The insiders are powerful, well-organized and represent a relatively closed club. They can relatively easily intimidate others by talking about a myriad of technical aspects, and about disaster that would accompany real change. The outsiders who support innovation are poorly organized even within their stakeholder groups, and there are only ad hoc and episodic contacts between them. There is no realistic possibility of creating the 'political will' for change given the current level of organization of outsider innovators.

Rather than propose their own list of ideas that would inevitably be inadequate, the GFI stakeholders defined four qualities that be embedded in a process that would produce the scale of change necessary. They proposed a global commission-like inquiry[6] to define the necessary changes and the path to them over 2 or 3 years. The process would be:

(1) Foundational: Change must be driven by addressing profound questions about the purpose of the financial system and the principles that direct its actions.
(2) Comprehensive: Change must encompass the connections between accounting systems, currencies, regulatory systems, economic structures and all parts of the financial system.
(3) Inclusive: Traditional insiders should be complemented by other groups including responsible investors, multi-stakeholder groups working on finance issues, asset owners, labor, NGOs and critical academics. And participation must be truly global.
(4) Systemic: True systemic risk is not only financial. The change must connect financial stability to the real economy, social equity, and environmental sustainability.

In fact, the multi-stakeholder essence of this strategy is reflected in the call by Lydenberg and Sinclair for:

> ...a reconceptualisation of the ways in which government, corporations, nongovernmental and quasi-governmental organisations and individuals collaborate in managing the interplay between markets and public policy. (Lydenberg and Sinclair 2009: 63)

Of course such a process is not going to develop overnight. There are two key preliminary steps, best developed at the same time:

---

[6]The World Commission on Dams was held up as an example that provides lessons. That was a 2-year, multi-stakeholder investigation to establish rules on the funding and development of large dams.

(1) Strengthening SRI as a *global* network is important to build global influence...just as the G7 is becoming the G20, SRI has to move beyond traditional geography and mindset. It is necessary to aggregate effort and increase alignment and focus of effort in order to influence something the scale of the GFS.

(2) Strengthening the connections between SRI and the other stakeholder groups pushing for real change will be necessary for the same reason; even a strong SRI global network will not be sufficient to have real influence on the GFS.

Practically, there are a number of large system development and change tools and methods that can be used. However, experience with those suggests they should focus at least initially on a third activity – which can be integrated into the first two: developing a comprehensive statement of principles for the operation of global finance and a strategy to give them real life (Waddell et al. 2009). Development of principles and support for their implementation by a wide range of issue stakeholders has proven a powerful strategy for a wide range of issues. This can be seen with Transparency International (corruption), the Forest Stewardship Council (FSC), the Marine Stewardship Council (MSC), the Global Reporting Initiative (GRI), The Access Initiative (TAI) and others.

Currently there are, of course, significant initiatives involving 'finance' and 'principles'. However, they share two enormous shortcomings. One is that they are not widely held or endorsed which both restricts their legitimacy and ability to be advanced. For example, the UNEP Finance Initiative and the Principles for Responsible Investment have statements to guide them, but they are the product of, and controlled by, those in the finance industry and inter-governmental organizations – and these two examples are UN-associated organizations which themselves have problems of legitimacy in the finance arena. These principles are also, by and large, a product of Western discussion. And, they are often directed either at specific institutions rather than being an overall frame.

The second short-coming is that existing principles are insufficiently comprehensive. For example, principles guiding regulators are framed very narrowly upon some financial aspects, and those focused upon 'sustainability' usually are weak on financial aspects. A statement about the purpose of finance is usually totally absent.

Defining and getting a global set of principles adopted is itself a significant task, but one that the stakeholders are well equipped for. Developing them will promote a global conversation that will bring out critical issues, in a way similar to, but much more powerful than, the World Commission on Dams at the end of the last century.

The principles then provide a platform for operationalization and application at the local and national levels. Today, the FSC principles are integrated into country forest regulations; Transparency has similar successes, including at the global level with the OECD; MSC has major retailer like Walmart commit themselves to buying only certified products; many of the world's largest companies use GRI's reporting framework; TAI is giving life to Principle 10 of the Earth Charter in 40 countries.

There are various concrete, doable ways for realizing that GFI is advancing with other stakeholders. The attraction of the stakeholders pressing for change is that collectively they are formidable: SRIs have deep knowledge at the product and institutional levels; progressive academics at the policy and theory levels; others bring the legitimacy of mass voice and pressure.

Conclusions

The global financial system is complex, but as with any system there are particular strategic leverage points. To realize change these must be identified and addressed. Of course, often the best course is not to try to change institutions themselves, but build up other ones that gradually become dominant. These are the type of strategic questions that are still well down the line.

The immediate question for the SRI community is whether it wants to rise to the GFS change challenge. Certainly no one would expect a majority of the community's attention to focus upon the Global Finance System, but if the SRI community is to play a role in fundamental finance system change it is difficult to see how it can avoid tackling the global public institutions in a globalized financial world.

For the Western economies where SRI is most strongly associated, one hopeful sign is the rising SRI focus upon the global issue of climate change. But one clear imperative is for SRI to build outside of its traditional geographic focus, and build engagement strategies with others who, in essence, share the SRI critique of Western markets. This includes Islamic financiers and sovereign wealth funds. This emphasizes the challenge for SRI itself to become truly global and change its own strategies.

References

Freeman, Robert. E. 1984. Strategic Management: A Stakeholder Approach. Boston, MA: Pitman.
Gersick, Connie J. G. 1991. Revolutionary change theories: a multilevel exploration of the punctuated equilibrium paradigm. Academy of Management Review 16: 10–36.
Held, David. 2009. LSE Government Department HotSeat interview by Justin Gest, 30 September 2009. Available at http://www2.lse.ac.uk/government/highlights/PODCAST/.../DHeld30_9_2009.pdf. Accessed 15 April 2010.
IIF. 2010. About IIF – Mission Statement. Retrieved February 1, 2010, from http://www.iif.com/about/. Accessed 15 April 2010.
Kuhn, Thomas. 1962. The Structure of Scientific Revolutions. Chicago, IL: The University of Chicago Press.
Louche, Celine and Steven Lydenberg 2006. Socially responsible investment: differences between Europe and the United States. Vlerick Leuven Gent Working Paper Series 22.
Lydenberg, Steven and G. Sinclair 2009. Mainstream or daydream? The future for responsible investing. Journal of Corporate Citizenship 33: 47–67.
Mitchell, Ronald K., B. R. Agle, et al. 1997. Toward a theory of stakeholder identification and salience: defining the principle of who and what really counts. Academy of Management Review 22: 853–886.
PRI. 2009. Principles for Responsible Investment. An investor initiative in partnership with UNEP Finance Initiative and the UN Global Compact. Available at www.unpri.org/principles. Accessed July 20, 2009.

Reinicke, Wolfgang. 1998. Global Public Policy: Governing Without Government? Washington, DC: Brookings Institution Press.

Reinicke, Wolfgang and F. M. Deng 2000. Critical Choices: The United Nations, Networks, and the Future of Global Governance. Toronto, ON: International Development Research Council.

Saiz, Ignacio. 2009. Rights in recession? Challenges for economic and social rights enforcement in times of crisis. Journal of Human Rights Practice 1: 277–293.

Stiglitz, Joseph. 2009. Principles for a new financial architecture. The Commission of Experts of the President of the UN General Assembly on Reforms of the International Monetary and Financial System. http://www.un.org/ga/president/63/commission/newfinancialarchitecture. pdf. Accessed 15 April 2010.

Waddell, Steven. 2003. Global action networks: A global invention for business to make globalization work for all. Journal of Corporate Citizenship 12: 27–42.

Waddell, Steven and Sanjeev Khagram. 2007. Multi-stakeholder global networks: Emerging systems for the global common good. Partnerships, Governance and Sustainable Development: Reflections on Theory and Practice, eds. P. Glasbergen, F. Biermann, and A. P. J. Mol, 261–287. Cheltenham: Edward Elgar Publishing.

Waddell, Steven, Sanjeev Khagram, Simon Zadek, and Sasha Radovich. 2009. Creating a global finance system for the 21st century: An action strategy. http://www.scalingimpact.net/projects/global-finance-initiative, iScale/GAN-Net.

Chapter 2
New Values in Responsible Investment

Neil Eccles

> *There's an old saying in Tennessee—I know it's in Texas,*
> *probably in Tennessee—that says, fool me once, shame*
> *on—shame on you. Fool me—you can't get fooled again.*
> (George W. Bush 17 September 2002)

Introduction

This chapter is a story of disquiet – I think we may have fooled ourselves. In it I trace the evolution of responsible investment (RI) from noble beginnings through to a current form which, rather cynically speaking appears to have been leached of much of the original good intent. I suggest how this shift in ethical posture may well have been the unintended consequence of the drive to mainstream RI, and more specifically of the approach that was adopted to achieve this mainstreaming. Essentially I argue that over time, RI has come to conform to the spirit of mainstream investment which has as a singular focus the pursuit of maximum risk adjusted return. Through this, any confrontation with the fiduciary duties paradigm based on the *Rational Man*[1] model of human character which apparently prevails in many legal jurisdictions (Freshfields et al. 2005) has been avoided. Unfortunately, it is fairly easy to demonstrate how this very paradigm of fiduciary duties is itself likely to be a source of irresponsible investment behavior. This is certainly the case in the context of a class of societal problems known as social dilemmas (Kollock 1998) in which individual rationality is at odds with collective rationality. Unfortunately, many of the most pressing societal problems facing us today are social dilemmas. Indeed, it is possible to trace the roots of the turmoil that characterized global economic systems

---

N. Eccles (✉)
University of South Africa, Pretoria, South Africa
e-mail: Ecclens@unisa.ac.za

[1] In 1977, Sen adjusted this title to 'Rational fools' (1977: 317)

W. Vandekerckhove et al. (eds.), *Responsible Investment in Times of Turmoil*,   19
Issues in Business Ethics 31, DOI 10.1007/978-90-481-9319-6_2,
© Springer Science+Business Media B.V. 2011

and financial markets starting in 2007 to a social dilemma. Somewhat simplistically speaking, a relatively small group of individuals took actions that were highly profitable individually, but which led to the erosion of a key public good in the form of stable economic and financial systems. The costs of fixing this erosion look set to be borne, not by these individuals alone, but by present and indeed future generations of taxpayers collectively. Climate change is another example.

Thus, by avoiding confrontation with the *Rational Man* fiduciary paradigm, we have left a (possibly the) major source of irresponsible investment behavior intact and even more problematically, have branded this as 'responsible investment'. In short, while there might well have been progress made in mainstreaming 'responsible investment', it is quite possible that not much progress has been made in terms of making mainstream investment more responsible. In a sense we have fooled ourselves and created a delusion of success.

But before I get ahead of myself, the first thing that anyone needs to do when they set out to tell stories about RI is to state what exactly they mean by RI. For the purposes of this chapter, I have intentionally chosen to define RI in the broadest possible sense. As such I take it to be any investment practice that integrates a consideration of environmental, social and governance (ESG) issues into decision making and ownership activities (Eccles et al. 2007). It would, however, be irresponsible of me not to acknowledge that this *choice* was made for convenience rather than because it represents any form of consensus view (academic or popular) on the concept. Indeed several authors (myself included) have on occasion suggested a far narrower definition than this (Eccles 2008, Eurosif 2008, Welker and Wood 2009).

The chapter is structured as follows. The next section characterizes pre-mainstreaming RI in which, despite notable evolution over time (deontological and utilitarian, religious and secular), returns were *potentially* constrained by clearly defined moral considerations. This is followed by a section in which I present an interpretation of the mainstreaming of RI (since 2005) as allowing moral consideration which is constrained by considerations of return rather than the other way around. I explain how this was convenient in the context of the *Rational Man* fiduciary paradigm and argumentatively possible. Crucial in this was the discursive affirmation that ESG issues are material. The section after that reopens that inquiry by considering pre-mainstream and mainstream RI against a matrix of return and morality combinations. I show how mainstream RI denies the existence of moral vs return scenarios that actually make up the social dilemma's we are facing today.

Responsible Investment – A Brief History

The debate regarding naming of RI activities is in a large part due to the marked changes in terms of participants, tactics and ethical posture that such activities have undergone over the years. The idea of RI is by no means a new one. In fact it is probably safe to say that since the beginning of investment, investors have considered ESG issues in one way or another. Certainly, Schueth (2003) notes that by early biblical times, formal guidance on investing morally was to be found in Jewish Law. Islamic Law dating to some centuries later also contains notable moral prescriptions on investing which persist today.

The Christian faith too was not to be outdone, and somewhat more recently than biblical times, John Wesley delivered his now famous sermon entitled 'The Use of Money' (Wesley 1760). In this he presented very clear moral guidance for the processes of: (a) acquiring money, (b) saving it, and (c) using it. Wesley's prescriptions in terms of acquisition in particular have relevance in terms of investment. The basic idea was that, while making money was generally deemed to be a good thing, this should not involve causing harm to body or mind of oneself or anyone else. While Wesley's sermon was theoretical, or prescriptive if you like, the anti-slavery movement of the late 1700s and 1800s, was an early example of the application of RI prescriptions. During this time, a number of religious institutions, most notably the Quakers, embarked on general social campaigns against the business of slavery. Besides political activities, these efforts also included extensive research into the business of slavery and investment adjustments. The simplest adjustments of course involved sacrificing prior investment in acquiring slaves through manumission.

The investment world of the 1700s and 1800s was of course a far cry from the more 'modern' investment world of the 1900s and 2000s. In this 'modern' investment period, the first mutual fund credited with giving formal expression to ethical investment prescriptions appears to have been the Pioneer Fund (Sparkes 2006). This was launched in the U.S. in 1928 and catered for the investment tastes of Temperance groups by integrating negative screens for alcohol in particular. Between the establishment of this fund and the mid 1960s there appears to have been a somewhat pedestrian increase in this genre of investing. By the 1960s a handful of similar funds existed around the world, for example, note the establishment of the first RI fund in Sweden in 1965 (Bengtsson 2008).

The late 1960s, however, heralded the emergence a new era in RI. This era was most notably marked by not one, but two significant RI 'movements': the anti-Vietnam war movement and the anti-apartheid movement. In their singular focus on very specific societal issues rather than on a whole raft of 'sin' screens, these movements were somewhat reminiscent of the heady days of the abolitionist movement. On a more philosophical level, they also bore more resemblance to the abolitionist movement than the early modern RI funds. In contrast with the early modern funds which were of the 'I won't participate in any investment that doesn't comply with my ethical views' type (a deontological approach if you like), this new era was characterised by a spirit of 'I'll use my investment to change the world' (a more utilitarian view) (Viviers et al. 2008a).

So in spirit, the new era of RI looked a bit like the abolitionist era. However, there were limits to this similarity, not least of which was the inclusion of tactical innovations that reflected the more modern reality of investment. Key amongst these was the use of shareholder resolutions. Indeed, the shareholder resolution filed at the 1969 AGM of Dow Chemicals regarding the production of the herbicide 'Agent Orange' which was used in the Vietnam war was one of the first such resolutions recorded (Sparkes 2006). By 1975 the Vietnam war was a thing of the past. The anti-apartheid struggle, however, had many years to run. In the end, by 1993/1994, it had arguably achieved the title of the largest RI movement ever seen. It had also proved to be a phenomenal testing ground for tactics which have become the cornerstone of modern RI.

The last important feature of this new era in RI was that although both of the RI movements that characterised it still had links to religious institutions, they also transcended the realms of specific religious groups. In particular, one didn't need to be a participant in any sort of organized religion to recognize the basic moral 'badness' of the apartheid system, or the psychosis of napalming villages in the Vietnam. In some ways this laid the groundwork for the more secular RI approach that is evident today.

So far so good. Despite the evolution of tactics, and the secularization of RI, the defining characteristic was that investment actions were premised on clearly defined moral considerations. These religious and more generally ethical responsible investors were willing to take *potentially* financially detrimental actions in order to pursue a specified moral outcome (Sparkes 2001). The only problem was that despite the obvious moral 'rightness' of these investment practices, RI as a whole still remained pretty marginalized. And this was a big problem. It was a big problem because of the issue of market elasticity whereby any constructive market signals that might be sent regarding ESG issues were simply absorbed in a swamp of amoral[2] investing (Munnel and Sunden 2004, Rivoli 2003). Furthermore it was a big problem because it meant that shareholder activism or engagement efforts were associated with a tiny minority of shareholders: the 'lunatic fringe' minority voice problem.

Mainstreaming RI

However, by the mid 2000s, winds of change were evident with regards to this niche character of RI. In 2005, the World Economic Forum in collaboration with AccountAbility, published the report entitled 'Mainstreaming Responsible Investment' (Zadek et al. 2005). Although the report itself noted that RI had 'yet to be embraced by the wider investment community' (Zadek:7), the investment mainstream was very strongly represented in the roundtables that culminated in its drafting. Household names including Citigroup, Credit Suisse, Goldman Sachs, J.P. Morgan, Merril Lynch, Morgan Stanley, and UBS to name a few were all there. Lehman Brothers was even represented. In the same year, Kofi Annan, the then UN Secretary General, invited a number of the world's largest asset owners to assist in drafting a set of principles which it was hoped would ensure a more responsible approach to investment. This effort culminated in the launch in April 2006 of the Principles for Responsible Investment (PRI) at the New York Stock Exchange. The launch signatories comprised a relatively intimate group of 20 of the world's largest

---

[2]Investment that does not consider moral distinctions or judgments (Viviers et al. 2008a)

pension funds, foundations and special government funds which at the time controlled an estimated US\$ 2 trillion in assets (UN Press Release 2006). If this initial support was promising, subsequent progress in recruiting signatories was nothing short of meteoric. By early 2009, the PRI reported some 538 signatories, with over US\$ 18 trillion in assets under management (PRI 2009a). This potentially represented close to a quarter of the total global assets behind an RI initiative. Indeed on the basis of these numbers it might well have been reasonable to conclude that by 2009, RI was well on its way to being mainstreamed. How can we explain this 'success' story? This question can be broken down into two sub-questions: (a) what was preventing the mainstream uptake of RI prior to the PRI?; and (b) how were these barriers removed?

In terms of the first of these, the key barrier appears to have been a paradigm – or at least elements of a paradigm – in the form of the prevailing (Western) economic paradigm. Central to this economic paradigm is a mythical person known as *Rational Man*. The conception of this character can be traced to rationalist philosophers of the seventieth century such as Descartes and Hobbes (Wishloff 2009). Essentially for reasons of mathematical convenience, *Rational Man* was defined as a normless, utility maximizing being. From adopting this model of human character it is a very short slippery slope to believing that the essence of investment must be the rational pursuit of maximum risk adjusted return. This is especially so if one assumes that whatever the particular social circumstance, the more money one has, the more utility one can buy on the open market. This is clearly diametrically opposed to the defining characteristic of RI up until the mid 1990s in which investments actions were explicitly informed by defined ethical considerations in a manner that could *potentially* yield reduced risk adjusted returns.

In and of itself, one would not necessarily expect some philosophical abstraction of human character to pose a barrier to a more constrained form of investment. There is plenty of anecdotal and empirical evidence to suggest that humans are in fact capable of a much richer range of behaviour than what *Rational Man* might recommend (Dierksmeier and Pirson 2009, Ostrom 1999). The pre-mainstreaming RI activity already described is an obvious example of this. The barrier arises because 'normal' humans are not actually making the bulk of investment decisions. In fact the bulk investment decision making authority has been surrendered (consciously or otherwise) to agents of 'normal' humans who are known as investment fiduciaries.

The relationship between these fiduciaries and 'normal' humans is governed by a cluster of duties sensibly called fiduciary duties. In the context of investment fiduciaries, despite some variation from one legal jurisdiction to another, at least one duty appears to be omnipresent: the duty to act in the best interest of the beneficiaries. Certainly this duty was common in all legal jurisdictions considered in the Freshfields Report (Freshfields et al. 2005) and one or two others that were not considered (e.g. South Africa according to Swart et al. 2009). So a key question on the minds of all fiduciaries should be: 'What are the best interests of the beneficiaries?' And this is where *Rational Man* becomes the essential barrier to pre-mainstreaming forms of RI. Submitting to *Rational Man* in formulating a position on best interests inevitably led to the 'best interests' duty being substituted with 'maximum risk adjusted return' as Viederman (2008) points out.

The legal opinion contained in the 2005 Freshfields Report essentially confirms this *Rational Man* fiduciary paradigm. The objective of the report was to answer the question: 'Is the integration of environmental, social and governance issues into investment policy .... voluntarily permitted, legally required or hampered by law and regulations; ...' (Freshfield: 6). It concluded that there are two circumstances under which the consideration of ESG issues by fiduciaries was permissible (and arguably required). The first is when considering these issues might reasonably allow the fiduciaries to 'more reliably predict the financial performance' (Freshfield: 13) of investments. The second is 'where a consensus (express or in certain circumstances implied) amongst beneficiaries mandates' (Freshfield: 13) such a consideration. In other words, the Freshfields Report concluded (in the jurisdictions covered) that *Rational Man* must be the model of human character that investment fiduciaries use unless the beneficiaries specifically stand up and say that this isn't their character. This then was the major barrier to mainstreaming RI.

Logically speaking, there are two possible ways in which overcoming this barrier might have been pursued. One would have been to overthrow the paradigm by defining the utility to be maximised as responsible behaviour rather than risk adjusted return. This equates to reinforcing or generalizing the second permissible circumstance in the Freshfields Report. Pre-mainstream RI was a proponent of this option. The other way to overcome the barrier would have been to remove the possibility that RI might constrain the pursuit of maximum risk adjusted return. This equates to the first permissible circumstance in the Freshfields Report. The passionate search for the business case both within the specific discipline of RI but also within the more general discipline of corporate social responsibility (CSR) is a clear indication of the popularity of this option.

It is insightful to briefly consider the academic literature describing this search for the business case. In terms of the general CSR business case literature, this has conveniently been subjected to a meta-analysis (Orlitzky et al. 2003). Within the body of literature that they considered (dating back as far as 1972) were studies that indicated the full spectrum of relationships between corporate social and corporate financial performance: positive, neutral and negative. However, combining all of the studies pointed to a generally positive statistical relationship between corporate social and corporate financial performance. On the basis of this Orlitzky et al. concluded that 'portraying managers' choices with respect to CSP and CFP as an either/or trade-off is not justified in light of 30 years of empirical data.' (Orlitzky: 427).

The RI business case literature also dates back at least as far as the 1970s (Vance 1975) and can be split into at least two broad methodological categories. The first category was based on the event studies method and so considered the effects of ESG events on investment performance. The anti-apartheid movement of the 1970s, 1980s and early 1990s in particular was a very fertile ground for this type of research given the huge number of events that it provided (e.g. Kumar et al. 2002, Meznar et al. 1998, Teoh et al. 1999). Once again, a sample of this broad body of empirical research has been subjected to a meta-analysis (Frooman 1997). In particular, Frooman considered event studies looking at acts of grave social irresponsibility or illegal behaviour. Quantitatively speaking, Frooman's analysis reinforced Orlitzky et al.'s conclusion by indicating that socially irresponsible behaviour appears to be negatively correlated with investment performance.

The second broad methodological category in the RI business case literature considers the financial performance of a vast array of responsible investments relative to the financial performance of appropriate 'irresponsible' benchmarks. Vance's paper in 1975 is one of the earliest examples of this approach but over the years methods have become increasingly robust and sophisticated. In recent years this avenue of research has been notably championed by Bauer and various collaborators (e.g. Derwell et al. 2005, Bauer et al. 2005, 2006, 2007). To my knowledge, no formal meta-analysis of this literature has been conducted to date. This is perhaps convenient since it draws attention to a more *qualitative* interpretation of the literature than that contained in the meta-analyses. From this perspective, what is perhaps most striking about this body of studies is that there are studies which indicate the full range of relative financial performance: out-performance (Derwall et al. 2005), under-performance (Girard et al. 2007) and no performance difference (Viviers et al. 2008b). And there are many studies that show combinations of these depending on the ESG issues under consideration (Bauer et al. 2005). This might suggest an alternative conclusion than that proposed by Orlitzky et al. as: 'sometimes there is an either / or trade-off in terms of CSP and CFP choices and sometimes there isn't.'

However, when advocating something, a 'yes' inevitably speaks louder than a 'maybe sometimes' and hence the more quantitative conclusion of a statistical business case as suggested in the meta-analyses has attracted more attention amongst advocates than the qualitative interpretation. And of course the quantitative conclusion was very convenient since it implied that the mainstream fiduciary paradigm based on *Rational Man* no longer had to be questioned in order to promote RI. Furthermore, the general findings suggested by the meta-analyses could be 'sexed-up' in text and discourse emphasizing how RI facilitated maximizing returns, while the more qualitative interpretation could be downplayed or ignored.

A fine example of this is the 'Show Me The Money' report compiled by the UNEP Finance Initiative Asset Management Working Group (UNEP FI 2006). Throwing aside the philosophical shackles of deductive logic, this report set out to achieve the 'simple objective: to unequivocally link ESG issues to financial value in such a manner that the mainstream value-driven investor can no longer disregard or dismiss them as irrelevant to investment performance' (UNEP FI: 8). And indeed the report concluded unequivocally that 'ESG issues are material' (UNEP FI: 11). End of story – the business case for *considering* ESG issues was declared!

This type of declaration paved the way for a profoundly new spirit of RI. Some have suggested that this is true 'responsible' investment (Eurosif 2008) and that everything that came before was ethical investment, or socially responsible investment or something else. Richardson (2009) has called this 'business case SRI'; Van Braeckel and Bontemps (2005/2006) called it 'materiality SRI'; and Viviers et al. (2008a) characterized it as 'ethical egoist responsible investment'. Whatever it might be called the basic result was that the ethical essence of earlier forms of RI was sold out (Richardson 2009) in favour of a completely egoist form. In this mainstream-able form of RI, ESG issues could be *considered* only in so far as they might be financially material and no further. There was no room in this for constraining individual greed and as such there was no conflict with the *Rational Man* fiduciary paradigm.

That the PRI were framed according to this philosophy of RI is fairly obvious from the rhetoric found on their public web site. As a starting point, they affirm the declaration that 'environmental, social and corporate governance (ESG) issues can affect investment performance' (PRI 2009b). On the basis of this they argue that 'the appropriate consideration of these issues [ESG issues] is part of delivering superior risk-adjusted returns' (PRI 2009b). Thus, the 'overall goal' of the PRI is: 'to help investors integrate a consideration of environmental, social and governance (ESG) issues into investment decision-making and ownership practices, and thereby improve long-term returns to beneficiaries.' (PRI 2009b). This then goes some way to explaining the meteoric uptake of the PRI within the investment mainstream.

But through the discursive fog associated with this mainstreaming success, a nagging question remains: if 'ESG issues are material' (UNEP FI 2006: 11); and if markets are at least a little bit efficient; and if participants in these markets are at least reasonably well described by the *Rational Man* abstraction; then why has it taken hundreds, if not thousands of years to make any real progress in mainstreaming RI behaviour?

The Materiality of ESG Issues

I submit that the answer to this question can be found by looking more closely at this thing which has become known as 'the materiality of ESG issues'. In much of the popular discourse on RI, 'the materiality of ESG issues' has taken on a singular characteristic as if ESG issues are a collection of items with different names, but a homogeneous pattern of materiality. This is a hopelessly inadequate assessment of the materiality of ESG issues.

To illustrate the inadequacy of this homogenized view of materiality it is useful to visualise a most basic range of logical materiality possibilities in a simple matrix (Fig. 2.1). The starting point for this simple representation of some possible *materialities* of ESG issues is the assumption that ESG issues are morally loaded. In other words, armed with a *consideration* of an issue, the investor is faced with a choice to respond through of their investment actions (whether they involve engagement or trading) in a responsible/moral way or an irresponsible/immoral way.[3] The responsible or moral path would lead to some sort of societal (or collective) good, while

---

[3]This is an extreme simplification of the realm of possibility but is still sufficient to illustrate the inadequacy of the homogenized view of the materiality of ESG issues. Adding complexity only reinforces the conclusion.

	Improved return	No effect	Reduced return
Responsible/Moral	a	b	c
Irresponsible/Immoral	d	e	f

Fig. 2.1 Some possible materialities of ESG issues

the irresponsible or immoral path would lead to some sort of societal (or collective) bad. The fact that I explicitly assume that ESG issues are *considered* removes the possibility of an amoral position on the matrix.

The investment actions taken in response to this consideration of the ESG issues (whether they involve engagement or trading) can theoretically affect the financial return that the investor receives in one of three ways. The first is that whatever investment action is taken may lead to an improved risk adjusted return. The second is that the investment action may lead to reduced risk adjusted return. Finally, despite the declaration that 'ESG issues are financially material' (UNEP FI: 11), it is entirely possible that the investment action may have absolutely no effect on the risk adjusted return.

This very simple dissection of some of the more obvious realms of possibility with respect to the materialities of ESG issues should hit a proverbial panic button when taken together with the shift in terms of ethical posture that has been so instrumental in helping to render RI mainstream-able (Richardson 2009, Swart et al. 2009, Viviers et al. 2008a). Of the six quadrants, only four ('a', 'b', 'e' and 'f') will lead to business case 'responsible investors' choosing the responsible option. Quadrant 'a' is the classic win-win scenario in which being responsible yields improved return. Howarth et al. (2000) for instance describe notable corporate cost savings associated with the certain energy efficiency initiatives in the U.S.[4] Quadrant 'f', is the corollary to this where being irresponsible results in financial penalties. Many such examples are contained in the Frooman (1997) meta-analysis. In quadrants 'b' and 'e' (LaPlante and LaNoie 1994), the business case 'responsible investor' is likely to kick him or herself for paying the inevitable costs associated with considering the issue, but having already invested in this consideration, there is no logical reason to choose the irresponsible path other than sheer spite.

This leaves two quadrants ('c' and 'd') in which a consideration of the ESG issue would theoretically lead the business case 'responsible investor' to rationally choose the irresponsible option. Worse still, investment fiduciaries would theoretically be *forced* to choose the irresponsible option under the prevailing *Rational Man* fiduciary paradigm. But do these logical possibilities actually exist in the real world? Very superficially, the answer is yes. Certain instances of pre-mainstream RI may have been examples of type 'c' while the vice funds of today can be regarded

---

[4]It is actually quite remarkable how difficult it is to find descriptions of single issue win – win situations other than the anecdotal kind of thing that finds its way into 'popular' CSR books. Generally the literature has focused on aggregate ratings/evaluations. Quadrant 'f' is much more commonly dealt with.

as illustrations of the validity of type 'd'. However, advocates of business case RI such as the PRI have in effect argued that neither 'c' nor 'd' exist, asserting that considering ESG issues '*will* contribute to improved corporate performance on environmental, social and governance issues'(PRI 2009b).[5] The implication is that considering ESG issues with a view to delivering maximum returns will deliver social responsibility. Two theoretical avenues of thought, namely long-termism (UN PRI 2009b) and universal ownership (Hawley et al. 2006), have commonly been invoked to lend support to this assertion.

Long-termism simply presents that over time, market failures will inevitably correct themselves such that excess returns gained from irresponsible investment in the short-term will be paid for in the future. Of course the time value of money and associated discounting of future spending pose something of a challenge to this argument.[6] Furthermore, in the modern investment context, a 20 year investment period is simply a series of 7300 odd investment days. Cynically speaking, it is entirely conceivable that through clever engagement and trading based on an '*appropriate consideration*' (PRI 2009b) of ESG issues, an investor could make short-term irresponsible returns, and then offload the asset onto an unsuspecting sucker[7] to pick up the future costs. And of course, in the case of investment fiduciaries, it would be their fiduciary duty to ensure that this took place.

Universal ownership is the idea that many investors (particularly large institutional ones) do not own little bits of the economy, but rather own a piece of the whole economy. The theoretical implication is that externalizing costs from one part of the portfolio onto the wider economy will be paid for elsewhere in the portfolio. However, the ideas of totally passive universal ownership and taking the trouble to consider ESG issues are somewhat difficult to reconcile with the egoist imperative of maximizing risk adjusted returns. If an egoist universal owner was going to go to the trouble and inevitable expense of considering ESG issues, then they would want to see a return on this effort. And a universal owner fiduciary would need to have a very good reason to believe that they would see such a return. One almost inevitable way in which they might try to realise this return would be to put the insight gained from the analytics effort to use in terms of the way investments in the portfolio were weighted. Combined with an appropriate engagement strategy, this could again result in maximizing irresponsible returns, while the broader economic costs are disproportionately picked up by other suckers in the economy. Perhaps we too easily assume RI escapes the pattern of suckers in the economy picking up the costs. In the next section I submit that this pattern amounts to a social dilemma and RI is not void of it.

---

[5]Emphasis added by the author.

[6]Darren Lee, Personal communication

[7]Of course this does imply some level of market inefficiency. Financial crises support the validity of this assumption.

RI and Social Dilemmas

Both long-termism and universal ownership are therefore susceptible to critique based on the existence of suckers in the economy, and therefore do not necessarily preclude the existence of quadrants 'c' and 'd' in Fig. 2.1. The existence of suckers in the economy points to the well documented class of societal issues known as social dilemmas as characterized by Kollock (1998). The transfer of the costs of being irresponsible from ESG savvy investors onto suckers could take the shape of one-to-one transfers in which case they would be referred to as 2-person dilemmas. Alternatively they could take the shape of one-to-many or many-to-many transfers in which case they would be referred to as N-person dilemmas. But all social dilemmas arise out of the fact that humans are a social species. This gives rise to a 'collective rationality', which in turn creates the possibility that individual rationality could be at odds with collective rationality (Kollock 1998). Or to frame this in the context of investment, it gives rise to the possibility that maximizing risk adjusted returns might require the investor or their fiduciary making choices that lead to the reduction of collective good (i.e. irresponsible or immoral choices). Social dilemmas then are the stuff of quadrants 'c' and 'd' in Fig. 2.1.

Crucially, social dilemmas (particularly N-person dilemmas) include many if not all of the most challenging sustainability problems that we face as a species (Kollock 1998). Examples include over-exploitation of environmental resources, economic inequality, and the erosion of public welfare systems. As already noted in the introduction, the turmoil that characterized global economic systems and financial markets starting in 2007 can be interpreted as emerging out of an inappropriately resolved social dilemma. Indeed, this is an example of a type of N-person dilemma that Kollock (1998) calls 'public good dilemmas'. In this example of a public good would be stable economic and financial systems. The root cause of the damage that was done to this public good was highly profitable to a select group of individuals prior to the bursting of the bubble. The huge cost of fixing the damage will however be borne by present and indeed future generations of taxpayers in general whether they benefited or not.

Other than the financial crisis, probably the most spoken about societal problem of our time, climate change also bears all of the trademarks of a public good social dilemma. Here, the public good is the climate from which all humans derive utility. However, the general consensus now holds that we are at a stage where preserving the public good is likely to require significant spending. Figuring out who individually is going to do this spending has to date proved somewhat difficult. Collective rationality says that we should all be flocking to pay whatever we can afford to protect the public good. Individual rationality says: 'let someone else pay'. The other commonly noted type of N-person dilemma is the 'tragedy of the commons' made famous by Hardin in his 1968 paper in the journal Science. Tragedy of the commons dilemmas differ from public good dilemmas in that they are characterized by 'subtractability' of the benefits. In other words, once someone uses the common good no-one else can. The classic example of this is the overexploitation of fisheries (Gordon 1954, Scott 1955). Such sustainability issues are the subject of RI initiatives.

Given the grave importance of many of the challenges associated with social dilemmas, and perhaps even more alluring, the apparent intractability inherent in any dilemma, it is hardly surprising that they have attracted the attention of academics as far back as the ancient Greeks (see Dawes 1980 and Kollock 1998 for reviews). Besides characterising them, the key academic consideration has been how to deal with them (Crowe 1969, Feeny et al. 1990, Hardin 1968, Ostrom 1999). Kollock (1998) provides a very comprehensive review of much of this research. He groups possible solutions discussed in the literature into three categories: (a) 'motivational solutions' which rely on the possibility that humans are not entirely egoist in nature; (b) 'strategic solutions' which rely on the ability of participants in dilemmas to collaborate in shaping the outcomes of the dilemmas; and (c) 'structural solutions' which involve changing the rules.

It is useful to consider each of these in a bit more detail, specifically in relation to the evolving practice of RI. As already noted, motivational solutions rely on the possibility that humans are capable of much a richer range of behaviour than that permitted by the *Rational Man* model. Within the investment context, the pre-mainstreaming RI was a perfect example of attempts at this type of solution. According to Kollock (1998) common conditions for such solutions to emerge and be successful include: specific social value orientations which permit collective rationality; strong group identity; and good communication. Given these, it is hardly surprising that over the years much of this type of RI activity was associated with various religious institutions. However, as I have already discussed at length, within the general investment setting, participation in this form of dilemma solution has generally been limited. And given the problems of market elasticity and 'lunatic fringe' minority voice, this has in turn rendered the efficacy of such solutions somewhat questionable. Unfortunately, the probability of limited efficacy has been shown to be a major barrier to the successful pursuance of any dilemma solution (Kollock 1998). Simply put, when you are pursuing some sort of collective good and you have just about no hope of achieving your purpose, your motivation is likely to wane, especially if this involves making personal sacrifices.

The second possibility for resolving social dilemmas is the cluster of solutions that Kollock (1998) calls 'strategic solutions'. In these, despite an assumed egoist character, participants in the dilemma nonetheless get it together and convince each other to behave in a manner that yields collective good. Such solutions apparently work best in dilemmas involving relatively small or intimate groups of participants (preferably 2-person dilemmas) who interact over a reasonably long time period in a transparent manner. These conditions are necessary because strategic solutions only work when participants are able to actually shape the outcome. Clearly, none of these conditions are particularly well met by the prevailing character of the investment world. In this world, there are huge numbers of participants who trade and engage, in and out of assets (and thus dilemmas) relatively quickly, and in a manner that is to all intents and purposes anonymous.

Arguably the most commonly advanced solutions to social dilemmas come from the category of solutions which Kollock (1998) terms 'structural solutions'. These change the rules of the game in such a manner that the individual and collective rationalities become aligned. Frequently, they involve invoking a Hobbesian Leviathan (Newey 2008) with 'external' top-down regulation, the classic formulation being to get governments to fix market failures (Mackenzie 2006). Certainly, structural changes could be envisioned in regards to fiduciary responsibilities. These could include steps to remove any legal constraints to behaving ethically associated with the *Rational Man* paradigm or somewhat more adventurous steps that might insist that investment fiduciaries behave ethically. This is the central argument of the campaign championed by Richardson (2007, 2008, 2009) in particular. And from comments contained in the follow up to the Freshfields Report commonly known as Fiduciary II (UNEP FI 2009) it would appear that this idea might be gaining some traction amongst law makers in at least one jurisdiction, the United Kingdom. But problems exist with such governmental 'structural solutions' (Kollock 1998, Ostrom 1999). Besides the obvious practical problems associated with monitoring or policing, there is also the important fact that many of the most pressing social dilemmas today play out on a global stage. And we simply do not as yet have anything nearing an effective global governance institution.

Conclusion

Which all brings me to a rather gloomy close to this chapter. In it I have traced how steps taken to give RI the *financial capacity* that it would need to have any significant influence, may ironically have leached it of much of the *ethical capacity* required to capitalize on this influence. I have argued that, the basic reason for this is that, in order to achieve mainstream-ability, we appear to have opted for accepting a *Rational Man* fiduciary paradigm as a basis for the practice of RI. Unfortunately this is precisely the greed-based paradigm that lies at the heart of socially malignant behaviour associated with the class of societal problems known as social dilemmas. And these problems are neither trivial nor obscure. On the contrary. Indeed, at least two of the most pressing contemporary societal problems at the time of writing this chapter (the global financial turmoil and climate change) are both examples. So, having fooled ourselves once (again?) we might well ask ourselves whether we should consider rolling back the changes? But clearly if all else stayed the same, this would simply result in the loss of the financial capacity gained. The challenge then is to somehow retain the gains made in terms of financial clout, and at the same time restore the ethical capacity. At the very least this will require a new fiduciary paradigm.

Acknwoledgement Writing this chapter was funded by Noah Financial Innovation. Many of the ideas presented here have emerged out of conversations with my colleagues Rene Swart and Kathleen van der Linde, as well as members of the advisory council of the Noah Chair in Responsible Investment: Deon Botha, Malcolm Gray, Julie Kotton, Corli le Roux, Raymond Ndlovu, John Oliphant, Victoria Ryan, Kevin Swart, and Christina Wood

References

Bauer, Rob, Jerome Derwall, and Rogér Otten. 2007. The ethical mutual funds performance debate: new evidence for Canada. Journal of Business Ethics 70: 111–124.

Bauer, Rob, Kees Koedijk, and Rogér Otten. 2005. International evidence on ethical mutual fund performance and investment style. Journal of Banking and Finance 29: 1751–1767.

Bauer, Rob, Rogér Otten, and Alireza T. Rad. 2006. Ethical investing in Australia: is there a financial penalty? Pacific-Basin Financial Journal 14: 33–48.

Bengtsson, Elias. 2008. A history of Scandinavian socially responsible investing. Journal of Business Ethics 82: 969–983.

Crowe, Beryl L. 1969. The tragedy of the commons revisited. Science 166(3909): 1103–1107.

Dawes, Robyn M. 1980. Social dilemmas. Annual Review of Psychology 31: 169–193.

Derwall, Jerome, Nadja Guenster, Rob Bauer, and Kees Koedijk. 2005. The eco-efficiency premium puzzle. Financial Analyst Journal 61: 51–63.

Dierksmeier, Claus and Michael Pirson. 2009. Oikonomia versus Chrematistike: Learning from Aristotle about the future orientation of business management. Journal of Business Ethics 88: 417–430.

Eccles, Neil S. 2008. Some lessons from South Africa's past. PRI Academic Network Conference. 17–19 September 2008. Maastricht.

Eccles, Neil S., Phillip Walker, Steve Nicholls, Graham Sinclair, and Derick de Jongh. 2007. The state of responsible investment in South Africa. Geneva: UNEP FI.

Eurosif. 2008. European SRI study. Paris: Eurosif.

Feeny, David, Fikret Berkes, Bonnie J. McCay, and James M. Acheson. 1990. The tragedy of the commons: twenty-two years later. Human Ecology 18: 1–19.

Freshfields Bruckhaus Deringer. 2005. A legal framework for the integration of environmental. Social and Governance Issues into Institutional Investment. Geneva: UNEP FI.

Frooman, Jeff. 1997. Socially irresponsible and illegal behavior and shareholder wealth: a meta-analysis of event studies. Business and Society 36: 221–249.

Girard, Eric, Hamid Rahman, and Brett Stone. 2007. Socially responsible investments: goody-two-shoes or bad to the bone? Journal of Investing 16: 96–110.

Gordon, H. Scott. 1954. The economic theory of common-property resources: the fishery. The Journal of Political Economy 62: 124–142.

Hawley, Jim P. and Andrew T. Williams. 2006. The universal owner's role in sustainable economic development. In Responsible Investment, ed. Rory Sullivan and Craig Mackenzie, 216–225. Sheffield: Greenleaf Publishing.

Hardin, Garrett. 1968. The tragedy of the commons. Science 162: 1243–1248.

Howarth, Richard B., Brent M. Haddad and Bruce Paton. 2000. The economics of energy efficiency: Insights from voluntary participation programs. Energy Policy 28: 477–486.

Kollock, Peter. 1998. Social dilemmas: the anatomy of cooperation. Annual Review of Sociology 24: 183–214.

Kumar, Raman, William N. Lamb, and Richard E. Wokutch. 2002. The end of South African sanctions, institutional ownership, and the stock price performance of boycotted firms: Evidence on the impact of social-ethical investing. Business and Society 41: 133–165.

LaPlante, Benoît and Paul Lanoie. 1994. The market response to environmental incidents in Canada: a theoretical and empirical analysis. Southern Economic Journal 60: 657–672.

Mackenzie, Craig. 2006. The scope for investor action on corporate social and environmental impacts. In Responsible Investment, ed. Rory Sullivan and Craig Mackenzie, 20–38. Sheffield: Greenleaf Publishing.

Meznar, Martin B., Douglas Nigh, and Chuck C.Y. Kwok. 1998. Announcements of withdrawal from South Africa revisited: making sense of contradictory event study findings. Academy of Management Journal 41: 715–730.

Munnel, Alicia H. and Annika Sunden. 2004. Social investing: pension plans should just say 'No'. http://www.aei.org/docLib/20040604_MunnellSunden.pdf Accessed 27 October 2009.

Newey, Glen. 2008. Hobbes and leviathan. London: Routledge.

Orlitzky, Marc, Frank L. Schmidt, and Sara L. Rynes. 2003. Corporate social and financial performance: a meta-analysis. Organization Studies 24(3): 403–441.

Ostrom, Elinor. 1999. Coping with tragedies of the commons. Annual Review of Political Science 2: 493–535.

PRI. 2009a. Annual Report of the PRI Initiative 2009. http://www.unpri.org/files/PRI%20Annual% 20Report%2009.pdf Accessed 1 September 2009

PRI. 2009b. Frequently asked questions. http://www.unpri.org/faqs/ Accessed 23 July 2009.

Richardson, Benjamin J. 2007. Do the fiduciary duties of pension funds hinder socially responsible investment? Banking and Finance Law Review 22: 145–201.

Richardson, Benjamin J. 2008. Socially responsible investment law: regulating the unseen polluters. Oxford: Oxford University Press.

Richardson, Benjamin J. 2009. Keeping ethical investment ethical: regulatory issues for investing for sustainability. Journal of Business Ethics 87: 555–572.

Rivoli, Pietra. 2003. Making a difference or making a statement? Finance research and socially responsible investment. Business Ethics Quarterly 13: 271–287.

Schueth, Steve. 2003. Socially responsible investing in the United States. Journal of Business Ethics 43: 189–194.

Scott, Anthony. 1955. The fishery: the objectives of sole ownership. The Journal of Political Economy 63: 116-124.

Sen, Amartya. 1977. Rational fools. Philosophy and Public Affairs 6: 317–344.

Sparkes, Russell. 2001. Ethical investment: whose ethics, which investment? Business Ethics: A European Review 10: 194–205.

Sparkes, Russell. 2006. A historical perspective on the growth of socially responsible investment. In Responsible Investment, eds. Rory Sullivan and Craig Mackenzie, 39–54. Sheffield: Greenleaf Publishing.

Swart, Rene, Neil S. Eccles and Kathleen van der Linde. 2009. The fiduciary responsibility of asset consultants and its influence on the practice of responsible investment in the South African pension fund industry. PRI Academic Network Conference, 1–3 October 2009, Ottawa.

Teoh, Siew H., Christopher P. Wazzan and Ivo Welch. 1999. The effect of socially activist investment policies on the financial markets: evidence from the South African boycott. Journal of Business 72: 35–89.

UN Press Release. 2006. United Nations Secretary-General Launches 'Principles for responsible investment' backed by World's Largest Investors. http://www.unpri.org/files/20060427_press/ un-unepfi-gc_press_20060427.pdf Accessed 9 October 2009.

UNEP FI. 2006. Show me the money: Linking environmental social and governance issues to company value. Geneva: UNEP FI.

UNEP FI. 2009. Fiduciary responsibility. Legal and practical aspects of integrating environmental, social and governance issues into institutional investment. Geneva: UNEP FI.

Van Braeckel, Dirk and Marc Bontemps. 2005/2006 Winter. SRI: the 'Materiality approach' versus the 'Sustainability approach'. Finance and the Common Good, 13–14.

Vance, Stanley C. 1975. Are socially responsible corporations good investment risks? Management review 64: 18–24.

Viederman, Stephen. 2008. Fiduciary duty. In Sustainable Investing. The Art of Long-Term Performance, eds. Cary Krosinsky and Nick Robins. London: Earthscan.

Viviers, S., J.K. Bosch, E. v.d.M. Smit and A. Buijs. 2008a. Is responsible investing ethical? South African Journal of Business Management 39: 15–25.

Viviers, S., J.K. Bosch, E. v.d.M. Smit and A. Buijs. 2008b. The risk-adjusted performance of responsible investment funds in South Africa. Investment Analysts Journal 68: 39–55.

Wesley, John. 1760. The Use of Money (http://www.jesus.org.uk/vault/library/wesley_use_of_ money.pdf Accessed 9 October 2009.

Welker, Marina and David Wood. 2009. Investor activism and the iron cage of the business case. PRI Academic Network Conference, 1–3 October 2009, Ottawa.

Wishloff, Jim. 2009. The land of realism and the shipwreck of idea-ism: Thomas Aquinas and Milton Friedman on social responsibilities of business. Journal of Business Ethics 85: 137–155.

Zadek, Simon, Mira Merme, and Richard Samans. 2005. Mainstreaming Responsible Investment. Geneva: World Economic Forum.

Chapter 3
The Legitimacy of ESG Standards as an Analytical Framework for Responsible Investment

Tim Cadman

Introduction

It has become fashionable in both the scholarly and corporate worlds to lay claim to being the first to have predicted the global financial crisis (GFC) of 2008. As the cliché goes, hindsight is a wonderful thing, and given this analysis it would seem axiomatic that commentators would identify the poor governance of international and domestic financial institutions as a leverage point for reform. And indeed they did – in 1999. In commenting on the lessons to be learned from the Asian financial crisis Jeffrey Garten, Dean of the Yale School of Management at the time, delineated a scenario virtually identical to the GFC, in which lenders and investors in an inherently unstable and overstretched financial system failed to read the signs, deluded themselves about the nature of the markets they were involved in, and fled at the first indication that the good times were over (Garten 1999). This led him to conclude that better governance of financial institutions and corporations was a solution that would help mitigate the next crisis. Yet 10 years later, analysts are still calling for global governance reform, and have extended their criticisms to include intergovernmental processes, which they consider to have lost their legitimacy (Bradford and Linn 2009).

Can any governance-related lessons be learned from the GFC and are there any parallels to be drawn with the rapidly expanding global 'responsible' investment (RI) market? In the case of the former, a huge range of complex and competitive products led investors to rely on entrepreneurs to attest to the legitimacy of the schemes in question, such as brokers, analysts and credit rating agencies (CRAs). In the case of RI, there are also varied and competing products in the market place, about which it is claimed, the consumer can rest assured, since there are 'disclosure' mechanisms, backed up by implementation consultants, and rating agencies. But it is incorrect to assume that the current practice of RI covers all its bases, as its focus is

T. Cadman (✉)
Faculty of Business, School of Accounting, Economic and Finance, University of Southern Queensland, Toowoomba, QLD, Australia
e-mail: tim.cadman@usq.edu.au

W. Vandekerckhove et al. (eds.), *Responsible Investment in Times of Turmoil*,
Issues in Business Ethics 31, DOI 10.1007/978-90-481-9319-6_3,
© Springer Science+Business Media B.V. 2011

on a very limited set of indicators, which are unable to demonstrate ethical corporate governance across the board. Even if it is accepted that RI addresses a limited set of corporate governance issues, there are problems in this regard too, since there is no consistent, universal agreement over what aspects of performance a company should be disclosing, or what exactly constitutes accountability, and so forth.

Following recent developments in contemporary governance theory and practice, this chapter argues from a social constructivist viewpoint that responsible invest-ment needs to be understood in inter-subjective terms, whereby the institutions within which social identities and interests operate are interactively constituted by means of collective intentionality (Barnett 2007, Ruggie 1998). Translated into more plain English terms, RI reflects the trends found across the field of sustainable devel-opment whereby non-government organizations (NGOs), stakeholders and other market-based actors are interacting within systems that have a wider focus than traditional 'top-down' institutions, and in which all actors play a role in institutional development. In the case of RI, maximising shareholder returns is supplemented by broader concerns about environmental-social governance (ESG) in financial prac-tice (Hawley and Williams 2005). Once it is accepted that the RI community is made up of a wide range of participants, from shareholders and other 'internal' interests to 'external' groups in civil society, and that these actors both shape and share ideas about investment, it becomes necessary to re-cast the governance frame-works through which claims about the legitimacy of RI are evaluated. On this view, the concept of 'universal ownership' is extended beyond large institutional investors to include interests traditionally seen as peripheral to business practice. By under-standing RI as being founded on stakeholder engagement in the broadest possible sense, fiduciary duty can be measured in terms of the levels of interaction and col-laboration in the development of environmental, social or economic outcomes. This allows for a less functionalist and less utilitarian – and in that sense a more ethical – model of governance quality.

This chapter investigates the changing identity of contemporary global gover-nance, most notably through the contribution of sustainable development and looks at how this has come to be reflected in the financial, and RI sector in particular. Given the ever-expanding range of RI products and the confusion and lack of con-sistency across the sector, it justifies the use of a governance quality framework to evaluate institutional performance and legitimacy. It argues that focussing on single aspects of governance, notably accountability and transparency, is an incomplete project, and presents an agenda for reform built upon a set of principles, criteria and indicators (PC&I) for evaluating institutional behaviour as a whole.

Contemporary Governance

Governance, understood as a mechanism for steering or coordinating policy making and implementation, has moved away from top-down, command/control admin-istrative models and is now typified by the social-political, and collaborative, nature of the interactions occurring within them (Kooiman 1993b, 2000). As a result, there has been an ongoing evolution towards the more abstract concepts of governance, based on the 'dynamic interplay between civil society, business and public sector' (Ruggie 2003). These new systems now sit alongside traditional, more legalistic, mechanisms (Fiorino 1999) and are exemplified by a range of new policy instruments, including voluntary agreements, management systems and market-based instruments such as emissions trading (Jordan et al. 2005). This development has been interpreted as being closely related to economic globalisation (Falkner 2003).

The environmental policy domain provides one of the best spaces available to study the emergence of new modes of governance that have arisen in response to globalisation (Arts 2006). This is because it is in the environment sector that some of the most extensive and innovative experiments in 'new' governance are to be found (Glück et al. 2005). What is occurring in this domain contains theoretically interesting reactions to some of the larger political and economic trends associated with globalisation and governance. It consequently provides one of the most useful lenses through which to scrutinise 'the increasing tendency for collaboration in many sectors where political and economic trade-offs also exist' (Overdevest 2004) and provides one of the best study areas for the involvement of civil society, private industry, and the state in the development of regulatory regimes (Mackendrick 2005).

Global governance provides for international collaboration and co-ordination in a system, which feeds into the macro (national), meso (programmatic) and micro (organisational) levels (Aguirre 2008, Bouckaert and Halligan 2008). Contemporary governance consequently shows a preference for interaction between decentralised networks made up of multiple actors functioning at multi-levels; environmental governance articulates this trend especially strongly (Haas 2001, Glück et al. 2005). Although 'governance without government' (Rosenau and Czempiel 1992) may still be some way off the 'government to governance transition' is well underway (Scholte 2008). Corporate and civic – primarily NGO driven – initiatives have especially contributed to the growth of a form of global governance consisting of 'mechanisms to reach collective decisions about transnational problems with or without government participation' (Haufler 2001).

The participation of non-state interests, economic, environmental and social, in global governance can be largely attributed to the United Nations Conference on Environment and development (UNCED), where business and NGOs in particular were active in shaping the agenda and outcomes (Birnie 2000). *Agenda 21*, the primary output of UNCED identified non-governmental interests as vital to participatory democracy, whilst simultaneously encouraging business to use the free market as a means for participation in sustainable development (UN 1993). Since UNCED, sustainable development has been implemented through a range of UN processes. These include the Commission for Sustainable Development (1992) and conventions on biodiversity (1992), climate change (1994), and desertification (1996). Since Rio, the UN has continued to promote sustainable development through a range of initiatives, including the Global Compact (2000). Other events of significance include the Millennium Summit (2001) and the World Conference on Sustainable Development (2002).

The phenomenon of collaboration and co-ordination is also evident in developments within *corporate* governance. In 1999, the World Bank and the Organization for Economic Co-operation and Development (OECD) co-founded the Global Corporate Governance Forum (GCGF) as a facility of the International Finance Corporation (IFC). The aim of the Forum is to encourage companies to invest, and behave, in a socially responsible manner (GCGF 2010). Ten years on, the proliferation of 'new' governance into corporate governance practice is visible, and it is now possible to speak of 'new corporate governance', which reflects the norms of contemporary governance theory including an orientation around such socially-oriented values as learning, consensus and trust (Hilb 2009). As companies become more global, they are increasingly reliant on non-state actors, who often have very different objectives from state agents. The capacity of these actors to work as change agents has necessitated their incorporation within some of the established institutions affecting the development of corporate governance. The World Bank through its Global Partnerships Programme, for example, now funds civil society interests (largely NGOs) to promote good governance by playing a watchdog role. The Bank estimates that this initiative has resulted in cost savings of USD $100 million by increasing transparency and avoiding corruption (World Bank 2006). Analysing the role of these interests is therefore essential in understanding the emergence of any future global corporate governance regime (Detomasi 2006). Governments have not been sidelined, however. In the light of the GFC, the state is again beginning to play a more interventionist role in global finance, but the observation nevertheless remains valid.

Responsible Investment and Environmental and Social Governance

The concept of 'ethical investment' has been around for some years, but became increasingly popular in the 1990s (Knowles 1997). The norm-building role of the United Nations Environment Programme Finance Initiative (UNEP FI) cannot be understated. UNEP FI is a typical institutional exemplar of a (global) public-private partnership (PPP), following the network model of new governance practice (UNEP FI 2009a), and consists of representatives from both the private financial sector and United Nations Environment Programme staff, governed by a joint steering committee. In 2003 its two main initiatives, relating to financial institutions and the insurance industry were combined to reflect the already existing collaboration between the two projects (UNEP FI 2009b). The mission of the programme is to 'identify, promote, and realise the adoption of best environmental and sustainability practice at all levels of financial institution operations' (UNEP FI undated). It currently consists of approximately 170 members, including fund managers, banks and insurers (UNEP FI 2009c). Institutions are expected to sign two UNEP statements confirming their commitment to the environment and sustainable development of the financial and insurance industries, and to agree to the recommendations submitted by UNEP to the World Summit for Sustainable Development (WSSD) in 2002. The statements represent 'aspirational voluntary declarations of intent' (UNEP FI 2009d), reflecting the norm of global environmental governance, established at UNCED, for voluntary self-regulated approaches to corporate accountability, responsibility and implementation (Clapp 2005). In 2005 it engaged in a process with the UN Global Compact and investment industry representatives to develop a set of principles for responsible investment (PRI) (Global Compact and UNEP FI 2009a). By 2007, 200 investment organisations from 25 countries had committed to the PRI, managing assets approaching USD 10 trillion (UNEP FI and UN Global Compact 2007).

The PRI initiative is aimed at integrating environmental and social governance (ESG) issues into the financial sub-sectors of asset owners, investment managers and professional service partners (Global Compact and UNEP FI 2009b). These cover elements required for reporting on environmental and social performance, referred to as sustainability reporting (UNEP FI 2009e). These reporting elements were identified and developed between 2003 and 2005 in collaboration with the Global Reporting Initiative (GRI), and building on the 2002 social performance indicators of SPI Finance. A working group was established, consisting of 11 financial institutions including the National Australia Bank and Bank of China, and eight 'stakeholder groups' including the Corporate Citizens Centre, Friends of the Earth and The Wilderness Society of Australia, which ran between 2006 and 2008 to pilot and review a draft version (UNEP FI 2009f).[1] The output, the *GRI Financial Services Sector Supplement*, it was envisaged, would 'become the sustainability reporting standard for the financial sector' (UNEP FI 2009g).

This supplement situates the notion of sustainability reporting against a background of 'transparency about economic, environmental and social impacts [as] a fundamental component in effective stakeholder relations, investment decisions, and other market relations' (GRI 2008: 6). Economic reporting concerns financial performance, market presence, indirect economic impacts, and investment in the community. Environmental reporting concerns a number of elements, including materials, energy, water, biodiversity, emissions, compliance and transport. Social reporting covers four sub-themes: labour and work practices, human rights, society, and product responsibility. Each of these activities is reported against a series of performance indicators (GRI 2008). By 2008 almost 25% of the Standard and Poor (S&P) 500 companies, and approximately 1,500 in total were using the GRI framework for the purposes of GRI reporting (Waddock 2008).

---

[1] It should be noted here that not all participants were particularly enthusiastic about the legitimacy of this working group. Two representatives from one national (Australian) environmental NGO questioned its credibility, one of whom dismissed its consultation processes as 'a classical example of tokenism', which had sought their views on sustainability, whilst permitting its members to continue destroying the environment as part of their daily corporate activities (personal interview conducted 23/09/09).

However, it is wrong to assume that RI, as normatively embedded within UNEP FI as it may appear, is a monolithic, or consistent, entity. It is governed by a plethora of initiatives that have arisen in the absence of any formal global corporate governance system. According to Waddock, there are a variety of institutions and assessment programmes, using a range of models to determine corporate social and environmental sustainability. These cover the gamut of institutional types, from state/government to market/economic and civil society. Certainly the UN-based models are significant, and omnipresent, including the PRI, but there are other significant initiatives, including a direct competitor, the Equator Principles, which functions as a system for benchmarking environmental and social issues in the determination, assessment and management of project financing. Such programmes then begin to blend into the less directly finance oriented, corporate social responsibility (CSR) schemes, such as the Private Voluntary Organization Standards, the Global Sullivan Principles, the OECD Guidelines for Multinational Enterprises and the International Non-Governmental Organizations Accountability Charter – to name but a few. There are also the International Standardisation Organisation's (ISO) 26000 series for corporate responsibility, Social Accountability International (SAI) SA8000 standards, and the AccountAbility AA 1000 series of standards. This vast array of schemes has resulted in a growing consulting industry to assist with implementation. These too vary in organisational type, and are located in both the business and non-profit sectors. There is also a further collection of think tanks, institutions, forums and other associations that seek to lobby, comment, and provide assistance on matters of sustainable development, including investment. There are also watchdogs and other activist organisations that are seeking to raise awareness regarding the activities of corporations, which do not have responsibility standards in place, and are simply engaging in 'greenwashing'. Beyond these again are the journals and magazines that cover the issues surrounding responsible investment and other initiatives; finally there are the ranking and rating agencies. The fact that there are now so many players and conflicting standards on the scene is resulting in confusion. There is clearly a need for some level of consolidation, but who will emerge as the dominant player, whether it be the GRI, the Global Compact, some other competitor, or any, is not yet clear (Waddock 2008).

However, this rapidly expanding plethora of competing systems has created confusion amongst governments, citizens and corporations alike, over which programmes to adopt and their associated costs and benefits. Despite the proliferation of such systems, there are no consistent rules or standards to guide them (Whitman 2005). Given their inconsistencies and differences in approach, it is therefore not always possible to determine which schemes offer genuine economic, environmental or social benefits, or merely 'greenwash'. This is problematic, since scholars have voiced wide-ranging criticisms regarding the legitimacy of contemporary global institutions (Dimitrov 2005). Whilst there are a number of organisations such as ISO and the International Social and Environmental Accreditation and Labelling Alliance (ISEAL), which accredit the activities of individual schemes, there are no best practice governance standards across the sustainable development policy domain, against which the performance of competing schemes can be evaluated. In the wake of the GFC, RI should pay greater attention to the governance of sustainable development, particularly given the sector's increasing engagement in emissions trading and 'offset' programmes. Governance standards will help avoid some of the uncertainties that interested parties currently experience regarding the legitimacy of a given system, and whether to lend it unwarranted credibility through their participation.

Emerging Governance Arrangements and Responsible Investment

The term 'governance arrangement' is used to refer to a range of specific mechanisms, influencing the execution of corporate governance (Bebchuk and Hamdai 2009). More broadly it is used to explain 'the interaction between various actors pursuing common goals' (Koenig-Archibugi 2006). Although theorists tend to concentrate on specific arrangements according to the preoccupations of their discipline, there are a number of recurring elements with which they are concerned. These relate primarily to four main issue areas. The foremost without doubt concerns responsible organisational behaviour, usually understood in terms of accountability and transparency. A second and almost equally significant area of concern is around the representation of different stakeholder interests within a given institution. Here the discussion is largely about issues of inclusiveness and equality, and whether all interests have the same economic or technical capacity to participate effectively. A third concern is centred upon decision-making, and the ways in which decisions are reached, and disagreements handled. The fourth major aspect of governance is the manner in which policies, programmes or standards are implemented, or put into practice. These institutional arrangements, identified across the fields of international relations, comparative politics and public administration, have a bearing on governance quality, and they are briefly reviewed here.

Accountability has become a central aspect of the quality of governance debate, since the rise of new actors and new institutions beyond the territorial confines of the nation state has necessitated a reconfiguration of conventional democratic methods of holding institutions to account (Held et al. 1999). Traditional 'vertical' systems of national democratic accountability have been supplemented by 'horizontal' accountability in which the external accountability of decision-makers is to the public at large, and is linked to what appears to be an associated attribute, transparency, expressed in terms of public access to information and decision making procedures (Kerwer 2006). Transparency is effectively a precondition for effective accountability, since it is impossible to hold an institution to account if its regulatory operations are not open to public view (Scholte 2004). There is universal agreement on the significance of accountability and transparency in 'traditional' corporate governance (Garten 1999, Hawley and Williams 2005, Detomasi 2006, Waddock 2008). Their relevance to what Hawley and Williams refer to as 'financial sustainability governance' is considerable, as they are currently the foremost indicators of governance quality, as in such programmes as the GRI.

While accountability and transparency are acknowledged as the place to begin the development of stakeholder relations (UNGC and GCGF 2009) the end point is not yet clear. Beyond the expectation that corporations should be 'accountable, responsible, transparent, and ecologically sustainable' (Waddock 2009) there is less clarity over what other governance arrangements underpin RI. Perhaps the most significant contemporary debate is what constitutes a 'stakeholder'. Here there is a normative expectation in traditional corporate governance that the term is synonymous with 'shareholder'. However, the more the influence of NGOs and other actors increases, the more encompassing the definition becomes. The GCGF and IFC for example identify a very wide range of actors in the constellation of 'multi-stakeholders'. These include local communities and citizens, private organisations, supply chain associates, governments, employees, investors (shareowners and lenders), customers and users, unions, regulatory authorities, and joint venture partners and alliances constitute a corporation's stakeholder base. Whilst the primary accountability of the board of a corporation is to its shareowners, taking a wider view of stakeholders, it is asserted, creates value and wealth for a company, reduces risk, yields opportunities for innovation, and heads emergent problems off at the pass. This sort of collaborative model generates new partnerships between businesses, NGOs and governments, and creates new services and products (GGCF and IFC undated). However, the extent to which the participation of these players in contemporary corporate governance is actually realised is moot, even if interest representation is considered an essential component of contemporary governance (Warren 2002). Interest representation is closely identified with the inclusion or inclusiveness of stakeholders, but it is also recognised as a currently unresolved problem, and a source of considerable institutional variation (Koenig-Archibugi 2006, Stiglitz 2003). Not including specific interests in global financial standards setting processes has been identified as resulting in legitimacy problems (Kerwer 2006). Theorists of democratic governance also argue that legitimacy is normatively expressed by equal participation in decision-making (Young 2000). Shareholders with a limited stake in decision-making cannot instigate changes in corporate laws if they cannot get sufficient proxies, no manner how legitimate their case (Bebchuk and Hamdani 2009). The US Securities Exchange Commission (SEC) has paid some attention this issue, and given the norm-shifting role of US financial regulation, this development is a space to be watched, since it is likely to have an impact on corporate governance standards at the global level (Hawley and Williams 2005).

In addition to inclusiveness and equality, the capacity (or resources) of different stakeholders within a given governance system is also an important indicator of governance quality. Here business is in a more privileged position than other less well-endowed interests (Scholte 2004). If the argument is accepted that multi-stakeholderism in RI has been extended to include public interests in civil society, there may be a need for a company developing a new RI programme to finance some level of external stakeholder involvement. To avoid conflicts of interest this should probably be limited to the provision of travel expenses – for remote stakeholders to attend meetings, for example. More importantly, however, there is a need for RI institutions to provide technical and infrastructural support to less well-endowed stakeholder groups if effective policy is to be created within decision-making processes (Mason 1999).

In terms of decision-making itself, there is general recognition that the exercise of democratic rights is problematic in traditional corporate governance – even if it is accepted that the maxim of profit maximisation means that some controlling interests may be afforded more rights in this regard than others (boards of directors versus external, civic, interests for example). There is considerable debate concerning the mechanics of corporate decision making and whether minority shareholders should be allowed to exercise the right to vote. Boards of directors can at times prohibit this – even when there is a clear case that it could improve corporate governance. Here the argument against broader enfranchisement is that minority interests could aggregate into a majority, overriding the board. In some jurisdictions the inequity of current arrangements has been recognised, and shareholders have been given a 'say on pay'. However, even with these changes, it is still possible for controlling interests to exercise their powers and block resolutions that they do not support (Bebchuk and Hamdani 2009).

When conflict occurs within negotiations, or as a result of complaints over procedure, several sources identify dispute-resolution as an important administrative mechanism in collective action institutions (Ostrom 1990, van Vliet 1993, Meidinger 2006). The inability to resolve conflicts has been identified as a key indicator of governance failure (Stoker 1998). Traditionally, disputes have related largely to matters which impact on shareholders' rights, board activities, and corporate governance although the trend for greater recognition of other interests is occurring here as well. Since judiciary enforcement is weak in many countries, legalistic mechanisms have not always proved effective, and companies have increasingly moved to alternative dispute resolution (ADR) mechanisms. This mediation-based approach has legal standing in some countries, and can help avoid litigation. Mediation is seen as advantageous since it seeks to promote interests over positions, and open discussion above secretive behaviour (Runeson and Guy 2007).

Implementation is widely understood as the process of putting policies and programmes into practice and is an important aspect of any RI scheme. In the domain of environmental policy, effective implementation has been identified as relating to both the behavioural- and problem solving abilities of an institution (Skjærseth et al. 2006). This perspective can be naturally extended to RI, since the very act of investing responsibly demonstrates the intention of shifting current investment behaviour away from unsustainable projects, and towards tackling environmental, social and economic problems. Here market-driven programmes such as carbon finance for example, with its stated intention of reducing overall global emissions through such initiatives as carbon offsetting, or emissions trading spring to mind. Given the inherently dynamic nature of environmentally related investments, such institutional approaches also need to incorporate a degree of flexibility to be resilient in the face of changing external circumstances (such as rising global temperatures). Non-resilient systems on the other hand can be negatively affected by such changes (Folke et al. 2005). The other side to effective implementation is enforcement and compliance. This can occur both via 'soft' instruments, of which RI is clearly an example, and 'hard' law, which inevitably impacts on RI via national financial regulations. However, voluntary codes of conduct are not generally known for their enforcement capacity. Consequently enforcement within the sector will continue to rely on both market forces and prescriptive regulation. (Hawley and Williams 2005).

After more than two decades of discussion about 'new' governance there is a well-articulated understanding in the academic literature about the main elements of contemporary governance such as responsibility, interest representation, decision-making and implementation. But this does not mean that scholars know exactly how all these criteria fit together; nor have companies adopted them comprehensively. Nevertheless, there has been some diffusion of these notions into the RI sector. The problem therefore remains as to how the other arrangements alluded to here can be taken into account when determining institutional performance. Here the application of principles, criteria to the evaluation of an institution's governance, rather than the programmes it implements, can be of value, and this idea is explored in more detail below.

Governance and Institutional Legitimacy

In short, the governance arrangements underpinning RI are still being developed, although it can be seen that global agencies, including UNEP FI, UNGC, GRI, IFC and GCGF are playing an influential role in norm building. The expectation for increased participation that these developments have brought about still pose some major problems for RI governance, both in terms of how to structure institutional responses in ways that effectively deal with the global problems encouraging the move towards responsible investment, but also how newly-enfranchised actors should be included in decision-making processes. Interaction is now occurring in non-spatial systems where multiple interests seek to make decisions whose impacts transcend boundaries so completely that it has become necessary to rethink current arrangements (Rosenau 2000, Arts 2006).

Much of the quality of governance debate revolves around the question of legitimacy, and whence it is derived. Two theories currently dominate. Legitimacy can be 'input oriented', that is, derived from the consent of those being asked to agree to the rules, and concerning such procedural issues as the democratic arrangements underpinning a given system. Legitimacy can also be 'output oriented', i.e. derived from the efficiency of rules, or criteria for 'good' governance and demonstrated by substantive outcomes (Kjaer 2004). Legitimacy can therefore be determined both according to the principles of democracy on the one hand and efficiency and effectiveness on the other (Bernstein and Cashore 2004).

However, given the nature of contemporary governance emphasised in the literature, quality of governance is best understood as being determined by the relationships between actors as they are expressed in an institution's structure and process, and the outcomes these interactions generate; the more these elements are balanced the more governable the system (Kooiman 2000). 'Good' governance in

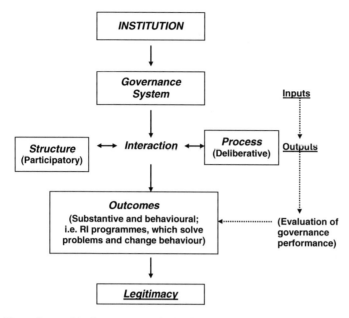

Fig. 3.1 Normative model of contemporary institutional legitimacy

this context should therefore be defined as the effective interaction between the structure, process and outcomes of a given institution. Contemporary governance is increasingly participatory in nature, with an increased role for multi-stakeholder dialogue, or deliberation, in content development and decision-making. Consequently, there have been calls for a more sociological conception of contemporary institutional legitimacy (Bernstein and Cashore 2004). This concept, which is to be understood normatively, given the extent and maturity of 'new' governance, is represented in Fig. 3.1.

In a sense, this model is an argument in figurative terms. What is being argued here is that contrary to the two previous schools of thought, which are divided into 'the means justify the ends' (input legitimacy) and 'the ends justify the means' (output legitimacy), this model stresses that the means and the ends are equally important. They are directly related and consequential to each other; both contribute to legitimacy. In other words, there's no point having a governance system, which is wonderfully participatory and deliberative, but constitutes nothing more than an endless 'talk fest'. In this case, it is not legitimate because it delivers no substantive agreements and longer term change (or solution to the problem at hand). Conversely, there's little point in 'delivering results' if participants in a given system are overridden, ignored, or excluded. In this case there is no collaboration and stakeholder participation is therefore of dubious legitimacy in terms of due process; consequently, there is likely to be no longer-term change in stakeholder behaviour, and the given problem is unlikely to be solved, as there is no broad-based 'buy in'.

Assessing Governance Performance

In this model, the legitimacy of an institution lies in the extent to which structure and process interact effectively, determined by the nature, role and extant of deliberations between stakeholders within the governance system. The system's performance can be evaluated, and a rating provided. The difference between the rating that would be delivered by such a model and existing methods is that such a rating is based on a holistic examination (inputs, outputs, and outcomes) of an institution's structures and processes, rather than individual corporate attributes. Once institutional legitimacy is understood in these terms, it is then necessary to determine exactly what institutional arrangements are being evaluated in the approach to rating as suggested here.

At present, the problem of competing approaches to evaluating corporate social responsibility, as noted above, is also visible in the RI sector. In the case of screening for example, there is an evolving debate over which method is preferable: some companies use negative screens (no alcohol, tobacco, firearms); others screen positively (best-in-class); others simply on the basis of the degree to which a company engages and involves multi-stakeholders (UNEP FI and Mercer 2007). This can lead to competing claims over which approach is best. This is a somewhat pointless conflict, given the fact that such screens are often internally generated, and/or following specific off-the-shelf products, driven as they are by varying ideological assumptions or divergent institutional imperatives.

The result is that there is considerable inconsistency in the RI sector regarding the legitimacy, or otherwise, of both the products being evaluated and the evaluation methods being used. A useful response to these problems of inconsistency is to envisage the evaluation of a governance system not in terms of specific attributes like transparency, but in terms of its structures and processes as a whole. In the following discussion, based on Cadman (2009), the various governance arrangements discussed above are brought together into a hierarchically consistent framework of principles, criteria and indicators (PC&I) of governance quality.

A *principle* is a fundamental rule, which serves as a basis for determining the function of a complete system in respect to explicit elements. A principle can also express a certain perspective, or value, regarding a specific aspect of the system as it interacts with the governance system. *Criteria* function at the next level down, and can be described as categories of conditions or processes, which contribute to the overall principle. They are intended to facilitate the assessment of principles that would otherwise be ideational and non-measurable. Criteria are not usually capable of being measured directly either, but are formulated to provide a determination on the degree of compliance. They are consequently linked to *indicators*, which are hierarchically lower, and which represent quantitative or qualitative parameters, and do describe conditions indicative of the state of the governance system as they relate to the relevant criterion. The value of a hierarchically consistent PC&I is that they are scalable and can be applied at multiple levels, and in individual contexts (Lammerts van Beuren and Blom 1997). The relationship between principles, criteria and indicators, and how the various governance arrangements discussed

Table 3.1 Hierarchical framework of PC&I for the assessment of governance quality

Principle	Criterion	Indicator
'Meaningful participation'	Interest representation	Inclusiveness
		Equality
		Resources
	Organisational responsibility	Accountability
		Transparency
'Productive deliberation'	Decision-making	Democracy
		Agreement
		Dispute settlement
	Implementation	Behavioural change
		Problem solving
		Durability

Source: Cadman, 2009

above can be formulated for assessing institutional performance, are laid out in Table 3.1.

In this framework the previously disparate components of 'good' governance have been brought together in a model in which participation is conceived as a fundamental aspect of institutional structure, whilst deliberation is central to the processes and procedures utilised by that institution.

'Participation as structure' is expressed by the principle of *meaningful participation*. This term is frequently associated with participation in much of the literature, and serves here as a normative, qualitative descriptor. This term first appears in the United Nations Declaration on the Right to Development, adopted by General Assembly resolution 41/128 of 4 December 1986 (Gaventa 2002). The principle has two associated criteria: *interest representation*, concerning who is involved in the governance system; and *organisational responsibility*, referring to the ethical behaviour of these interests as they interact with each other and external parties. Interest representation is evaluated by three indicators: *inclusiveness*, referring to participants' levels of access; *equality*, concerning the weight, or balance of power, between participants; and the availability of *resources* (technical, economic or institutional), which ensure that participants' interests are properly represented. The second criterion, organisational responsibility, is evaluated by two indicators accountability and transparency. *Accountability* has two components: the extent to which the participants are vertically accountable to management and other actors within the organization; and horizontally accountable to their clients and the public at large. *Transparency* refers to the extent to which the activities of the institution in question are open, visible, and accessible to scrutiny by actors within the institution, and the wider community.

'Deliberation as process' is expressed by the principle of *productive deliberation* (Dryzek and Braithwaite 2000). This principle is more than a statement about the democratic legitimacy of a process, as it refers both to the quality of deliberations, as they occur within the system, as well as the quality of the outcomes, or products, of those deliberations. The principle of productive deliberation is captured by two criteria: decision making and implementation. *Decision making* refers to the existence of measures to reach agreement, the manner in which decisions are made, and how disagreements are handled, and is evaluated by three indicators: democracy; agreement; and dispute settlement. *Democracy* concerns the extent to which a system can be deemed as functioning democratically and whether those engaged in deliberations are expressing the 'will of the people' (i.e., the wishes of their constituents), rather than a specific democratic mode. *Agreement*, like democracy, refers not so much to the merits of one method over another (e.g. voting vs. consensus), but the degree to which deliberation is encouraged or checked. Finally, *dispute settlement* focuses on whether the institution has procedures to settle disputes and whether these are effective. *Implementation* concerns the putting into practice of the substantive outputs generated and is evaluated by means of the indicators of behaviour change, problem solving and durability. *Behaviour change* is used to determine whether the implementation of agreements, or substantive outcomes results in changed behaviour regarding the problem that the system was created to address. *Problem solving* refers to the extent to which the system has solved the problem it was created to address (in this case irresponsible, or unsustainable, investment). Here *durability* is interpreted as referring to systemic resilience, as well as flexibility and adaptability (whilst still ensuring a degree of consistency).

The advantage of this framework for analysing the quality of governance over single, dual- or multi- criteria approach is that it establishes a strong hierarchical logic between the elements commonly used to assess governance quality. It thus makes explicit how key governance concepts such as democracy, accountability and transparency are articulated with each other. Notably, the framework does not directly include the concept of legitimacy, a key criterion used by many analysts to assess governance quality. This is because the framework conceptualises legitimacy as the final end point of institutional performance, which is determined by the successful interaction between the structural and procedural components of the governance system, as Fig. 3.1 has outlined above.

Problems with the 'Single Criterion' Approach to Governance Quality

A major implication of the governance quality framework advanced in this chapter is that determining the legitimacy of an institution on the basis of individual criteria is problematic. Corporate social responsibility, for example, with its emphasis on accountability and transparency addresses only a restricted set of governance quality indicators. If CSR is adopted as the sole expression of a company's commitment to environmental, social and economic performance, other significant aspects of institutional behaviour can be overlooked. Enron made much of its commitment to corporate social responsibility, and was assiduous in publicly reporting on its social and environmental activities. But this 'fig leaf' approach to accountability and transparency contributed very little to the company's overarching philosophy and objectives (Baker 2007). There are more contemporary examples. The Extractive Industries Transparency Initiative (EITI), for example, seeks to promote transparency through public reporting on what payments oil, gas and mining companies make to governments, and what governments do with these revenues. This is a multistakeholder programme, and includes civil society, which participates in the design, monitoring, evaluation and discussion of local procedures. Although acclaimed as a ground-breaking initiative, only three of the 24 signatory companies have moved to full disclosure in all countries where they are active, and only two of the 21 participating governments had produced fully audited and reconciled reports (Doane and Holder 2007).

A similar approach is to be found in the RI sector. The fact that the Royal Bank of Scotland was an active supporter and promoter of the Global Compact, UNEP's Finance Initiative and the Equator Principles – and was also audited under the AA1000 AccountAbility Principles Standard – did not prevent it from what can now be seen with hindsight as involvement in irresponsible investments (RBS 2008). Of course, no company can be insulated from the vagaries of global capital, and not even exemplary behaviour can protect all institutions in all contexts, but there is a real danger that focussing on single elements of 'good' behaviour, such as public disclosure, can be used as a surrogate for a more profound commitment to governance quality. If the actions of the Royal Bank of Scotland Group (RBS) are explored in more detail for example, it is possible to see the use of vague and equivocal language in its 2008 report; for example it 'considered' the Global Reporting Initiative and 'sought to cover the principles of the Global Compact' (RBS: 11). One of the more profound problems here is the voluntary nature of such non-state approaches to governance, one that is explicitly promoted by UNEP FI for instance is that the commitments to sustainability made by the signatories to the Initiative represent nothing more than 'aspirational voluntary declarations of intent' (UNEP FI 2009d). When corporations and governments band together to form voluntary private-public initiatives to reassure the public of their commitment to 'good' governance, it is difficult to determine the legitimacy of these assurances when they are based on such a restricted set of assessment criteria.

Conclusions

The recent financial crisis should encourage RI stakeholders to pay greater attention to considerations of institutional governance when making investment-related decisions. This chapter has explored the changing nature of governance at the global level and its impacts on traditional corporate conceptions, particularly in terms of the role accorded to non-economic participants. In recent decades ever-increasing numbers of environmental and social interests have become involved in the development of a wide range of sustainable development-related initiatives, including investment. When it comes to analysing the quality and legitimacy of governance practice within these divergent institutions, it has become necessary for scholars to develop more cross-disciplinary approaches than before. As the world comes to grips with a range of global problems, and social political interactions increasingly shift to non-state contexts, governance standards have the potential to become an important means by which legitimacy can be evaluated. Such standards will make it easier for potential participants to determine whether they should engage in a given programme or not. It will avoid some of the uncertainties that interested parties currently experience over the legitimacy of a given institution, and whether to lend it credibility through participation. In this context, standards for the determination of quality of governance could act as a surrogate, substitute or supplement to territorially-based regulatory frameworks. In view of the inconsistency in the literature over what constitutes 'good' governance, and the claims financial institutions make for themselves – and entrepreneurs make on their behalf – such global standards are in fact essential. This goes for any sector, including the financial sector and the RI sector.

The RI sector, based as it is on the PRI (a voluntary set of agreements) does not have any formal standards for accrediting RI activity. Financial analysts and investors tend to develop and use their own in-house screens (or other mechanisms) for determining the degree to which various materialities might affect their choice (or development) of a certain product. The justification for such an approach might be that there are so many different categories of investor out there (from church groups to conventional banks) that it is impossible to determine any kind of universal approach, and it is best left to the analysts to develop their own ratings. However, different entities place different emphases on ESG: just E or S or G or combinations thereof. Governance is seen as being merely another criterion, rather than a fundamental, of RI. This is resulting in a great deal of inconsistency between what RI assessment/accreditation programmes might consider relevant for determining investment practice (accountability, or disclosure, or one, or both, or others), and the indicators by which these are assessed. It is worth giving some consideration to what such inconsistencies might mean for emerging RI markets, such as carbon finance. Playing devil's advocate, the question might be asked as to how this makes RI any better than the various financial mechanisms used by the banks and other ventures, that have been blamed for the GFC. How, with the proliferation of potentially 'toxic' programmes in the market, can the sector avoid a collapse of confidence in the legitimacy of RI? In view of such possible dangers, standards for determining the quality of ESG across the sector will probably become essential. Such an assertion is based on the view that ESG is not just as a side-component of RI, but the basis for sustainable development in the 'post greenhouse' era.

References

Aguirre, Daniel. 2008. The Human Right to Development in a Globalized World. Aldershot and Burlington: Ashgate.

Arts, B. 2006. Non-state actors in global governance: New arrangements beyond the state. In New Modes of Governance in the Global System: Exploring Publicness, Delegation and Inclusiveness eds. Mathias Koenig-Archibugi, and Michael Zürn, 177–200. Basingstoke and London: Palgrave Macmillan.

Baker, Mallen. 2007. Corporate social Responsibility – companies in the news: Enron. Mallenbaker website. http://www.mallenbaker.net/csr/CSRfiles/enron.html. Accessed 23 January 2010.

Barnett, Micael. 2007. Social constructivism. In the Globalization of World Politics: An Introduction to International Relations, eds. John Bayliss, Steve Smith and Patricia Owens, 160–173. Oxford: Oxford University Press.

Bebchuk, Lucia and Assaf Hamdai. 2009. The elusive quest for global governance standards. University of Pennsylvania Law Review 157: 1263–1317.

Bernstein, S. and Benjamin Cashore. 2004. Nonstate global governance: Is forest certification a legitimate alternative to a global forest convention? In Hard Choices, Soft Law: Combining Trade, Environment, and Social Cohesion in Global Governance, eds. John Kirton and Michael Trebilcock, 33–63. Aldershot: Ashgate Press.

Birnie, P. 2000. The UN and the environment. In United Nations, divided world: the UN's roles in international relations, ed. Adam Roberts and Benedict Kingsbury, 327–383. Oxford: Oxford University Press.

Bouckaert, Geert and John Halligan. 2008. Managing Performance: International Comparisons. Abingdon: Routledge.

Bradford, Colin and Linn, Johannes. 2008. The G-20 Summit: could the financial crisis push global governance reform? Borokings Institute website. http://www.brookings.edu/opinions/2008/1024_g20_summit_linn.aspx. Accessed 21 September 2009.

Cadman, Timothy. 2009. Quality, legitimacy and global governance: A comparative analysis of four forest institutions. PhD dissertation. School of Government, University of Tasmania, Tasmania, Australia.

Clapp, Jennifer. 2005. Global environmental governance for corporate responsibility and accountability. Global Environmental Politics 5: 23–34.

Detomasi, David. 2006. International regimes: The case of western corporate governance. International Studies Review 8: 225–251.

Dimitrov, Radoslav. 2005. Hostage to norms: States, institutions and global forest politics. Global Environmental Politics 5: 1–24.

Doane, Deborah and Alison Holder. 2007. Why corporate social responsibility is failing children. London: Save the Children and The Corporate Responsibility (CORE) Coalition.

Dryzek, John and Valerie Braithwaite. 2000. On the prospects for democratic deliberation: Values analysis applied to Australian politics. Political Psychology 21: 241–266.

Falkner, Robert. 2003. Private environmental governance and international relations: Exploring the links. Global Environmental Politics 3: 72–87.

Fiorino, Daniel. 1999. Rethinking environmental regulation: Perspectives on law and governance. The Harvard Environmental Law Review 23: 441–469

Folke, Carl, Thomas Hahn, Per, Olsson, and Jon Norberg. 2005. Adaptive governance of social-ecological systems. Annual Review of Environment and Resources 30: 441–473.

Gaventa, John. 2002. Making rights real: Exploring citizenship, participation and accountability. Journal of International Development Studies 33: 1–11.

Garten, Jeffrey. 1999. Lessons for the next financial crisis. Foreign Affairs 78: 76–92.

Glück, P. J. Rayner and B. Cashore. 2005. Changes in the governance of forest resources. In Forests in the Global Balance, eds. G. Mery, R. Alfaro, M. Kaninnen, and M. Lobovikov, 51–74. Helsinki: IUFRO.

Global Corporate Governance Forum. 2010. Global corporate governance forum: Better companies, better societies. Global Corporate Governance Forum website. http://www.gcgf.org/. Accessed 23/10/2010.

Global Corporate Governance Forum and International Finance Corporation. Undated. Stakeholder Engagement and the Board: Integrating Best Governance Practices. Washington, DC: Global Corporate Governance Forum and International Finance Corporation.

Global Compact and UNEP FI. 2009a. The principles for responsible investment. UNPRI website. http://www.unpri.org/primciples/. Accessed 23 February 2009.

Global Compact and UNEP FI. 2009b. Signatories to the principles for responsible investment. UNPRI website. http://www.unpri.org/signatories/. Accessed 23 February 2009.

GRI. 2008. Sustainability Reporting Guidelines & Financial Services Sector Supplement. Amsterdam: Global Reporting Initiative.

Haas, Peter. 2002. UN conferences and constructivist governance of the environment. Global Governance 8: 73–91.

Hawley, James and Andrew Williams. 2005. Shifting ground: Emerging Global Corporate-Governance Standards and the Rise of Fiduciary Capitalism. Environment and Planning 37: 1995–2013.

Haufler, Virginia. 2001. A Public Role for the Private Sector: Industry Self-Regulation. Washington, DC: Carnie Endowment for International Peace.

Held, David, Anthony G. McGrew, David Goldblatt, and Jonathan Perraton. 1999. Global transformations: Politics, Economics and Culture. London: Polity Press.

Jordan, Andrew, Rudiger Wurzel and Anthony Zito. 2005. The rise of 'new' policy instruments in comparative perspectives: Has governance eclipsed government? Political Studies 53: 441–469.

Hilb, Martin. 2009. New corporate governance in the post-crisis world. Private Sector Opinion 16: 3–11.

Kerwer, Dieter. 2006. Governing financial markets by international standards. In New Modes of Governance in the Global System: Exploring Publicness, Delegation and Inclusiveness, eds. Mathias Koenig-Archibugi and Michael Zürn. Basingstoke and London: Palgrave Macmillan.

Kjaer, Anne. 2004. Governance. Cambridge: Polity Press.

Koenig-Archibugi, M. 2006. Introduction: Institutional diversity in global governance. In New Modes of Governance in the Global System: Exploring Publicness, Delegation and Inclusiveness, eds. Mathias Koenig-Archibugi, and Michael Zürn, 1–30. Basingstoke and London: Palgrave Macmillan.

Kooiman, J. 1993a. Findings, speculations and recommendations. In Modern Governance: New Government Society Interactions, ed. Jan Kooiman, 249–262. London: Sage.

Kooiman, J. 1993b. Social-political governance: Introduction. In Modern Governance: New Government Society Interactions ed. Jan Kooiman, 1–8. London: Sage.

Kooiman, J. 2000. Societal governance: Levels, models, and orders of social-political interaction. In Debating Governance: Authority, Steering and Democracy, ed. Jon Pierre, 138–166. Oxford: Oxford University Press.

Knowles, Ross. 1997. Ethical Investment. Sydney: Choice Books.

Lammerts van Beuren Erik and Esther Blom. 1997. Hierarchical Framework for the Formulation of Sustainable Forest Management Standards. Leiden: The Tropenbos Foundation.

Mackendrick, Nora. 2005. The role of the state in voluntary environmental reform: A case study of public land. Policy Sciences 38: 21–44.

Mason, Michael. 1999. Environmental Democracy. New York, NY: St Martin's Press.

Meidinger, Errol. 2006. The administrative law of global private-public regulation: The case of forestry. European Journal of International Law 17: 47–87.

Ostrom, Elinor. 1990. Governing the Commons: The Evolution of Institutions for Collective Action. Cambridge: Cambridge University Press.

Overdevest, Christine. 2004. Codes of conduct and standard setting in the forest sector: constructing markets for democracy? Relations Industrielles/Industrial Relations 59 (1): 172–197.

Rosenau, J. 2000. Change, complexity and governance in a globalising space. In Debating Governance: Authority, Steering and Democracy, ed. Jon Pierre, 167–200. Oxford and New York, NY: Oxford University Press.

Rosenau, James and Ernst-Otto Czempiel. 1992. Governance Without Government: Order and Change in World Politics. Cambridge: Cambridge University Press.

Royal Bank of Scotland. 2008. Sustainability Report 2008. Royal Bank of Scotland website. http://www.rbos.net/microsites/sustainability-report-2008/default.htm. Accessed 2 January 2010.

Ruggie, John. 1998. What makes the world hang together? Neo-utilitarianism and the social constructivist challenge. International Organization 52: 855–885.

Ruggie, John. 2003. Taking embedded liberalism global: The corporate connection. In Taming Globalisation: Frontiers of Governance eds. David Held and Mathias Koenig-Archibugi, 93–129. Cambridge: Polity Press.

Runeson, Eric and Guy, Marie-Laurence. 2007. Mediating Corporate Governance Conflicts and Disputes. Washington, DC: Global Corporate Governance Forum and International Finance Corporation.

Scholte, Jan. 2004. Civil society and democratically accountable global governance. Government and Opposition 39: 211–233.

Scholte, Jan. 2008. From Government to governance: New Roles for EU Diplomats. In Global Governance and Diplomacy, eds. Andrew Cooper, Brian Hocking, and William Maley, 39–62. London and Basingstoke: Palgrave Macmillan.

Skjærseth, Jon, Olav Stokke Olav, and Jørgen Wettestad. 2006. Soft law, hard law, and effective implementation. Global Environmental Politics 6: 104–120.

Stiglitz, Joseph. 2003. Globalization and development. In Taming Globalisation: Frontiers of Governance, eds. David Held and Mathias Koenig-Archibugi, 47–67. Cambridge: Polity Press.

Stoker, Gerry. 1998. Governance as theory: five propositions. International Social Science Journal 50 (155): 17–28.

UN. 1993. Agenda 21: Programme of Action for Sustainable Development, Rio Declaration on Environment and Development, Statement of Forest Principles. New York, NY: United Nations Publications Department of Public Information.

UNEP FI. 2009a. Regional activities. UNEP FI website. http://www.unepfi.org/regional_activities/index.html. Accessed 23 February 2009.

UNEP FI. 2009b. About UNEP FI. UNEP FI website. http://www.unepfi.org/about/structure/index.html. Accessed 23 February 2009.

UNEP FI. 2009c. What we do. UNEP FI website. http://www.unepfi.org/index.html. Accessed 23 February 2009.

UNEP FI. 2009d. Our signatories. UNEP FI website. http://www.unepfi.org/signatories/statements/index.html. Accessed 23 February 2009.

UNEP FI. 2009e. Sustainability reporting. UNEP FI website. http://www.unepfi.org/work_streams/reporting/index.html. Accessed 23 February 2009.

UNEP FI. 2009f. UNEP FI/GRI working groups. UNEP FI website. http://www.unepfi.org/work_streams/gri_working_groups/index.html. Accessed 5 March 2009.

UNEP FI. 2009g. Publications – sustainability reporting. UNEP FI website. http://www.unepfi.org/publications/reporting/index.html. Accessed 5 March 2009.

UNEP FI. Undated. UNEP FI Japan group: Environment and finance. No location: UNEP FI.

UNEP FI and Mercer. 2007. Demystifying responsible investment performance. No location: UNEP FI and Mercer.

UNEP FI and UN Global Compact. 2007. The working capital report. No location: UNEP FI and UN Global Compact.

Van Vliet, M. 1993. Environmental regulation of business: Options and constraints for communicative governance. In Modern Governance: New Government Society Interactions, ed. Jan Kooiman. London: Sage.

Waddock, Sandra. 2008. Building a new institutional infrastructure for corporate responsibility. The Academy of Management Perspectives 22: 87–108.

Warren, Michael. 2002. What can democratic participation mean today? Political Theory 30: 677–701.

Whitman, Jim. 2005. The Limits of Global Governance. Abington: Routledge.

World Bank. 2006. Good Governance: Community Mobilization to Combat Corruption, Annex 10, 145–146. No location: World Bank.

Young, Iris. 2000. Inclusion and Democracy. Oxford: Oxford University Press.

Chapter 4
Reputational Penalties in Financial Markets: An Ethical Mechanism?

Peter-Jan Engelen and Marc van Essen

Introduction

Responsible investment (RI) and responsible corporate behaviour received a lot of attention during the last decade in the corporate social responsibility (CSR) literature (McWilliams and Siegel 2001, 2006). After the U.S. and European financial markets were being troubled in the early 2000s by several major scandals like Enron, Worldcom, Tyco and Parmalat, financial ethics received a lot of attention by the public as well. Irresponsible corporate behaviour can occur in different ways such as corruption, market abuse, fraud, insider trading, ecological harm, racial or sexual discrimination. Examples include foreign briberies to get supply contracts (Volkswagen), insider trading ahead of a profit warning (EADS), lower salaries for female employees (Wal-Mart), and worker's conditions in Indonesia (Nike).

One often heard argument with SRI activists is that through responsible investment one can stimulate good corporate behaviour and 'punish' corporations for misconduct because they will be excluded from the opportunity set of investors. An important issue in the responsible investment debate is the distribution of responsibilities. What is the role of governments, banks, investment funds, customers, rating agencies and other stakeholders? This chapter provides some insight into how the functioning of the financial market itself – regardless of any moral intention – induces corporations to behave responsibly with regard to some of the issues that are of concern for RI as well. We review the literature on the relationship between the discovery of irresponsible corporate behaviour and its stock price reaction. We answer questions such as do stock markets exercise any disciplinary role for corporate misconduct? Do stock markets sanction certain types of maleficence and ignore others? When can we rely on reputational penalties (financial markets) and when do we need to rely on legal penalties (court-imposed or administrative sanctions by supervising agencies)?

P.-J. Engelen (✉)
Utrecht University, Utrecht, The Netherlands
e-mail: P.J.Engelen@uu.nl

W. Vandekerckhove et al. (eds.), *Responsible Investment in Times of Turmoil*,
Issues in Business Ethics 31, DOI 10.1007/978-90-481-9319-6_4,
© Springer Science+Business Media B.V. 2011

It is no surprise to see that the global financial crisis has led to calls for greater corporate accountability and heightened controls over public corporations (Harper and Ho 2009). In order to prevent similar episodes governments around the world announced changes in regulations and increase the enforcement to restore confidence. This chapter summarizes the literature on whether investors through financial markets 'punish' certain corporate practices.

We have written this chapter in a language which is morally loaded. For example, we write that markets and investors punish or sanction, and we write that corporations misbehave. We realize this may come over as inaccurate or scientifically invalid, but we chose to do so in an attempt to make our findings more relevant to RI supporters and policy makers, as the discourse around RI is a morally loaded one. It is of course not true that markets 'punish' or 'reward'. Markets do not act; investors do. Fluctuations in stock prices are simply an aggregate of a huge number of buy-and-sell decisions. In this chapter, we do not assume that investors include non-financial considerations into their investment decision. It suffices for us that they consider issues and corporate behaviour that will have a material impact on the corporate bottom line. Thus, what we seek to find out is which corporate behaviours will have a negative impact on their financial performance. Hence we get some insight into which corporate misbehaviour is dealt with through a morally blind process – stock market – and which corporate misbehaviours need to be tackled through other means such as RI and legal penalties. However, it is still too early to draw far-reaching conclusions on an increased disciplinary role for investors or for RI after the crisis. A recent study shows that investors are more sensitive to disciplining corporate misconduct when it receives more press coverage. Lumsdaine (2009) finds indications that greater Bloomberg news readership attention was associated with lower equity returns of large bank stocks in the beginning of the financial crisis.

We will examine what types of corporate misconduct are disciplined through the market mechanism and complement or even substitute public enforcement of legal penalties. We will also show the limitations of relying on reputational penalties and demonstrate for what types of misconduct reputational penalties are ineffective. For types of the latter case more reliance on legal penalties might be necessary. It can give supervising agencies and the legislator guidance on what types of corporate conduct to focus on, while being able to rely more on financial markets for disciplining other types of misconduct.

The answer to these questions is complementary to the CSR literature which examines the link between good business practices and firm financial performance (Pava and Krausz 1996, McWilliams and Siegel 2000, Roberts and Dowling 2002). A meta-analysis of 52 empirical studies by Orlitzky et al. (2003) finds a positive relationship between corporate social performance and corporate financial performance. Examining stock market penalties for corporate misconduct is therefore the mirror image of good business practices and looks into any negative relationship between corporate misconduct and firm financial performance. In contrast to CSR indexes that measure a wide range of different aspects, the empirical studies in this chapter focus on a precisely observable event of corporate misbehavior. Such analysis can therefore contribute to better insights into measuring the impact of responsible corporate behavior.

Traditionally most of the literature focuses on court-imposed penalties to induce companies to behave responsible. Besides criminal and civil sanctions, market-based penalties might complement or substitute those legal penalties to reach an optimal level of sanctions to deter corporate misconduct or irresponsible behavior. Reality shows that corporations not only face court-imposed penalties, but also incur market-based sanctions for corporate misconduct. Although different terms can be found in literature to refer to the stock market penalizations (stock equity losses) such as 'loss of goodwill', 'loss of brand name capital' or 'loss of faith', we prefer to use the term 'reputation penalty' since it is the most widely used term.

In the remainder of the chapter we first visit theoretical reputation models in Section 'Reputation Models'. Before moving to empirical studies on the impact of reputational penalties, we discuss the methodological issue of measuring the reputational penalty in Section 'Measuring the Reputational Penalty'. Section 'Product Unsafety and Product Recalls' presents studies measuring the stock price impact of product recalls and news about product unsafety. In the next section we focus on empirical studies on the reputational penalties for corporate maleficence such as fraud, environmental violations, insider trading, financial misrepresentations and discrimination. In the conclusions, we round up this chapter with an overview of the empirical findings and an answer to the question how effectively different types of corporate misconduct are sanctioned through financial markets.

Reputation Models

The reputational literature starts with the models of Klein and Leffler (1981), Shapiro (1982, 1983) and Lott (1988) and define reputation in terms of customer expectations about product quality. In those models atomistic customers update their expectations about product quality of a seller when they receive news about product defects or product unsafety. They will switch to another seller with higher quality products or they will keep buying products from the same seller at a lower price. This loss of cash flow that occurs due to changing customer behavior is called a reputational penalty. This mechanism induces companies to maintain product quality at a high level because the market mechanism internalizes the cost of corporate misconduct in repeating business transactions. While the original Klein and Leffler model offers a discrete choice between cheating and not cheating on product quality, Lott (1988) extends this model to a stochastic decision process. Alexander (1999) points out that this reputation mechanism is not limited to a seller-customer framework but can be applied to a wide range of settings of repeated transactions. Besides customers other related parties such as suppliers or employees can change their implicit and explicit contracts with the company.

Reputational losses are actually the downward revised present values of lower future net sales or higher future costs of capital. In an efficient capital market, this will be translated in a lower stock price. While legal penalties include fines, damage payments and compliance costs, reputational penalties might include lower company's profits due to lost socially conscious customers (lower purchases, consumer boycotts), due to more expensive suppliers (less trade credit) or due to more expensive labor force (lower job satisfaction, absenteeism, lower job performance, higher job turnover) (Posnikoff 1997, Viswesvaran et al. 1998, Vitell and Davis 1990).

Figure 4.1 shows the channels of the stock market penalization in more detail. The market price on the stock exchange is actually an equilibrium price of expectations of investors about the value of the company through the mechanism of supply and demand. It is an aggregation of the reputational penalties the stakeholders impose on the company through different channels. Socially conscious customers will impose a reputational penalty on the company by buying fewer products leading to lower expected revenues, which in turn leads to a lower stock price. In a similar way, socially conscious employees and suppliers will lead to increased costs and thus to a lower stock price. Reputational penalties might also show up in the discount rate through higher costs of capital from debtholders as well as equity holders. The latter means that stock market investors might demand a higher required rate of return (cost of equity) to reflect a higher company risk. The observed stock market penalization is thus a monetary translation and 'summary' of all underlying penalization channels instead of an active punishment by socially conscious investors. The mechanism of 'reputation penalties' does not even have to assume the presence of RI investors for stock market reaction when these issues have material impact.[1]

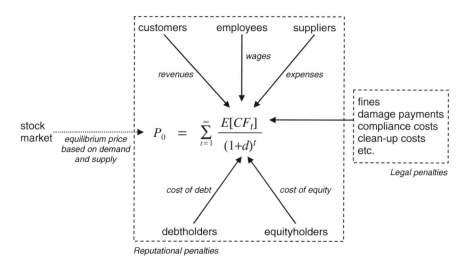

Stock price = present value of all future expected cash flows

Fig. 4.1 Channels of stock market penalization. Legend: P_0 = current stock price; CF_t = cash flows at time t; d = discount factor; E[.] = expected value operator; t = time parameter

---

[1]The chapter by Sandberg in this volume suggests that the investment decisions taken by RI investors have no impact on stock prices. We show here that the presence of RI investors is unnecessary to induce corporations to behave responsible on a number of issues, provided that there are primary stakeholders of the corporations who sanction the corporate misbehavior by altering

The reputational penalty companies pay for corporate maleficence also depends on the nature of the party incurring damage from the misconduct. The reputational penalty seems to work effectively in case the damaged party is a related party, such as customers, suppliers, employees and alike. It does not seem to work well in case of unrelated or third parties. Related party misconduct involves customers, suppliers or other related parties who stop dealing with the company or change the terms to do business with the company. All these parties have implicit and explicit contracts with the company through repeated transactions that can change in future (Alexander 1999). In terms of the Klein and Leffler model, this means that companies lose the quasi-rents they can earn when customers pay premium prices for high quality products. Other related parties such as suppliers might charge more stringent credit terms; or employees might become more expensive to hire or to keep with the company. This will be translated in lower cash flow terms, being the present value of lower future sales or higher future (capital) costs, and thus in a lower stock price. In this way, the corporate misconduct is partly or fully internalized by means of the reputational penalty (Karpoff and Lott 1993). If the misconduct only induces external costs on parties that do not deal directly with the company, the reputational penalty seems negligible since it cannot be directly incorporated through stock prices.

Measuring the Reputational Penalty

Although most empirical studies presented below show a negative stock price reaction upon the announcement of corporate irresponsible behavior, it does not automatically answer the question about the magnitude of the reputational penalty.[2,3]

---

their interactions with that corporation, for example withholding discretionary effort (employees), renegotiating payment periods (suppliers), or changing brand (customers). Hence, resonating with the critique of Eccles in his chapter in this book, if issues are material they will be sanctionned by the market. If they are not material, they can be of concern to RI.

[2]Before the negative news about the irresponsible behavior reaches the market, the stock price is at its equilibrium level P_{before} in Figure 5.2. After the news release the stock price drops to a new equilibrium level P_{after}. In an efficient market this stock price adjustment is permanent, since prices will only adjust if new information reaches the market. Measured as abnormal returns, this implies a significant negative return on the announcement date and zero abnormal returns on all other trading days. If the stock market penalization on the announcement date would only be temporarily, one would have to observe a post-announcement abnormal return drift in the opposite direction (while no new information arrives to the market). In the conventional post-event windows of about 10–20 trading days after the announcement date, most studies do not show such trend. More background information on the efficient market hypothesis and the dissemination of information on financial markets can be found in Engelen (2005) and Engelen and Kabir (2006).

[3]The downward revision of the stock price is the result of supply and demand on the stock market. Translated in financial economics terminology, the revision reflects either lower expected future cash flows or a higher required cost of equity (discount rate). Although it would be interesting to see what type of investors set the new market price at the margin (e.g. SRI investors or regular investors), no empirical study shows the identity of the marginal investors around the announcement of corporate misconduct.

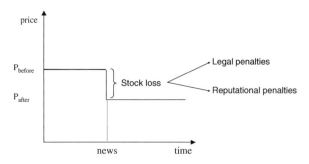

Fig. 4.2 Stock price reaction upon the announcement of corporate misconduct

The empirical difficulty is to distinguish between the level of the expected legal penalty and the level of the reputational penalty, since the stock price decline on the announcement date of the illegal practice reflects both.

Figure 4.2 shows that in event studies the equity loss is typically measured as the (cumulative) abnormal return over the event window and captures the joint impact of expected legal penalties and reputational loss. Therefore assumptions have to be made to assign part of the stock price decline to the effect of the legal penalty and part to the effect of the reputational penalty. Karpoff et al. (2005) assume that the imposed legal penalty is an unbiased estimate of the size of the expected legal penalty at the announcement moment in press. If the lost market value on this date exceeds the value of the legal penalty, they attribute the difference to the reputational penalty.

Figure 4.3 illustrates the process of determining the magnitude of the reputational penalty. If one assumes the ex-post imposed legal penalties to be equal to the ex-ante expected legal penalties, the residual of the equity loss can be attributed to the reputational penalty.[4] Figure 4.3 shows how this process works as communicating vessels. For instance, following this procedure, Karpoff and Lott (1993) find that the

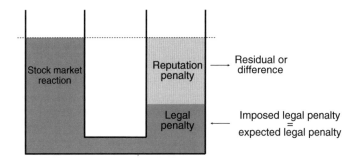

Fig. 4.3 Legal versus reputational penalties as communicating vessels. Source: Engelen (2009)

---

[4]Legal penalties can include fines, damage payments, compliance costs or cleanup costs (depending on the type of misconduct).

equity loss for fraud consists for about 90% of reputational penalties and for about 10% of expected legal penalties. This process rests upon the assumption of rational expectations, according to which investors fully anticipate the legal penalties at the moment of the announcement of the illegality.

The magnitude might vary across different types of corporate maleficence. Figure 4.4 shows the findings of Karpoff et al. (2005) who demonstrate the equity loss for environmental violations only to consist of expected legal penalties and not of any reputational penalty. In contrast, Engelen (2009) shows illegal insider trading practices by CEOs in five European countries only to exhibit reputational penalties for the involved companies (Fig. 4.5).[5]

At first sight, it might seem as if a reputational penalty of 1% (measured as an abnormal return) on the announcement date is quite small. The severity of such a 'small' penalty becomes clearer when translates in absolute values. For a company with a market capitalization of 10 billion dollars, a 1% penalty corresponds

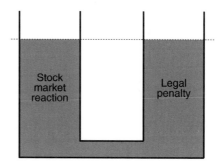

Fig. 4.4 Legal versus reputational penalties for environmental violations. Source: Engelen (2009)

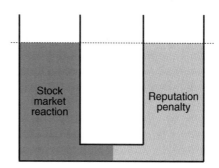

Fig. 4.5 Legal versus reputational penalties for illegal insider trading. Source: Engelen (2009)

[5]We discuss these results in more detail in section 5.4.

with a loss in market value of 100 million dollars on a single day.[6] Companies in the 10 billion dollar market value bracket are, for instance, Carlsberg, Solvay, Lagardere or Telekom Austria. For bigger companies such as Nestle, BP or Wal-Mart in the 200 billion dollar market value bracket the loss would even be more severe in absolute value.[7]

Product Unsafety and Product Recalls

If one assumes that producing and selling defective products is an example of socially irresponsible corporate behavior (inappropriate quality checks or ignoring bad news from the work floor or customers for too long), one expects to see a negative stock price reaction upon the announcement of product recalls or the disclosure of unsafe products or service practices. The market penalty could display the link between shareholder wealth and socially irresponsible corporate behavior (Davidson and Worrell 1992).

Drug Recalls

Examining product recalls for drugs and automobiles during the seventies, Jarrell and Peltzman (1985) find considerable stock market losses for producers of recalled products (a negative abnormal return of 6.12% for a 10-day event window for drugs). The stock price decline is substantially larger than the direct costs of recalling defective products: 'The stock market is imposing a substantial goodwill loss on a firm over and above the product-specific costs' (Jarrell and Peltzman: 524). This can be interpreted as a reputational penalty imposed by the stock market. In contrast with Jarrell and Peltzman, Dranove and Olsen (1994) attribute the negative stock price reaction to increasing compliance costs with more stringent drug testing.

Mitchell (1989) focuses on the case-study of the 1982 Tylenol product recall by Johnson & Johnson. This case study complements earlier studies on product recalls since it examines the impact of external parties on the company's reputation. It shows that the stock price decline due to the product tampering far exceeded the direct costs, which was largely due to the loss of brand-name capital. This reputational loss reflects the lower expected quasi-rents from future sales since customers were no longer willing to pay a premium price for superior product quality such as safety. Even when the company itself did not lower the product quality below the expected level, its reputation was hurt badly since the incident revealed that it did not provide a safe packaging which could have prevented the tampering. Dowdell et al. (1992) focus on the Tylenol case as well and find that during the first nine trading days after the incident only Johnson & Johnson experienced significantly equity

---

[6]A market value of 10 billion dollars can be considered as a mid-cap company, and would be too small to be included in the Top 500 of world wide companies.
[7]Figures at the end of 2008.

losses, while its competitors were essentially unaffected. Other studies confirm the negative stock price impact for drug recalls (Ahmed et al. 2002, Cheah et al. 2007).

Air Crashes

Air crashes are excellent instances to test whether companies are sanctioned through investment markets for offering unsafe products and services. A case study on airline safety can be found in Chalk (1986), who analyses the impact of the 1979 DC-10 crash (and subsequent grounding) at Chicago's O'Hare Airport on the stock price of McDonnell Douglas. The data suggest that the losses suffered by shareholders largely exceed any estimates of regulatory and liability costs (lawsuits and other costs related to legal proceedings). The author concludes that market forces have a significant impact on the company through a reputational penalty of its stock price. Such a reputational penalty can induce firms ex-ante to invest in product safety. Using a larger sample of manufacturer implicated air crashes, Chalk (1987) finds a negative stock price reaction of the shares of the involved manufacturer (either Boeing, Lockhead, or McDonnell Douglas). Air crashes that did not implicate the manufacturer did not exhibit any market reaction. Again the cumulative abnormal return over the first four trading days of –3.8% was larger than FAA fines, investigation costs and alike. The difference is again attributed to a reputational penalty.

Borenstein and Zimmerman (1988) examine a sample of 74 airline crashes between 1962 and 1985 and find a statistically significant loss in equity value of 1% or $4.5 million. This study fails to link adverse consumer reaction to the equity loss. The weak consumer response can be explained by the fact that consumers do not seem to infer much more information from an airline crash. This would limit the use of a reputational penalty. Chance and Ferris (1987) report an average stock market loss of –1.2% on the day of the crash for airline companies and a cumulative loss of about –2% after 1 month.

Mitchell and Maloney (1989) fine-tune the analysis whether airline crashes cause any stock market reaction by comparing a sample of at-fault crashes with a sample of no-fault crashes. The former includes crashes due to pilot error and improper maintenance and signal airline negligence. Hence, a negative stock price reaction of the airline carrier is expected to account for the increased probability of accidents and the impact of the airline's brand name capital. The latter category includes crashes due to manufacturer error or miscellaneous causes not controlled by the airline (e.g. bad weather, air traffic control error). No impact on the airline carrier's reputation is expected in such cases. The empirical results indeed show no stock price reaction for no-fault crashes and a clear impact of approximately –2.5% for at-fault crashes. Taking into account increases in insurance premium, about 42% of this stock market decline can be attributed to a reputational loss. The results show that a reputational penalty is an effective mechanism to prevent fraudulent firms to cheat on product safety.

Automobile Recalls

While consumers can observe many of the factors that characterize the quality of a vehicle, they cannot observe the integrity of the production process of the car producer. This stand of literature examines whether the valuation effects on the stock market of recall campaigns can function as a credible (negative) signal regarding the integrity of the production process (Barber and Darrough 1996).

While Jarrell and Peltzman (1985) find stock market losses for automobile recalls in the period 1975–1981 of –1.60% over an event window of 10 trading days around the recall announcement, Hoffer et al. (1988) reanalyze their data set and question the valuation effects. Barber and Darrough (1996) expand this data set by including a longer time period (1973–1992) and three Japanese car producers (Honda, Nissan, and Toyota) in addition to the three American car producers (Chrysler, Ford, and General Motors). The stock market reacts indeed significantly negatively to the recall announcements (–0.32% for the U.S. companies and –0.69% for the Japanese companies).[8] Since the price decline is not in line with the costs of the product recalls, Barber and Darrough argue that the reputational penalty is substantial and 'documents [. . .] a direct link between product reliability and shareholder wealth. The stock market imposes a penalty on a manufacturer that produces defective vehicles' (p.1098).

Similarly, Rupp (2004) examines automobile recalls in the period 1973–1998 and finds a negative stock price reaction which is larger than the direct recall costs. Rupp attributes this to a reputational penalty which comprises a substantial portion of the equity losses caused by recall announcements. This study furthermore focuses on different attributes of the recalls. Using twelve categories (e.g. air bags, bumpers, etc.), he analyses which defective components have a more serious stock price impact. He finds no evidence that government-imposed recalls are sanctioned more severely by the markets than manufacturer-initiated recalls (see also Rupp 2001, and Rupp and Taylor 2002). Other studies focusing on different attributes include Barber and Darrough (1996) showing that results hold for both U.S. and Japanese automakers and Hoffer et al. (1994), who examine the impact of vehicle age, defect severity and the nationality of the manufacturer.

In 2000 Bridgestone Corporation recalled 6.5 million of a class of Firestone radial tires after vehicle rollover incidents at high speed, particularly with the Ford Explorer SUV. Govindaraj and Jaggi (2004) try to calculate the different components of the negative stock price reaction of –10.57% on the announcement day. The equity loss of –64.39% over the first 27 trading days corresponds with 10 billion U.S. dollars. This decline is not in relation to the direct recall costs. Only when taking into account worst-case estimates of direct and indirect costs, litigation costs, regulation compliance costs and reputational costs, the authors succeed in reconstructing an amount close to the equity loss. About 13% of the negative

---

[8]The difference in price reaction between U.S. and Japanese car producers is not statistically significant.

stock price reaction is associated with a reputational cost, although it might be a conservative estimate.

Other Product Recalls

While drugs, air carriers and automobiles are examples of product recalls in heavily regulated industries, some studies focus on other product recalls in less regulated or non-regulated industries. Recalls of cosmetics, electronics, consumables, rubber, automotive parts, toys and small appliances are all included in the sample of Pruitt and Peterson (1986) covering the period 1968–1983. These recalls, on average, had an impact on the stock market of about –0.70%. The equity loss is not in relation to the direct recall costs, implying that indirect cost such as litigation costs or reputation costs explain the stock price decline.

Davidson and Worrell (1992) confirm the negative stock market reaction based on a sample of 133 non-automobile product recalls between 1968 and 1987 in the U.S. They find that product recalls involving the replacement or the refund of the purchase price are associated with a higher negative reaction than recalls involving a repair or a check of the product. No difference is found between government-ordered and voluntary recall announcements.

Salin and Hooker (2001) and Thomsen and McKenzie (2001) examine equity losses around food recalls. The former find a clear negative stock reaction for the smallest firms, but not for the biggest firms, although conclusions should not be pushed too far given their extremely small sample size. The latter report a stock market penalization of 2% for class 1 recalls, but no significant impact for less severe hazards (class 2 and 3 recalls).

Computer virus announcements are associated with negative abnormal returns if there is a direct link with a responsible IT vendor which introduced wares embedded with viruses (e.g. installation disk contains a virus) (Hovav and D'Arcy 2005). This is the typical case of a product recall. However, they do not find any negative market reaction for press announcements involving IT products that are vulnerable to viruses (e.g. Microsoft Outlook more vulnerable for spreading certain viruses). The lack of any industry-wide effect is not surprising since those press articles only refer in general terms to certain software to be more susceptible to viruses at the occasion of a virus incident.[9] Similar results are reported by Mitchell and Maloney (1989) who find no stock price reaction for air crashes for which the airline is not directly responsible. Only for air crashes where the airline carrier is directly at fault are penalized. Industry-wide effects are difficult to predict anyway: for automobile recalls Jarrell and Peltzman (1985) find a negative effect on competitors, while Barber and Darrough (1996) find no impact and Govindaraj and

---

[9]The market structure of the software market and the dominance of Microsoft obviously distort the results as well. Microsoft was involved in 54 of the 92 cases in their sample.

Jaggi (2004) find a positive impact. Dowdell et al. (1992) find no effect on competitors for drug recalls, only the introduction of new stringent regulation had an industry-wide negative impact.

Campbell et al. (2003) examine 43 IT security breaches between 1995 and 2000 and find a highly significant negative market reaction for those breaches that relate to violations of confidentiality, while no-confidentiality IT security breaches are not associated with a significant market reaction. Similarly, Hovav and D'Arcy (2003) show that in general the market does not sanction companies that experience Denial-of-Service (DOS) attacks.

The occurrence of accidental deaths with an indication of possible fault or liability by the company causes average cumulative excess returns of about –2% (Broder 1990). These shareholder losses 'exceed the average property damage or increase future insurance costs of an accident, and that loss of goodwill [...] must be an important component of this decline' (Broder: 60). Broder shows that prior expectations about the riskiness of the product have an impact on the magnitude of the stock market loss. Using relative risk categorizations such as low risk products (food), medium risk products (railroad, hotels) and high risk products (airlines) he reports a different influence. The lower the a priori risk expectation, the greater the upward revision in the risk perception and therefore the greater the market loss (Broder 1990).

Prince and Rubin (2002) examine the impact of news on private product liability litigation (filing, losing or other) in the drug and automobile industry on the company's stock price. The observed equity loss corresponds with a worst-case scenario of out-of-pocket costs (upper-bound). Since stock markets can be assumed to rationally expect future costs and litigation outcomes, the difference between the worst-case scenario costs and the expected costs can be attributed to a reputational penalty. If the market would overreact to the expected costs and assume a higher cost, the reputational cost will be lower. The observed market impact is the largest for the filing subsample. This is in line with theory on efficient markets and empirical observations of earlier studies. It is therefore no surprise that Garber and Adams (1998) do not find any significant results by focusing on verdicts only.

The empirical results from the product recall and product safety literature suggest that stock markets react negatively to news that affects a firm's reputation. It shows that stock markets can induce corporations to take responsibility with respect to product quality and safety. The next section analyzes whether reputational penalties can be found with respect to more pronounced cases of corporate irresponsible behavior such as fraud, bribery or environmental violations.

Corporate Maleficence

We first examine the empirical studies which investigate different types of corporate maleficence in an aggregate sample, before moving to empirical studies focusing on one specific type of corporate misconduct to make results easier to interpret.

Aggregate Studies

Criminal indictments into illegal political payoffs and price fixing during the seventies were the object of an empirical study in Straachan et al. (1983). They report a negative impact for price fixing indictments. Similar results are found by Skantz et al. (1990).

Davidson and Worrell (1988) examine the daily returns of a sample of 131 announcements of illegal U.S. business practices during the period 1970–1979. Their sample includes illegalities such as bribery, criminal fraud, tax evasion, illegal political contributions and criminal antitrust violations. They find a significant abnormal return of –0.87% on the day before the publication and a non-significant abnormal return of –0.21% on the publication date. They conclude that the market reacts negatively on the day the news reaches the market.

In a similar way, Reichert et al. (1996) examine a U.S. sample of 83 announcements of filing of formal indictments against companies for corporate illegalities at firm level during the period 1980–1990. The aggregate sample shows a stock price decline on the announcement date (abnormal return of –1.38%).

Rao and Hamilton (1996) examine a sample of 58 events from 1989 through 1993 in the U.S. on bribery, employee discrimination, environmental pollution, insider trading and business ethics. They find a monthly abnormal return of –5.67% for the full sample on the announcement moment of the publication in financial press. Given the sample size, no subsample analysis was performed for each type of corporate misconduct. Between 1988 and 1992, Gunthorpe (1997) examines 69 U.S. cases of formal investigations into fraud, bribery, price fixing, breach of contract and alike. Again, the full sample shows a negative abnormal return of –1.33% on the announcement date.

Using a dataset on criminal offenses by 78 U.S. corporations, Alexander (1999) finds a stock market penalty for a wide range of illegalities such as contract violations, bribes, fraudulent bids, FDA violations, safety violations, illegal antitrust practices, export violations and environmental and wildlife offenses. Over a 2-day period around the announcement in press she measures a significant –2.84% abnormal return. Correcting for legal penalties, she attributes the difference to a reputation penalty.

However, pooling all types of corporate maleficence in one sample as is the case in the above aggregate studies makes the results difficult to interpret. Markets might react differently to different types of corporate misconduct. For instance, financial markets might react negatively to accounting fraud, but positively to bribery. Accounting fraud could be considered as bad business practice (decrease of cash flows), while bribery might be considered as good business practice to obtain important business contracts in certain countries (increase of cash flows). Moreover, financial markets might react more strongly to certain types of corporate misconduct than to others (e.g. fraud versus environmental violations). Any aggregation across all types of maleficence could make the results difficult to interpret since the price impacts of different illegal categories might offset each other, and thus, a smaller overall abnormal return is observed.

While the above studies used an aggregate sample of a diverse range of corporate misconduct, the scope of the following studies is more focused by examining different types of fraud.

Misleading Advertising

Peltzman (1981) examines the impact of Federal Trade Commission's (FTC) charges on false and misleading advertising on companies' stock prices and finds strong results for complaints. In a period of three trading days before and one trading day after the complaint an excess mean loss of 3.12% is observed. Since the total advertising expenses rarely account for more than 1% of a company's total assets or sales, 'we have to suspect that the adverse effects on a company go beyond those on the market for the specific product' (p. 418). Other papers on misleading advertising include Sauer and Leffler (1990), Rubin et al. (1988) and Mathios and Plummer (1989). Garbade et al. (1982) show a negative stock price decline of about 6% on the announcement of the filing of an antitrust suit by the Justice Department of the FTC.

Fraud

Over the period 1981–1987 Karpoff and Lott (1993) examine 132 U.S. cases of frauds of customers, suppliers, employees, government and investors and find that public announcements of corporate fraud in press leads to an average decline of 1.34% of the stock price. On a subsample of 15 companies they collected information on the level of the legal penalties and find that the stock market loss is in no relation to the expected penalties. They interpret the stock price decline therefore as a reputational penalty imposed by the financial market.

Environmental Violations

Environmental violations can be penalized through explicit legal sanctions imposed through regulatory, civil and criminal proceedings (such as fines, payments to damaged parties, compliance costs and cleanup expenses) and reputational penalties. Karpoff et al. (2005) examine 478 U.S. environmental violations over the period 1980–2000 to determine to what extent reputational penalties impose a significant cost on violating firms. For the full sample they find a stock market loss of 1.00% over a 2-day period and for the allegations subsample a 2-day abnormal return of −1.69%.

Using smaller sample sizes, earlier researchers show a significant negative price reaction (−1.5% in Klassen and McLaughlin 1996) or no significant price reaction (Lanoie and Laplante 1994, Lanoie et al. 1998). Examining the impact of news coverage of toxic release inventory data Hamilton (1995) finds a negative stock market reaction of about −1% over the first five trading days. Dasgupta et al. (2001) find a similar equity loss when examining environmental complaints.

Most of these studies only measure a negative stock price reaction and assume it as evidence that financial markets sanction environmental violations. However, they conduct no attempt to sort out the effect of legal penalties versus reputational penalties. To make strong conclusions about any reputational penalty imposed by environmental violations it is necessary to calculate which part of the stock market loss can be attributed to legal penalties and which part to reputational penalties. Of the above environmental studies, only Karpoff et al. (2005) conduct this valuation exercise. Using detailed information on a subsample of 148 violations with respect to fines, damage awards, compliance and cleanup costs, they find that the equity loss constitutes only of expected legal penalties. Estimates for reputational penalties do not differ significantly different from zero. This implies that 'firms do not on average experience reputational loss when they violate environmental regulations' (Karpoff: 668) and that 'legal penalties, and not reputational penalties, are the primary deterrents to environmental violations' (Karpoff: 655).

Accounting Misrepresentation

Companies pay substantial reputational penalties for cooking the books. Karpoff et al. (2008) examine 585 U.S. firms for financial misrepresentation between 1978 and 2002. Financial accounting misconduct is penalized by a very heavily equity loss. According to their measurement 24.5% of the equity loss can be attributed to market adjustment to reflect the correct fundamental value of the company's financial situation, 8.8% can be associated with expected legal penalties and no less than 66.6% is due to a reputational penalty. Or in absolute dollars terms: 'For every dollar of inflated value when a firm's books are cooked, firm value decreases by that dollar when the misrepresentation is revealed; in addition, firm value declines an additional 36 dollar cents due to fines and class action settlements *and $2.71 due to lost reputation*' (Karpoff: 606). Karpoff et al. (2008) clearly show that legal penalties are only a small part of the total losses suffered by these firms. The reputational penalty is obviously far more important.

Insider Trading

Engelen (2009) shows that companies are penalized in financial markets for the illegal insider trading practices of their managers. He observes a clear negative abnormal return on the day of the newspaper announcement of the illegal insider trading practice of about −1.50%. Illegal insider trading offers a unique opportunity to measure the reputational effect (see infra). Any legal penalty is attributed to the individual level, being the manager which is caught for illegal insider trading. Legal penalties are normally not imposed at the company level. The stock price therefore does not anticipate any legal penalty paid by the company and, by definition, any stock price reaction should reflect lost reputation only. This empirical study shows that financial markets impose a reputational penalty of about one and a half percent on companies whose managers engage in illegal insider trading.

Conclusions

The empirical literature confirms the theoretical reputation model of Klein and Leffler (1981), which predicts that reputational penalties induce companies to maintain product quality at a high level because the market mechanism internalizes the cost of corporate misconduct in repeated business transactions. The empirical studies on product recall and product safety suggests that stock markets react negatively to news that affects a firm's reputation. It shows that stock markets can induce corporations to take responsibility with respect to product quality and safety.

The empirical studies on corporate maleficence furthermore show that this reputation mechanism is not limited to a seller-customer framework but can be applied to a wide range of settings of repeated transactions. Besides customers, other related parties such as suppliers or employees can change their implicit and explicit contracts with the company. We find strong negative stock price declines in aggregate samples for a wide range of corporate misconduct, including bribery, tax evasion, illegal political contributions, employee discrimination, environmental pollution, and criminal antitrust violations.

Legend: Information on environmental violations is obtained from Karpoff, Lott and Wehrly (2005), on tire recalls from Govindaraj and Jaggi (2004), on drug recalls from Mitchell (1989), on airline crashes from Mitchell and Maloney (1989), on financial misrepresentation from Karpoff et al. (2008), on fraud from Karpoff and Lott (1993) and on illegal insider trading from Engelen (2009).

Similar results are found for more focused samples of fraud, financial misrepresentation, insider trading and misleading advertisements. For instance, for financial representation the legal penalties are only a small part of the total losses suffered by these firms and the reputational penalties prove to be far more important. Reputational penalties are thus an important channel to induce corporations to behave responsible. The empirical literature clearly shows that investors on financial markets take responsibility and use their powers to punish certain corporate practices.

However, reputational penalties do not perform effectively under all circumstances. The literature supports a clear distinction between related party and third party maleficence. Karpoff et al. (2005) show that environmental violations impose no reputational penalty since there are no directly related parties involved (see Fig. 4.6). Karpoff and Lott (1993) find a reputational penalty of 90% of the equity

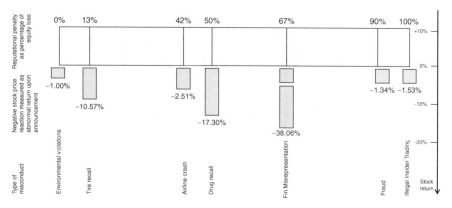

Fig. 4.6 Reputational penalty as percentage of equity loss for different types of corporate misconduct. Source: Engelen (2009)

loss for party related misconduct as fraud of stakeholders, fraud of the government and financial reporting fraud. As predicted by theory, they do not find any reputational penalty for regulatory violations without direct involvement of related parties (e.g. check-kiting scheme). Figure 4.6 shows percentages between 13 and 42% for product recalls and 67% for financial misrepresentation. A 100% reputational penalty is found for illegal insider trading cases (Engelen 2009).

The distribution of responsibilities in inducing companies to behave responsible is an important issue for questions of CSR. Perhaps it even became more important after the recent financial crisis. Since the crisis showed limitations of monitoring by internal governance systems, by external monitors such as rating agencies and regulators, this chapter discusses the role of investors on financial markets. The empirical results reviewed in this chapter suggest that the morally blind process of stock price allocation through financial markets functions as a supervisor of related party misconduct such as financial misrepresentation, fraud of stakeholders, insider trading and product quality and safety. Financial markets clearly penalize these types of irresponsible corporate behavior by imposing a reputational penalty which is often a multiple of the legal penalties. For third party misconduct, reputational penalties work less effectively. In those cases legal penalties are much more important to force companies to behave responsibly.

These findings have a distance resonance with Eccles critique in this book on the mainstreaming of RI. In his chapter, Eccles seems to regret that RI justifies itself by claiming its materiality. Perhaps Eccles would agree with us that our findings show that if corporate misbehavior is regarded by investors as material, there is no need for RI to concern itself with it. Morally blind investors will, through the aggregate of their investment decisions, sanction these firms and hence incentivize them and other to behave more responsible. If corporate misbehavior is not deemed as material by investors, then governments and RI initiatives need to step in.

References

Ahmed, Paravez, John Gardella, and Sudhir Nanda 2002. Wealth effect of drug withdrawals on firms and their competitors. Financial Management 31: 21–41.

Alexander, Cindy. 1999. On the nature of the reputational penalty for corporate crime: Evidence. Journal of Law and Economics 42: 489–526.

Barber, Brad and Masako Darrough. 1996. Product reliability and firm value: The experience of American and Japanese automakers.1973–1992. Journal of Political Economy 104: 1084–1099.

Chalk, Andrew. 1986. Market forces and aircraft safety: The case of the DC-10. Economic Inquiry 24: 43–60.

Chalk, Andrew. 1987. Market forces and commercial aircraft safety. Journal of Industrial Economics 36: 61–81.

Chance, Don and Stepen Ferris. 1987. The effect of aviation disasters on the air transport industry. Journal of Transport Economics and Policy 21: 151–165.

Cheah Eng, Wen Chan, and Corinne Chieng. 2007. The corporate social responsibility of pharmaceutical product recalls: An empirical examination of U.S. and U.K. markets. Journal of Business Ethics 76: 427–449.

Dasgupta, Susmita, Benoit Laplante, and Nlandu Mamingi. 2001. Pollution and capital markets in developing countries. Journal of Environmental Economics and Management 42: 310–335.

Davidson, Wallace and Dan Worrell. 1988. The impact of announcements of corporate illegalities on shareholder returns. Academy of Management Journal 31: 195–200.

Davidson, Wallace and Dan Worrell. 1992. The effect of product recall announcements on shareholder wealth. Strategic Management Journal 3: 467–473.

Dowdell, Thomas, Suresh Govindaraj, and Prem Jain. 1992. The tylenol incident, ensuing regulation, and stock prices. Journal of Financial and Quantitative Analysis 27: 283–301.

Dranove, David and Chris Olsen. 1994. The economic side effects of dangerous drug announcements. Journal of Law and Economics 37: 323–348.

Engelen, Peter Jan. 2005. Remedies to informational asymmetries in stock markets. Antwerpen: Intersentia Publishers.

Engelen, Peter Jan. 2009. The reputational penalty for illegal insider trading. Paper presented at the Academy of Management Conference August 2009, Chicago U.S.

Engelen, Peter Jan and Rezaul Kabir 2006. Empirical evidence on the role of trading suspensions in disseminating new information to the capital market. Journal of Business, Finance and Accounting 33: 1142–1167.

Garbade, Kenneth, William Silber, and Lawrence White. 1982. Market reaction to the filing of antitrust suits: An aggregate and cross-sectional analysis. The Review of Economics and Statistics vol 64(4): 686–691.

Garber, Steven and John Adams. 1998. Product and stock market responses to automotive product liability verdicts. Brookings Papers on Economic Activity: Microeconomics 1998: 1–44.

Govindaraj, Suresh and Bikki Jaggi. 2004. Market overreaction to product recall revisited: The case of firestone tires and the Ford explorer. Review of Quantitative Finance and Accounting 23: 31–54.

Gunthorpe, Deborah. 1997. Business ethics: A quantitative analysis of the impact of unethical behavior by publicly traded corporations. Journal of Business Ethics 16: 537–543.

Hamilton, James. 1995. Pollution as news: Media and stock market reactions to the toxics release inventory data. Journal of Environmental Economics and Management 1: 98–113.

Ho, Virginia. 2009. Enlightened shareholder value: Corporate governance beyond the shareholder-stakeholder divide. Indiana Legal Studies Research Paper No. 1476116. Available at SSRN: http://ssrn.com/abstract=1476116. Accessed April 2010.

Hoffer, George, Stephen Pruitt, and R. J. Reilly. 1988. The impact of product recalls on the wealth of sellers: A reexamination. Journal of Political Economy 96: 663–670.

Hoffer, G. E., S. W. Pruitt and Robert Reilly. 1994. When recalls matter: Factors affecting owner response to automotive recalls. The Journal of Consumer Affairs 28: 96–106.

Jarrell, Gregg and Sam Pletzman. 1985. The impact of product recalls on the wealth of sellers. Journal of Political Economy 93: 512–536.

Karpoff, Jonathan and John Lott Jr. 1993. The reputational penalty firms bear from committing criminal fraud. Journal of Law and Economics 26: 757–802.

Karpoff, Jonathan, John Lott Jr., and Eric Wehrly. 2005. The reputational penalties for environmental violations: Empirical evidence. Journal of Law and Economics 48: 653–675.

Karpoff, Jonathan, Scott Lee, and Gerald Martin. 2008. The cost to firms of cooking the books. Journal of Financial and Quantitative Analysis 43: 581–611.

Kashyap, Anil, Raghuram Rajan, and Jeremy Stein. 2008. Rethinking capital regulation. Working Paper. Available at: http://kansascityfed.org/publicat/sympos/2008/KashyapRajanStein.03,12, 09.pdf. Accessed April 2010.

Klassen, Robert and Curtis McLaughlin. 1996. The impact of environmental management on firm performance. Management Science 42: 1199–1214.

Klein, Benjamin and Keith Leffler. 1981. The role of market forces in assuring contractual performance. Journal of Political Economy 89: 615–641.

Lanoie, Paul and Benoite Laplante. 1994. The market response to environmental incidents in Canada: A theoretical and empirical analysis. Southern Economic Journal 60: 657–672.

Lanoie, Paul, Benoite Laplante, and Maité Roy. 1998. Can capital markets create incentives for pollution control? Ecological Economics 26: 31–41.

Lott, John Jr. 1988. Brand names, ignorance, and quality guaranteeing premiums. Applied Economics 20: 165–176.

Lumsdaine, Robin. 2009. What the market watched: Bloomberg news stories and bank returns as the financial crisis unfolded. Working paper. Available at SSRN: http://ssrn.com/abstract= 1482019. Accessed April 2010.

Mathios, Alan and Mark Plummer. 1989. The regulation of advertising by the federal trade commission: Capital market effects. Research in Law and Economics. ed. by R. Zerbe, Greenwich: JAI 2: 77–93.

McWilliams, Abagail and Donald Siegel. 2000. Corporate social responsibility and financial performance: Correlation or misspecification? Strategic Management Journal 21: 603–609.

McWilliams, Abagail and Donald Siegel. 2001. Corporate social responsibility: A theory of the firm perspective. Academy of Management Review 26: 117–127.

McWilliams, Abagail and Donald Siegel. 2006. Corporate social responsibility: Strategic implications. Journal of Management Studies 43: 1–18.

Mitchell, Mark. 1989. The impact of external parties on brand-name capital: The 1982 Tylenol poisonings and subsequent cases. Economic Inquiry 27: 601–618.

Mitchell, Mark and Michael Maloney. 1989. Crisis in the cockpit? The role of market forces in promoting air travel safety. Journal of Law and Economics 32: 329–355.

Orlitzky, Marc, Frank Schmidt, and Sara Rynes 2003. Corporate social and financial performance: A meta-analysis. Organization Studies 24: 403–441.

Pava, Moses and Joshua Krausz. 1996. The association between corporate social responsibility and financial performance: The paradox of social cost. Journal of Business Ethics 15: 321–357.

Peltzman, Sam. 1981. The effects of FTC advertising regulation. Journal of Law and Economics 24: 403–448.

Posnikoff, Judith. 1997. Disinvestment from South Africa: They did well by doing good. Contemporary Economic Policy 15: 76–86.

Prince, David and Paul Rubin. 2002. The effects of product liability litigation on the value of firms. American Law and Economics Review 4: 44–87.

Pruitt, Stephen and David Peterson. 1986. Security price reactions around product recall announcements. Journal of Financial Research 9: 113–122.

Rao, Spuma and Broke Hamilton III. 1996. The effect of published reports of unethical conduct on stock prices. Journal of Business Ethics 15: 1321–1330.

Reichert, Alan, Michael Lockett, and Ramesh Rao. 1996. The impact of illegal business practice on shareholder returns. The Financial Review 31: 67–85.

Roberts, Peter and Grahame Dowling. 2002. Corporate reputation and sustained superior financial performance. Strategic Management Journal 23: 1077–1093.

Rotthoff, Kurt. 2009. Product liability litigation: An issue of merck and lawsuits over Vioxx. SSRN working paper, http://ssrn.com/abstract=115-1271. Accessed April 2010.

Rubin, Paul, Dennis Murphy, and Gregg Jarrell. 1988. Risky products, risky stocks. Regulation 1: 35–39.

Rupp, Nicholas. 2001. Are government initiated recalls more damaging for shareholders? Evidence from automotive recalls, 1973–1998. Economics Letters 71: 265–270.

Rupp, Nicholas. 2004. The attributes of a costly recall: Evidence from the automotive industry. Review of Industrial Organization 25: 21–44.

Rupp, Nicholas and Curtis Taylor. 2002. Who initiates recalls and who cares? Evidence from the automobile industry. Journal of Industrial Economics 123–149.

Salin, Victoria and Neal Hooker. 2001. Stock market reaction to food recalls. Review of Agricultural Economics 23: 33–46.

Sauer, Raymond and Keith Leffler. 1990. Did the federal trade commission's advertising substantiation program promote more credible advertising? American Economic Review 80: 191–203.

Shapiro, Carl. 1982. Consumer information, product quality, and seller reputation. The Bell Journal of Economics 13: 20–35.

Shapiro, Carl. 1983. Premiums for high quality products as returns to reputations. The Quarterly Journal of Economics 659–679.

Skantz, Terrance, Dale Cloninger, and Thomas Strickland. 1990. Price-fixing and shareholder returns: An empirical study. Financial Review 25: 153–163.

Stefou, Marina. 2009. Does the financial crisis teach us anything about corporate governance? Working Paper. Available at SSRN: http://ssrn.com/abstract=1480224. Accessed April 2010.

Straachan, James, David Smith, and William Beedles. 1983. The price reaction to (alleged) corporate crime. Financial Review 18: 121–132.

Thomsen, Michael and Andrew McKenzie. 2001. Market incentives for safe foods: An examination of shareholder losses from meat and poultry recalls. American Journal of Agricultural Economics 3: 526–537.

Yahanpath, Noel and Tintu Joseph. 2009. Factors that contributed to global financial crisis (GFC) and the role of shareholder wealth maximization in GFC. Working Paper. Available at SSRN: http://ssrn.com/abstract=1460355. Accessed April 2010.

Chapter 5
The Financial Performance of RI Funds After 2000

Olaf Weber, Marco Mansfeld, and Eric Schirrmann

Introduction

More and more investors integrate social and environmental criteria into their investment decisions (Kasemir et al. 2001). Thus the number of investment funds in the socially responsible investment (SRI) sector has increased correspondingly. In 2007 there were 313 SRI funds available in Europe (Eurosif 2007). Those funds strive for satisfying the needs of the investors with respect to social and environmental impacts (Koellner et al. 2007). But do those funds offer a satisfying financial return as well? How did those financial products perform financially in times of turmoil like in the past years? Additionally to their performance with respect to sustainability, the environment, or ethical criteria, SRI funds are expected to perform financially in a sustainable way as well. Only then they guarantee a positive long term financial return and acceptable financial risks.

A study by Koellner et al. (2007) showed that between 2000 and 2004 SRI funds did outperform comparable conventional products not only in terms of environmental impacts, but with respect to financial return as well. However this study used data in a so-called bull phase with increasing stock prices. At that time especially environmental sectors like the renewable energy sector performed very well (Weber et al. 2008). But Galema et al. (2008) could find a significant impact of socially responsible investment on stock returns as well. In contrast to that, other studies could not find significant differences in risk-adjusted returns between SRI funds and conventional portfolios (Bauer et al. 2005).

Mahler et al. (2009) analysed the performance of companies committed to corporate social responsibility practices especially in bear phases and found that those companies achieved above average performances in those phases. On the other side Scholtens (2008) showed that rather the financial success of a company causes better performance in corporate social responsibility than vice versa. Other scholars

O. Weber (✉)
School of Environment, Enterprise and Development, University of Waterloo,
Waterloo, ON, Canada
e-mail: oweber@uwaterloo.ca

W. Vandekerckhove et al. (eds.), *Responsible Investment in Times of Turmoil*,
Issues in Business Ethics 31, DOI 10.1007/978-90-481-9319-6_5,
© Springer Science+Business Media B.V. 2011

like Barnett and Salomon (2006) stress the large heterogeneity between different SRI funds depending on the type of social and environmental screening criteria and strategies. They confess that the financial performance of SRI funds varies with the types of social screens used.

Generally, phases of turmoil are characterized by high market price fluctuations and high risks for investors. Thus the question is whether SRI funds react in those phases differently compared to conventional funds. Koellner et al. (2007) did not find significant differences in the volatility between SRI funds and their conventional counterparts. But special analyses on the performance of SRI funds especially in times of turmoil are rare. A Canadian study for the years 2007 and 2008 showed that Canadian SRI funds performed similar to their conventional counterparts (Shin 2009). Kropp (2008) found that SRI funds even outperformed mainstream funds in 2009. A study by the Social Investment Forum (2009) for the time between August 2008 and August 2009 resulted in a slight outperformance of SRI funds to the MSCI World Index as well. Based on those studies, we hypothesized that SRI funds show similar results in times of turmoil as well.

But what could be reasons for a different performance of SRI funds compared to their conventional counterparts? A number of academic surveys have identified a positive correlation between environmental performance – environmental strategies, environmental management practices, emissions – and financial performance of firms (Annandale et al. 2001, Dasgupta et al. 2002, Dowell et al. 2000, Klassen and McLaughlin 1996, Nakao et al. 2007). This positive relation has an influence on the performance of SRI equity funds that mainly invest in companies with good environmental and/or social performance.

On the one hand a group of analyses suggests that a positive environmental performance can be associated with neutral to positive economic (Ilnitch and Schaltegger 1995, Schaltegger and Figge 2000) or financial performance (Benson et al. 2006, Elsayed and Paton 2009, Kreander et al. 2005). On the other hand there are empirical studies that do not show a clear positive relation between CSR performance of firms and their financial performance (Margolis and Walsh 2001, Wagner et al. 2001). Based on the first group of studies an outperformance of SRI funds is suggested for all market phases. The latter group of studies proposes a strong correlation with conventional products or indices. In those cases influences like regions, sectors, services, regulations (Bleischwitz 2004), market capitalization (Cerin and Dobers 2001), price-to-book ratio (Galema et al. 2008) or other influences play a more important role than CSR performance.

Thus the following study concentrates on the following questions:

1. Is there a significant difference in the financial return between a portfolio of SRI funds and a conventional index during times of turmoil?
2. Is there a relation between financial and sustainability ratings based on the past performance of funds and the return of an SRI fund portfolio in times of turmoil?

Methods

In order to analyse differences in the financial return between a portfolio of SRI funds and a conventional index during times of turmoil we calculated t-tests, standard deviation, and coefficient of variation.

To analyse the relation between financial and sustainability ratings based on the past performance of funds and the return of a SRI fund portfolio in times of turmoil we performed a multivariate linear regression model. Those models are used to analyze the influence of different independent variables like CSR indicators on a dependent variable like the financial performance (Margolis and Walsh 2001, Weber et al. 2008). To analyze similarities between the SRI funds and the MSCI World Index we calculated correlations (Campbell et al. 1997). The MSCI World Index was selected because the funds in the sample are equity funds based in Europe, North-America, Asia-Pacific, South Africa and Latin America and no other, better fitting, index could be used in due time.

The standard deviation and the coefficient of variation (Lee et al. 1999) were used to measure the risk of the SRI fund portfolio. The coefficient of variation (cv) allows determining how much standard deviation is assumed in comparison to the amount of return. Thus it represents a risk adjusted measurement taking into account both, market price fluctuation and return. The cv is useful for investors basing their investment on a risk-return trade-off (Geczy et al. 2005).

In addition to analysing the financial performance of the SRI fund portfolio during the whole time period from November 2001 to June 2009 we split the data in two phases, the bull phase from April 2003 to May 2007, and the bear phase between June 2007 and March 2009. We separately analysed the performance during those phases as well. The two phases were selected to gather two time series that are long enough to use comparative statistics on a monthly basis. We tested the selection of the two phases using the Chow breakdown test.

Database

Monthly performance data of 151 from 229 mutual funds that classified themselves as sustainable, environmental, ethical, or social in the Bloomberg database was used. The first month was December 2001. The last entry is end of June 2009. Monthly return data was taken from the Bloomberg database. The sample of 151 funds consisted of those funds that offered monthly performance data for the whole time period. Furthermore we rated those funds with respect to their financial and sustainability performance. Monthly data has to be interpreted with a wider confidence interval than weekly or daily data. One month with extremely good or bad performance can influence the time series significantly. However Martin et al. (1997) stated that monthly data can be used to measure relative risk and return rankings.

As mentioned above, we analysed funds that classified themselves as sustainable, environmental, ethical, or social in the Bloomberg database. However a self-assessment does not mean that a fund qualifies for an investment of a sustainability fund-of-funds or satisfies the requirements of socially responsible investments. Thus, additionally we rated the funds with respect to their financial and sustainability performance in the past in a standardized way on a scale from 1 to 5 with 1 as the worst and 5 as the best rating. The ratings were done once for every fund. The financial rating and the sustainability rating are equally weighted. However, there is a possibility that the rating of a fund changes, i.e. when the fund management changes. If a fund is rated for a second time the latest rating was selected. To rate the funds with respect to their financial performance, the fund management skills (i.e. alpha, beta, Sharpe ratio etc.) and the cumulative performance compared to the funds' benchmarks were rated. Secondly, a consistency analysis for bullish and bearish market phases was done. As a third step the risk adjusted performance was rated against the respective benchmark as well. The weighting of the financial criteria were 15% for the fund management skills, 30% for the cumulative performance, 20% for the consistency, 25% for the risks and 10% for the costs.

The sustainability rating based on the analysis of the research quality (number of qualified researchers, sustainability concept), the portfolio quality (environmental and social performance, product sustainability and controversies of the invested companies, sustainability rating of sectors measured on the basis of company and sector data of a CSR rating agency), the engagement of the fund management company (policy and forms of engagement) and the transparency according to the Eurosif transparency guidelines of (Eurosif 2004). The portfolio quality was rated using the Centre Info ESG Equity Research database for the CSR performance of companies. Information about the research quality was gathered by analysing the available publications of the respective funds and by contacting the fund management by telephone, email and mail. The weights for the sustainability ratings were 30% for the research quality, 40% for the portfolio quality, 20% for engagement and 10% for transparency.

Results

After presenting the descriptive statistics we will give an overview about the financial returns between 2002 and 2009 followed by a comparison between the MSCI World Index and SRI funds. Afterwards, we concentrate on the analysis of the bear and bull phases between 2002 and 2009. In order to specify relevant variables and to explain the performance difference on the basis of fund characteristics we constructed a regression model that is presented after having analysed of the bull and bear phase. The analysis is completed by calculating and testing the standard deviation and the coefficient of variation as measures of risk.

Descriptive Statistics

The financial and sustainability ratings as well as the financial return for the whole time series are presented in Table 5.1. The sustainability ratings are significantly

Table 5.1 Descriptive values of the financial and sustainability rating and for the financial return

–	Financial rating	Sustainability rating	Financial return
Mean	3.18	3.83	0.20
Median	3.10	3.88	0.15
Standard Deviation	0.95	0.52	0.23
Kurtosis	2.04	2.61	6.29
Skewness	−0.07	−0.32	1.44

higher than the financial ratings (t-test, $p < 0.00001$, df $= 150$, $t = 6.8$). Given a sample of self-declared SRI funds the result could be expected.

The correlation between sustainability rating, financial rating, and financial return is presented in Table 5.2. The results show that there is a positive correlation between the financial rating and the financial return. The sustainability rating correlates negatively to the financial rating and to the financial return.

Furthermore we allocated the regions where the funds are domiciled. The result is presented in Table 5.3. Thus we see that the majority of funds in the sample are located in Europe.

Table 5.2 Correlation between sustainability rating, financial rating and financial return

–	Financial rating	Sustainability rating
Sustainability rating	−0.21*	–
Financial return	0.31*	−0.23*

*Indicates a significant correlation with $p < 0.01$

Table 5.3 Location of the funds

Region	Frequency
Europe	106
Asia/Pacific	13
North America	26
South Africa	1
Latin America	1
Missing	4
Total	151

Financial Returns

In Fig. 5.1 we present the monthly returns of the SRI funds starting December 2001 compared to the MSCI index. A t-test for the return of the SRI funds vs. the MSCI World Index was significant ($p < 0.00001$, df $= 90$, $t = 16.3$) and showed that the

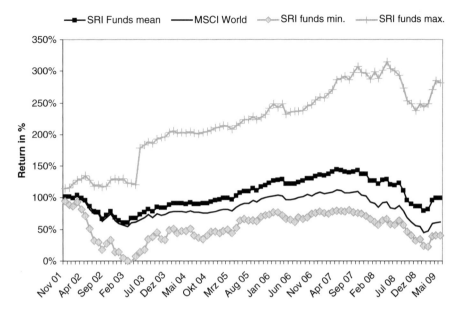

Fig. 5.1 Monthly returns of different groups of funds and of MSCI World Index Generally the SRI funds managed to reach a value of 99.4% compared to the starting date end of 2001 meaning that an investment at the end of 2001 resulted in a loss of 0.6%

SRI fund-portfolio had a higher return during all periods compared to the MSCI World Index. The standard deviation for the SRI fund portfolio is s = 25.05% vs. s = 17.25% for the MSCI World Index. The high standard deviation of the returns indicates a time of turmoil.

Bull and Bear Phases

The monthly returns of the SRI fund portfolio and the MSCI World Index between 2001 and 2009 can be split into different phases of upward and downward development. The bull phase represents the period of increasing returns and the bear phase represents the period of decreasing returns. To analyse the performance of the funds and the MSCI World Index for the bull and bear phases we selected two sections to represent the upward and the downward development. Those are the months from April 2003 to May 2007 representing the upward development and the months from June 2007 to March 2009 representing the downward development. To test whether the selection of the different phases was adequate we used a breakpoin *t*-test (Chow-test). The test resulted in significant differences of the regression models of the bull and the bear phases and the whole time series ($F = 1352$, $k = 3$, $n = 66$, $p < 0.0001$).

Figure 5.2 shows the performance of the funds during the bull phase. Again MSCI World shows a lower return compared to the mean of the SRI funds. The

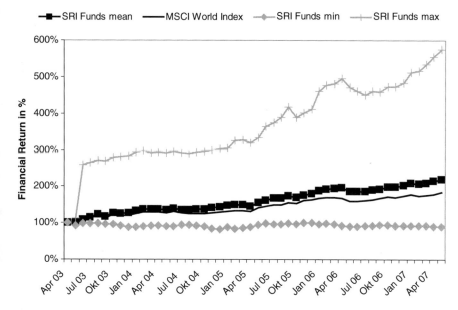

Fig. 5.2 Monthly returns of MSCI World and the SRI funds in the bull phase

means for the returns of MSCI World Index ($\bar{x} = 149.7\%$) and the SRI Funds ($\bar{x} = 159.3\%$) are significantly different (t-Test, $p < 0.0001$). The difference at the end of the bull phase is 40.4%. Thus, the portfolio of SRI funds shows a significantly higher financial return as the MSCI World Index.

The returns for the SRI fund portfolio and for the MSCI World Index in the bear phase are presented in Fig. 5.3. The means for the returns of MSCI World Index ($\bar{x} = 75.7\%$) and the SRI Funds ($\bar{x} = 82.0\%$) are again significantly different (t-test, $p < 0.0001$). The difference at the end of the bear phase is 13.3%. Though we found significant differences between the SRI funds and the MSCI World Index in both phases, the difference is significantly smaller in the bear phase than in the bull phase (t-test for the differences between the SRI fund portfolio and the MSCI World Index with the phases as independent variable: $p < 0.00001$, $t = 4.87$, df $= 69$).

The Relation Between Financial and Sustainability Ratings and the Financial Performance of SRI Funds

In order to analyse whether there is a relation between financial and sustainability ratings based on the past performance of funds and the return of SRI fund portfolio in times of turmoil we calculated a multivariate regression model as dependent variable we used the mean return of the SRI funds for each month of the time series. Thus the model analyses the relation between financial and sustainability ratings

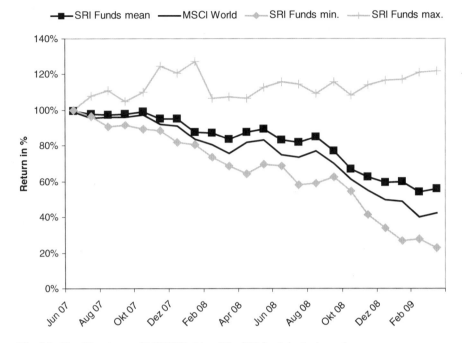

Fig. 5.3 Monthly returns of MSCI World and the SRI funds in the bear phase

based on the past performance of funds and the return of SRI funds in times of turmoil. The resulting model was significant ($p = 0.0001$, $r^2 = 0.12$). The β-weights of the variables are presented in the following function:

$$\text{finret}_{\text{SRIfunds}} = 0.067 \times \text{finrat} - 0.074 \times \text{susrat} + 0.266$$

with finret = financial return of the SRI funds; finrat = financial rating; susrat = sustainability rating.

Thus the result shows that the financial rating of the SRI funds is positively related to the financial return of the funds during a time of turmoil. In contrast to that, the sustainability rating of those funds has a negative relation to their financial performance.

Correlation Between SRI Funds and the MSCI World Index

Even if significant differences between MSCI World and the SRI funds were found in the 'Financial Returns' section, it seems that there are similarities with respect to the trend of the financial returns. Thus we analysed the correlation between the SRI fund portfolio return and the MSCI World Index return. The results are presented in Table 5.4.

Table 5.4 Correlation between the SRI fund portfolio and MSCI World Index for the whole time series (all), the bull phase (April 2003 to May 2007) and the bear phase (June 2007 to March 2009)

Time series	Correlation	Sig.
Nov 2001 to June 2009	0.88	< 0.00001
Apr 2003 to May 2007	0.99	< 0.00001
June 2007 to Mar 2009	0.99	< 0.00001

The correlation between SRI funds and MSCI World Index for the whole time series is $r = 0.88$. The correlation in the shorter bull and bear phases is even higher.

Standard Deviation and Coefficient of Variation

The standard deviation is a measure of the risk of investments. Thus the lower the standard deviation the smaller is the financial risk of a fund especially in bear phases in which the standard deviation is often caused by negative deviations form the mean. Thus, it is interesting to compare the standard deviation of the SRI fund portfolio and the MSCI World Index in different phases. The standard deviations for bull and bear phases are presented in Table 5.5. A F-test for differences of standard deviations showed significant results for the bull phase ($p = 0.02, f = 1.98$, df = 48) and for the whole time series ($p = 0.006$, f = 1.79, df = 90) showing that the standard deviation of the SRI fund portfolio is higher than the standard deviation of the MSCI World Index. For the bear phase we did not find significant differences for the standard deviation ($p = 0.36, f = 0.67$, df = 21).

In order to analyze the relation between standard deviation and average returns, the coefficient of variation (cv) is used as a measure of the relation between risk and return. It is calculated as following:

$$cv = \frac{\sqrt{s^2}}{\bar{x}} \times 100$$

The higher the coefficient of variation the higher the risk compared to the return. We calculated the coefficient of variation for the MSCI World Index and for the SRI fund portfolio. The results are presented in Table 5.6.

Table 5.5 Standard deviation of MSCI World Index and the SRI fund portfolio in bull and bear phases and for the whole time series including F-tests for differences of the standard deviations

Phase	MSCI world index	SRI funds	Sig.
Bear	21.09%	20.57%	0.36
Bull	13.85%	19.86%	0.02
Nov 2001 to June 2009	29.94%	34.26%	0.006

Table 5.6 Coefficients of variation of the MSCI World Index and the SRI fund portfolio including the results of a *t*-test

Phase	MSCI world index	SRI funds	Sig.
Bear	26.7%	19.4%	< 0.00001
Bull	16.2%	20.7%	< 0.00001
Nov 2001 to June 2009	21.4%	23.3%	< 0.00001

Table 5.6 shows that the coefficient of variation is significantly lower for the SRI fund portfolio than for the MSCI World Index in the bear phase ($p < 0.00001$, $t = 8.1$, df $= 21$), but higher in the bull phase ($p < 0.00001$, $t = 18.8$, df $= 48$). That means the risk-return ratio of the SRI fund portfolio is higher in bull phases compared to the MSCI World Index, but lower in bear phases. This is valid for the whole time series as well, because the coefficient of variation of the SRI fund portfolio is significantly higher than the coefficient of variation for the MSCI World Index.

Discussion and Conclusions

We analysed the financial return of 151 SRI funds and the MSCI World Index during a phase of turmoil between December 2001 and June 2009 using correlations, statistical tests and multiple regression models. Furthermore we calculated the standard deviation and the coefficients of variation of an SRI fund portfolio and compared them with the MSCI World Index.

The first question we wanted to answer was whether there are significant differences in the financial return between a portfolio of SRI funds and a conventional index during times of turmoil. We found that SRI funds had a significantly higher return than the MSCI World Index, though the correlation between both is very high as well. This suggests a high influence of external conditions on the performance of company shares and goes in-line with the results of O'Sullivan and Sheffrin (2003). Restrictions on the database did not allow calculating models like the Fama-French model or Capital Asset Pricing models that could have resulted in higher impacts of the sustainability rating of the funds on their financial return (Galema et al. 2008).

However, analysing performance of the SRI fund portfolio, we could show that the selected SRI funds reached a significantly higher return than the MSCI World Index during the whole time of measurement between December 2001 to June 2009 and in the bull and bear phase respectively. This corresponds to other studies (Annandale et al. 2001, Dasgupta et al. 2002, Dowell et al. 2000, Klassen and McLaughlin 1996, Koellner et al. 2007, Kropp 2008, Nakao et al. 2007, Shin 2009) showing an outperformance of SRI investments compared to conventional portfolios. The finance literature on this question shows mixed results. There are studies showing no difference between SRI and conventional investment (Bauer et al. 2005, Bello 2005), while in other studies SRI portfolios under-performed compared to a conventional portfolio (Geczy et al. 2005, Renneboog et al. 2008b). Another study found an outperformance of SRI investments compared to their conventional counterparts based on book-to-market regression (Galema et al. 2008). Thus, the results on the performance of SRI are still inconclusive.

But being rated well with respect to being socially responsible does not guarantee a good financial performance (Bleischwitz 2004, Cerin and Dobers 2001). Thus a multivariate regression analysis with the financial and sustainability rating of the funds was done in order to answer the question whether there is a relation between financial and sustainability ratings based on the past performance of funds, and the return of SRI funds in times of turmoil. As dependent variable we used the difference between the monthly returns of the SRI fund portfolio and the MSCI World index. The positive β-weight of the financial rating in the regression model suggests that there is a positive relation between SRI funds that get a positive financial rating, including consistency analyses for different market phases and financial risk analyses, and their financial return in times of turmoil. In contrast to that, the sustainability rating of the funds did even have a negative β-weight. Thus, to rely only on sustainability or social responsibility analyses did not have a positive effect on the financial return of funds as also Hamilton et al. (1993) suggest. It is possible to create a well-performing SRI portfolio by adding an in-depth financial analysis to the sustainability analysis what is in-line with a number of studies (Milevsky et al. 2006, Waddock and Graves 2000) and thus contradictory to Benson et al. (2006) mentioning that an outperformance of SRI funds is not stable over time, or Renneboog et al. (2008a) who found that SRI investors were unable to identify the funds that will outperform their benchmarks.

Having analyzed the performance in different phases, the mean outperformance of the SRI fund portfolio was significantly higher in the bull phase. The SRI fund portfolio performed negatively with respect to financial performance in the bear phase as well, but could outperform the MSCI World Index.

High correlation between the SRI fund portfolio and the MSCI World Index suggests stressing similarities instead of the differences. This is valid for the time between December 2001 to June 2009 as well as for the bull and bear phases. This result again favours high influences of external impacts like the general financial market performance, regional, sector and other influences on the performance of SRI funds.

Thus investing in SRI funds in times of turmoil could result in a better financial return than the MSCI World Index if an analyst is able to perform a financial rating of those funds. However, the influence of social responsibility on the financial return of company shares is not strong enough to avoid the influence of general financial market tendencies. Socially responsible investing needs to be based on in-depth financial analysis to create a positive financial return for the investor in times of turmoil as well.

Annex: List of Funds Used in the Analysis

Fund name	Financial rating	Sustainability rating
3 Banken-Generali – 3 Banken Nachhaltigkeitsfonds	4.4	4.3
Aberdeen Investment Funds ICVC – Ethical World Fund	4.0	3.6
Adviser I Funds – Meridio Green Balance	2.8	4.5
AEGON ICVC – Ethical Equity Fund	4.8	2.9
Allchurches Investment Funds – Amity Fund	4.7	3.8
AMP Capital Sustainable Share Fund	4.9	3.9
Ariel Appreciation Fund	3.1	3.7
Ariel Fund	1.5	3.4
Asahi Life Socially Responsible Investment Fund – Asunohane	1.9	3.1
ASN Aandelenfonds	2.7	3.6
ASN Milieu Waterfonds	2.8	3.8
Australian Ethical Large Companies Share Trust	4.0	3.9
Ave Maria Catholic Values Fund	3.6	2.5
Aviva Investors Investment Funds ICVC – Aviva Investors Sustainable Future Corp	3.4	4.2
Aviva Investors Investment Funds ICVC – Aviva Investors Sustainable Future Euro	4.0	4.8
Aviva Investors Investment Funds ICVC – Aviva Investors Sustainable Future Manag	3.6	4.1
Aviva Investors Investment Funds ICVC – Aviva Investors Sustainable Future UK Gr	3.2	4.2
Aviva Investors Investment Funds ICVC – Aviva Investors UK Ethical Fund	3.3	4.6
Aviva Investors Sustainable Future Pan-European Equity Fund	3.1	4.7
AXA Euro Valeurs Responsables	3.1	3.8
AXA UK Investment Company ICVC – Ethical Fund	1.9	3.2
Banco Etisk Norden	3.0	3.9
Banco Etisk Sverige	2.6	4.2
Banco Etisk Sverige Special	2.7	4.3
Banco Euro Top 50	1.8	4.3
Banco Hjalp	3.0	4.2
Banco Ideell Miljo	3.3	4.2
Banco Svensk Miljo	3.0	3.9
Bankhaus Schelhammer &Schattera – Superior 3 – Ethik	2.7	4.8
BlackRock Global Funds – New Energy Fund	4.1	2.7
BT Institutional Australian Sustainability Share Fund	2.9	4.0
BT Wholesale Ethical Share Fund	4.1	4.0
Calvert Capital Accumulation Fund	1.8	4.4
Calvert Large Cap Growth Fund	2.7	4.2
Calvert Social Investment Fund – Bond Portfolio	2.4	3.6
Calvert World Values International Equity Fund	3.2	4.1
Carlson Sverigefond	2.3	4.0
Challenger Socially Responsive Share Fund	2.7	3.9
CIS Sustainable Leaders Trust	3.9	4.2

Fund name	Financial rating	Sustainability rating
Credit du Nord Etoile Partenaires	4.0	3.2
Credit Mutuel Finance CM Valeurs Ethiques	2.0	4.2
Dexia Sustainable EMU	2.3	4.4
Dexia Sustainable Europe	2.1	4.1
Dexia Sustainable North America	2.0	3.6
Dexia Sustainable Pacific	1.4	4.2
Dexia Sustainable World	2.1	4.0
DnB NOR Gront Norden	2.7	3.9
DnB NOR Miljoinvest	3.6	4.4
Domini Social Bond Fund	2.9	4.3
Domini Social Equity Fund	2.1	4.2
Dr. Hoeller PRIME VALUES Income	3.2	4.3
Ecofi Investissements Choix Solidaire SICAV	4.0	3.2
Ecofi Investissements Epargne Ethique Actions	2.4	4.2
Ecureuil Benefices Responsable	2.3	3.9
Erste Sparinvest – ESPA Stock Umwelt	4.1	4.4
ESPA VINIS Stock Austria	3.8	2.9
Ethical Growth Fund	2.8	3.9
Ethical Special Equity Fund	4.8	3.4
Europe Gouvernance	1.9	3.7
F & C Investment Funds ICVC III – UK Ethical Fund	4.3	3.8
Federal Gestion Federal Actions Ethiques	2.4	3.2
Federis Gestion d'Actifs Federis ISR Euro	3.0	3.4
FORTIS L FUND – Equity Socially Responsible Europe	2.5	4.0
Green Century Balanced Fund	4.4	3.5
Green Century Equity Fund	2.6	4.2
Green Effects NAI-Werte Fonds	4.5	4.2
Groupama Asset Management Euro Capital Durable	2.9	3.7
Henderson Global Care Funds – Global Care Growth Fund	2.7	4.4
Henderson Global Care Funds – Global Care UK Income Fund	4.9	4.0
Henderson Global Fund – Industries of the Future Fund	2.7	4.3
Hunter Hall Global Ethical Trust	4.3	3.0
Hunter Hall Value Growth Trust	3.9	2.8
IDEAM – Integral Development Asset Management Eurosocietale	4.5	3.9
IN.Flanders Index Fund	3.9	3.4
ING Sustainable Investments – Wholesale Australian Shares Trust	3.8	3.6
Investors Summa SRI FundTM	2.6	3.5
Julius Baer Multipartner – SAM Sustainable Water Fund	4.5	3.7
Jupiter Environmental Income Fund	4.3	4.1
KBC Eco Fund – Alternative Energy	3.9	4.3
KBC Eco Fund – Sustainable Euroland	1.8	4.4
KBC Eco Fund – Water	4.9	3.7
KBC Eco Fund – World	3.9	3.6

Fund name	Financial rating	Sustainability rating
KBC Institutional Fund – Ethical Euro Equities	2.8	4.5
KLP AksjeNorge	4.4	3.3
Lazard Objective Ethique Socialement Responsable	3.9	3.4
LBPAM Actions Developpement Durable	2.1	3.6
Legal & General Ethical Trust	4.6	2.7
LKCM Aquinas Growth Fund	3.0	3.0
LKCM Aquinas Value Fund	3.3	3.0
MACIF Gestion MACIF Croissance Durable Europe	2.7	4.6
MACIF Gestion MACIF Croissance Durable France	2.1	4.4
MACIF Gestion MACIF Obligations Developpement Durable	2.7	3.3
Meeschaert Asset Management MAM Actions Ethique	1.5	4.2
Meritas Jantzi Social Index Fund	3.0	3.4
Miljo Teknologi	1.6	4.0
Mitsubishi UFJ Eco Partners – Midori no Tsubasa	1.5	3.5
MMA Praxis Value Index Fund	3.9	3.5
Natixis Asset Management Natixis Impact Actions Euro	2.3	3.6
Neuberger Berman Socially Responsive Fund	4.1	3.7
New Alternatives Fund Inc/fund	2.9	4.3
Nomura Global Environment RF Rainbow Fund	3.6	3.2
Oasis Crescent Equity Fund	5.0	2.8
Oekoworld – Oekovision Classic	3.9	4.1
Ohra Milieutechnologie Fonds	3.7	3.4
OHRA New Energy Fund	3.4	3.7
Orkla Finans Nordic	4.3	3.0
Orsay Croissance Responsable	2.7	4.0
Parnassus Equity Income Fund	2.4	3.5
Parnassus Fund/The	1.8	4.1
Pax World High Yield Bond Fund	3.0	3.4
Perennial Institutional Investment Trusts – Socially Responsive Shares Trust	4.0	3.7
Pictet Funds Lux – Water	4.2	2.7
Pictet-Ethos CH – Swiss Sustainable Equities	2.6	4.9
Pioneer Funds – Global Ecology	4.4	3.7
Professionally Managed Portfolios – Portfolio 21	3.9	4.7
Real FIA Ethical II	3.6	2.9
Sarasin Asset Management Sarasin Euro Mid-Caps Expansion Durable	3.1	3.6
Sarasin Asset Management Sarasin Europe Expansion Durable	2.9	4.5
Sarasin Investmentfonds SICAV – Sarasin OekoSar Portfolio	1.9	4.6
Sarasin Investmentfonds SICAV – Sarasin Sustainable Equity Global	2.0	4.8
Sarasin Multi Label SICAV – New Energy Fund EUR	3.8	4.6
Scottish Widows UK and Income Investment Funds ICVC – Environmental Investor	3.9	3.7

Fund name	Financial rating	Sustainability rating
SEB Fund 1 – SEB Ethical Europe Fund	3.6	2.8
SEB Gyllenberg Forum	3.9	3.9
SEB OekoLux	3.4	4.6
SEB Ostersjofond/WWF	2.7	3.6
Sentinel Sustainable Core Opportunities Fund	4.1	3.3
Sentinel Sustainable Growth Opportunities Fund	1.7	3.2
SGAM Invest Europe Developpement Durable	2.3	3.5
Skandia Ideer for Livet	4.3	3.5
SNS Duurzaam Aandelenfonds	2.0	4.2
Sompo Japan Green Open – Bunanomori	2.2	3.5
St James's Place Ethical Unit Trust	3.4	4.0
Standard Life Investment Co – UK Ethical Fund	3.6	4.1
Stewardship Growth Fund	4.9	3.8
Stewardship Income Fund	4.6	3.7
Swedbank Robur Sverigefond MEGA	4.0	4.2
Swisscanto CH Equity Fund Green Invest	3.6	3.9
Swisscanto LU Portfolio Fund Green Invest Balanced	4.5	3.8
Swisscanto LU Portfolio Fund Green Invest Equity	4.5	4.4
Taifook SRI Asia Fund	2.0	2.9
The Flex-funds Total Return Utilities Fund	4.0	3.5
Triodos Meerwaarde Aandelenfonds N.V.	4.0	4.2
UBS Lux Equity Fund – Eco Performance	2.2	3.4
UBS Lux Equity Fund – Global Innovators	4.2	4.2
Vontobel – Raiffeisen Futura Global Stock	2.9	3.7
Vontobel – Raiffeisen Futura Swiss Franc Bond	2.0	4.0
Vontobel – Raiffeisen Futura Swiss Stock	4.1	4.2
Vontobel Fund – Global Trend New Power	1.0	3.6
Walden Social Equity Fund	2.8	4.1
Winslow Green Growth Fund	1.4	4.2

References

Annandale, David, John Bailey, Ely Ouano, Warren Evans, and Peter King. 2001. The potential role of strategic environmental assessment in the activities of multi-lateral development banks. Environmental Impact Assessment Review 21: 407–429.

Barnett, Michael L. and Robert M. Salomon. 2006. Beyond dichotomy: The curvilinear relationship between responsibility and financial performance. Strategic Management Journal 27: 1101–1122.

Bauer, Rob, Kees Koedijk, and Roger Otten. 2005. International evidence on ethical mutual fund performance and investment style. Journal of Banking and Finance 29: 1751–1767.

Bello, Zakri Y. 2005. Socially responsible investing and portfolio diversification. The Journal of Financial Research XXVIII: 41–57.

Benson, Karen L., Timothy J. Brailsford, and Jacquelyn E. Humphrey. 2006. Do socially responsible fund managers really invest differently? Journal of Business Ethics 65: 337–357.

Bleischwitz, Raimund. 2004. Governance of sustainable development: Co-evolution of corporate and political strategies. International Journal of Sustainable Development 7: 27–43.

Campbell, John Y., Andrew W. Lo, and A. Craig Mackinlay. 1997. The Econometrics of Financial Markets. Princeton, NJ: Princeton University Press.

Cerin, Pontuns and Peter Dobers. 2001. What does the performance of the Dow Jones sustainability group index tell us? Eco-Management and Auditing 8: 123–133.

Dasgupta, Susmita, Benoit Laplante, Hua Wang, and David Wheeler. 2002. Confronting the environmental Kuznets curve. Journal of Economic Perspectives 16: 147–168.

Dowell, Glen, Stuart Hart, and Bernard Yeung. 2000. Do corporate global environmental standards create or destroy market value? Management Science 46: 1059–1074.

Elsayed, Khaled and David Paton. 2009. The impact of financial performance on environmental policy: Does firm life cycle matter? Business Strategy and the Environment 18: 397–413

Eurosif. 2004. Eurosif transparency guidelines for the retail SRI fund sector. Eurosif. http://eurosif. org. Accessed January 2010.

Eurosif. 2007. SRI funds service. Eurosif. http://www.eurosif.org. Acessed January 2010.

Galema, Rients, Auke Plantinga and Bert Scholtens. 2008. The stocks at stake: Return and risk in socially responsible investment. Journal of Banking and Finance 32: 2646–2654.

Geczy, Chistopher C., Robert F., Stambaugh, and David Levin. 2005. Investing in socially responsible mutual funds. SSRN eLibrary. http://papers.ssrn.com/sol3/papers.cfm?abstract_id= 416380. Accessed 30 March 2010.

Hamilton, Sally, Hoje Jo, and Meir Statman. 1993. Doing well by doing good? The investment performance of socially responsible mutual funds. Financial Analysts Journal 49 (November–December): 62–66.

Ilnitch, Anne and Stefan Schaltegger. 1995. Developing a green business portfolio. Long Range Planning 28: 29–38.

Kasemir, Bernd, Andrea Süess, and Alexander J. B. Zehnder. 2001. The next unseen revolution. Pension fund investment and sustainability. Environment 43: 8–19.

Klassen, Robert, D. and Curtis P. McLaughlin. 1996. The impact of environmental management on firm performance. Management Science 42: 1199–1214.

Koellner, Thomas, Sangwon Suh, Olaf Weber, Corinne Moser, and Roland W. Scholz. 2007. Environmental impacts of conventional and sustainable investment funds compared using input-output life-cycle assessment. Journal of Industrial Ecology 11: 41–60.

Kreander, N., R. H. Gray, D. M. Power, and C. D. Sinclair. 2005. Evaluating the performance of ethical and non-ethical funds: A matched pair analysis. Journal of Business Finance and Accounting 32: 1465–1493.

Kropp, Robert. 2008. SRI funds post losses, but hold their won in relative performance: www. socialfunds.com.

Lee, Cheng, John Lee, and Alice Lee. 1999. Statistics for Business and Financial Economics (2 ed.). Singapore, London: World Scientific Publishing.

Mahler, Daniel, Jeremy Barker, Louis Besland, and Otto Schulz. 2009. 'Green' Winners – The performance of sustainability-focused companies during the financial crisis. Chicago: A.T. Kearney. http://atkearney.com. Accessed 30 March 2010.

Margolis, Joshua D and James P. Walsh. 2001. People and Profits? The Search for a Link Between a Company's Social and Financial Performance. Mahwah NJ, London: Lawrence Earlbaum Associates, Publishers.

Martin, George, David McGarthy, and Thomas Schneeweis. 1997. Return interval selection and CTA performance analysis. Derivatives Quarterly Summer: 73–82.

Milevsky, Moshe, Anchar Aziz, Allen Goss, Jane Comeault, and David Wheeler. 2006. Cleaning a passive index: How to use portfolio optimization to satisfy CSR constraints. The Journal of Portfolio Management (Spring): 110–118.

Nakao, Yuriko, Akihiro Amano, Matsumura Kanichiro, Kiminori Genba, and Makiko Nakano (2007). Relationship between environmental performance and financial performance: An empirical analysis of Japanese corporations. Business Strategy and the Environment 16: 106–118.

O'Sullivan, Arthur and Steven M. Sheffrin. 2003. Economics: principles in action. Upper Saddle River, NJ: Pearson Prentice Hall.

Renneboog, Luc, Jenke ter Horst, and Chendi Zhang. 2008a. The price of ethics and stake-holder governance: The performance of socially responsible mutual funds. Journal of Corporate Finance 14: 302–322.

Renneboog, Luc, Jenke ter Horst, and Chendi Zhang. 2008b. Socially responsible investments: Institutional aspects, performance, and investor behavior. Journal of Banking and Finance 32: 1723–1742.

Schaltegger, Stefan and Frank Figge. 2000. Environmental shareholder value: Economic success with corporate environmental management. Eco-Management and Auditing 7: 29–42.

Scholtens, Bert. 2008. A note on the interaction between corporate social responsibility and financial performance. Ecological Economics 68: 46–55.

Shin, Melissa. 2009. The death of short-termism. The dawn of a new economic age. Corporate Knights Winter 2009: 34–40.

Social Investment Forum. 2009. Socially responsible mutual fund charts: Financial performance. Retrieved October, 1st, 2009, 2009, from www.socialinvest.org

Waddock, Sandra A. and Samuel B. Graves. 2000. Performance characteristics of social and traditional investments. Journal of Investing 9: 27–38.

Wagner, Marcus, Stefan Schaltegger, and Walter Wehrmeyer. 2001. The relationship between the environmental and economic performance of firms. What does theory propose and what does empirical evidence tell us? Greener Management International 34(Summer): 95–108.

Weber, Olaf, Thomas Koellner, Dominique Habegger, Henrik Steffensen, and Peter Ohnemus. 2008. The relation between sustainability performance and financial performance of firms. Progress in Industrial Ecology 5: 236–254.

Chapter 6
Responsible Investment by Pension Funds After the Financial Crisis

Riikka Sievänen

Introduction

Responsible investment is a deliberate choice of pension funds, also in times of turmoil. This chapter reports on exploratory research into how pension funds are affected by the financial crises with respect to their approach to responsible investment. In general, better governance, regulations and transparency in the financial market are called for by the pension funds.

The main focus of the recent literature on responsible investment is on financial performance in connection with responsible investments (Renneboog et al. 2008a, Galema et al. 2008). The results of this literature suggest that there is no significant difference between the financial returns of responsible investments compared to conventional investments. A further finding (Renneboog et al. 2008a) is that responsible investors are not willing to accept lower returns for responsible investing. This then is a possible explanation for the suggestion made by Louche (2004) and Sparkes and Cowton (2004) that responsible investment is becoming mainstream. It appears that the reasons to invest in a responsible manner – better governance, regulations and transparency (Eurosif 2009, Bengtsson 2008) – can be linked to the underlying causes for the current financial crisis (see for example Hellwig 2009, McSweeney 2009, Dăianu and Lungu 2008, Crouchy et al. 2007). Hence, our interest is in how pension funds reflect responsible investment in times of turmoil. More specifically, the aim of this contribution is to answer the following questions in an exploratory way: (1) How does the financial crisis impact on pension funds, and (2) How is the impact related to their approach to responsible investment.

The chapter is structured as follows. In Section 'Literature Review' we build a framework based on a literature review. After that Section 'Data and Methodology' describes our methodology In Section 'Results', we organize the findings based on two viewpoints. First we report interview results with ten pension funds regarding the financial crisis. As to the second viewpoint, we investigate how our framework

R. Sievänen (✉)
Department of Economics and Management, University of Helsinki, Helsinki, Finland
e-mail: riikka.sievanen@helsinki.fi

W. Vandekerckhove et al. (eds.), *Responsible Investment in Times of Turmoil*,
Issues in Business Ethics 31, DOI 10.1007/978-90-481-9319-6_6,
© Springer Science+Business Media B.V. 2011

reflects the positions of our interviewees regarding the financial crisis. We discuss this further in Section 'Preliminary Conclusions and Further Considerations' where we synthesize our findings to sketch an answer to our research questions: how the financial crisis impacts the pension funds, and how this is related to their approach to responsible investment.

Literature Review

The aim of this literature review is to find out which underlying factors of the crisis are connected with the motives to invest in a responsible manner. We recognize that several authors suggest the same factors in slightly different forms, through different contexts. We try to find suitable headings for these factors, and comprehend that headings like transparency about the value of the funds, liabilities, and risk management and governance and regulations can be connected to the motives to invest in a responsible manner.

The first context is that of systemic risk. For example, Hellwig (2009) analyzes what went wrong in the implementation of the mortgage securitization mechanism and links this to two factors of systemic risk: systemic interdependency and lack of transparency. Keys et al. (2009) study the quality of mortgage loans. They argue, supported by Van den Heuvel (2009), that the lack of regulations has a significant impact: the mortgage lenders and brokers have a belief in their market share, which encourages stronger risk taking and looser standards. As most of the existing regulations are not targeted to capture the problem of moral hazard, the lack of this quality increases the problem. The authors suggest the problem of moral hazard seems to be controlled better by 'skin in the game' regulations that strongly encourage the brokers to examine the quality of the loans due to the requirement to compensate losses. They confirm their argument by referring to Kleiner and Todd (2007), who find stronger state broker laws are linked to lower competition and loans of better performance (Niinimäki 2009). From the context of systemic risk we directly pick up transparency and regulations. Risk management, governance and the value of the funds are also included to this context indirectly.

The second context is that of accounting. Transparency about the value of the funds takes a central place here, but further factors such as liabilities, risk management, governance and regulations are relevant too. McSweeney (2009) discerns the main contributions of accounting that result in additional corporate vulnerability. The author suggests accounting can support the delusion of continuous growth and biased valuation of the capital. These factors combined with the possibility of excessive pay-outs from corporations result in corporate vulnerability. In addition, McSweeney (2009) identifies three characteristics of the financial markets which enable the present crisis. First, the financial markets have the tendency to create information leading to market failure instead of failure-avoiding. Second, the regulations are not adequate, and unbalance is encouraged by financial markets. Third, financial markets make its participants behave imprudently. McSweeney (2009) argues that these characteristics of the contribution of accounting, and the disbelief in the financial market failure together directed the crisis.

The third context is that of the characteristics of the financial markets. Dăianu and Lungu (2008) classify the underlying causes of the crisis into structural and cyclical factors, on a macro and micro economic level. An example of the structural causes is the increased role of the complex financial markets. Another example is the use of new risk-spreading yet transparency-reducing financial instruments. The authors argue that in the present crisis the cyclical factors – very low credit risk across all instruments and very low risk-free interest rates – are similar to earlier crises. Dăianu and Lungu suggest that for example solving conflicts of interest among market participants and improving transparency regarding disclosure requirements and risk-bearing of the market participants would help. In addition, the authors recommend improving regulations regarding the banking institutions and controlling frameworks that would regulate the involved institutions as a whole. Cumming and Johan (2007) also come up with transparency and regulations as a solution in their study regarding private equity funds. They suggest the current private equity fund regulations hinder institutional investor participation especially due to limited transparency.

A fourth group includes various aspects. Crouhy et al. (2008) consider investment management, lax underwriting standards and poor risk management by financial institutions as reasons that advance the crisis. Also mentioned are lack of market transparency, limitation of extant valuation models and complexity of financial instruments. The authors suggest the regulators did not understand the implications of the changing environment for the financial system. Furthermore, a recent OECD working paper stresses the role of good governance (Yermo 2008).

Thus we see that the literature from different contexts related to the financial crisis list similar factors in slightly different forms. Hence we retain for our framework the following factors: transparency about the value of the funds, liabilities, risk management, governance, and regulations. These might also play a role as motives to engage in responsible investment, given that these factors receive more attention from RI actors.

Responsible investment aims at appropriate transparency of the investments. This is because investors need to ensure the investment targets match their responsible investment criteria. In the Scandinavian context, the revelation of non-acceptable investments was the promoter of responsible investment (Bengtsson 2008). The concept of transparency is logical when discussing institutional investors and responsible investment. These investors need to ensure the investment objects fulfill their responsible investment strategies. To obtain this information, the corporate social responsibility (CSR) policies and practices of companies provide non-financial information to investors. For example, Hockerts and Moir (2004) find the growth of responsible investment has led the companies to provide better information about their CSR related activities and in this way the management's actions have become more visible.

Benson and Humphrey (2008) find that the portfolios and management styles of responsible investment funds are different from those of conventional funds. They conclude the responsible investment fund flow is less sensitive to returns than conventional flows. Also Renneboog et al. (2008b) present findings that are related to different management styles: responsible investment funds include companies which have high ethical and social, and strict stakeholder criteria. Several authors find responsible investment funds, portfolios and indices perform not in a significantly different way from their peers (Kempf and Osthoff 2007, Benson et al. 2006, Derwall et al. 2005, Orlitzky et al. 2003, Abramson and Chung 2000). However, contradictory evidence exist as well (Fowler and Hope 2007). Galema et al. (2008) study the difference between theoretical and empirical literature. In general, the former indicates a relation between responsible investment and stock returns, and the latter does not find one. They find that responsible investment is to be associated with a lower book-to-market ratio, which means the alphas do not capture responsible investment effects (Galema et al. 2008). A question closely related to financial performance is whether responsible investors are prepared to receive lower returns than conventional investors. Renneboog et al. (2008a) find this is not the case. This finding is supported by Wen (2009), who finds one of the central drivers of institutional investors' responsible investment is their financial expectations. In contrast to the large number of studies about financial returns and CSR, the amount of studies linking the financial crisis, responsible investment and institutional investors is very modest. An exception is Quarter et al. (2008), who mention the interest in stronger control in public pension funds' investments in challenging financial times. They conclude that the way in which public pension funds react to the financial crisis may have an impact on responsible investment.

Data and Methodology

To find out how the financial crisis relates to pension funds' responsible investment, we did exploratory research on pension funds in Belgium and Finland. The intention is not primarily to compare these two countries or draw conclusion based on cultural differences. We base the choice of these two countries on the very different development phases regarding the popularity of responsible investment. The Eurosif (2008) SRI study shows that in Belgium the total responsible investment management market (AUM €238.8 billion) represents 48% of the Belgian asset management market. Out of the 13 countries included in Eurosif study, Belgium has the highest market share of its domestic asset management industry in 'broad' responsible investments which include simple negative screening, engagement and integration strategies. The size of the total responsible investment management market in Finland is AUM €67.4 billion. The Eurosif report lists the reasons for the inertia being the lack of asset managers and institutional investors promoting responsible investment. In addition, until now responsible investment and corporate responsibility have not received much attention from NGOs and the media in Finland (Eurosif 2008).

We interviewed ten pension fund representatives: five from Belgium and five from Finland. Their job titles were: Pension Fund Manager, CFO (3), Senior Adviser, Managing Director (2), Financial Manager, Head of Investments, and

Administrative Manager. The pension funds were chosen primarily on the basis of the size of their portfolio. The aim was not to include the five biggest ones from each country but to have a mixture of different types of 'median' sized pension funds. The Belgian pension funds were sized within the range of €100,000,000 to €1,500,000,000 AUM, were responsible for the pension cover of 45,000 employees in average, and had 500 pensioners in average. The figures for Finland were respectively: €600,000,000– €15,000,000,000 AUM, 200,000 and 120,000. These figures are based on the annual reports of the year 2008. Seven of the pension funds are related to a corporation or to part of a public sector. Out of the corporation pension funds, the majority were in B2B business, and two in B2B and retail business. Two pension funds also cater for the pensions of the entrepreneurs. Only one of the funds is targeted at employers from several private industry sectors. Two funds focus on the pensions of one specific sector.

We conducted two rounds of interviews, one in Spring and the beginning of Summer of 2009 and one in the Autumn of 2009. The first round of interviews was carried out face-to-face. Each interview lasted for about an hour. At the beginning of each interview the interviewee was informed about the purpose of our exploratory research, and confidentiality was guaranteed. We recorded each interview and sent drafts of this chapter containing citations, interpretations and conclusions to the interviewees for them to agree. We used a semi-structured questionnaire to guide our interviews, but let the interviewees take the discussion where they wanted in order to receive a genuine viewpoint on each of their funds' situation. The questionnaire included questions asking the interviewees about which considerations are at play when pension funds decide on whether or not do deploy activities within the field of responsible investment. In the interviews of the first round, the approach of pension funds to responsible investment was the key topic. We used simple classification to analyze the results, and compare them to the framework we set up based on our literature review.

The second round of interviews was conducted with the same persons as in the first round. These interviews were carried out over the telephone, and last 15–30 min. Again, drafts of this chapter containing citations, interpretations and conclusions were sent to the interviewees for their agreement. The second round of interviews focused on the impact of the financial crisis. We asked the following questions about the financial crisis:

1. Has the financial crisis impacted your pension fund's thoughts about responsible investment? If it has, in which ways?
2. Has the financial crisis impacted your pension fund's way of doing responsible investment? If it has, in which ways?
3. How has the financial crisis influenced your pension fund's portfolio composition? How permanent are these possible changes?
4. How does the crisis affect the way you view the responsibilities of your fund against the sponsor(s), the employees who pay a premium, and the persons who receive a pension?
5. What would you – with hindsight – have wanted to do in another way?

The added value of the first round was that interviewees spontaneously commented on the financial crisis. Thus, we were able to collect interview data that could not be found by asking straightaway about the financial crisis directly. More specifically, in our analysis we picked up all the comments in which the financial crisis is mentioned directly or the link to the financial crisis was clear. We also triangulated our data from the two rounds of interviews with data from the annual reports of the pension funds to complement our interpretation of the interview data.

Results

We organize the results according to two approaches: the five questions and the framework developed in Section 'Literature Review' (see Fig. 6.1). The first three sub-sections focus on five interview questions. We also integrate considerations from the framework and where applicable, from the annual reports. The two remaining sub-sections focus on the framework: transparency about the value of the funds, liabilities, and risk management and governance and regulations. In these two last sub-sections, we use the data from both interview rounds in an illustrative way: the five questions and the spontaneous comments from the interviews where the approach to responsible investment was the key topic.

Fig. 6.1 Framework for the analysis of the pension funds

Thoughts and Actions Regarding Responsible Investment During the Financial Crisis

In the interviews, each pension fund representative clearly states the financial crisis does not impact their attitude towards responsible investment. Three interviewees tell about the actions their organizations take due to the crisis. Risk related action points are mentioned by three, strategic asset allocation by two pension funds.

> ...About responsible investment...the financial crisis has impacted us on a number of...aspects of our investment strategy...on diversification, on the types of asset classes...on counterparty risk, which was a risk that we sort of ignored before...we have a different look now at the (responsible investment) models that we use, the rating agencies we're looking at them differently... (PF 001)

> The only difference is that maybe...we have been going through our investments more strongly and closely during the last months. So, we have made a stricter screening regarding

the items in the portfolio because we were afraid of having a position like Lehman etc. in our portfolio... (PF 003)

The first comment includes an extensive list of factors, the second comment fewer. We can link all these factors to the framework. Both cited pension funds face a decrease in the value of the funds. The list of the impacts communicates about the changes that take place in their internal governance and risk management processes. The pension funds do not directly mention a possible change in their internal regulations. However, the change in the internal governance would logically mean updates in internal regulations too. Transparency is not mentioned directly either. However, mentioning Lehman can, from our point of view, be interpreted to mean investments with too little transparency.

The interviewees also bring up comments that relate to the financial crisis and responsible investments. One conventional pension fund interviewee from Belgium says:

...We have mostly...spoken about the strategic asset allocation, and the risk profile but...we...didn't speak about the responsible investments...as a solution or as a problem...because of the financial crisis. (PF 004)

We think the comment above simply communicates responsible investment is not considered as a relevant item in the financial crisis discussion. The same conclusion is disclosed by a Finnish peer. The following Finnish pension fund, where responsible investment view point is taken into account says:

...Of course it is so that it (responsible investment) is not necessarily the primary focus when the world is going through perhaps the worst financial crisis ever.... (PF 008)

Both comments are logical if we take into account the magnitude of the crisis. The pension funds may need to put additional efforts in keeping the situation in control. Interestingly, two Finnish pension funds with established responsible investment strategies consider the financial crisis strengthens the responsible investment strategy they have:

...Our strategy regarding responsible investments works in this situation in the same way as before the financial crisis...I have said that the financial crisis if anything, is an evidence that responsible investment matters, and attention should be paid on it. (PF 009)

...In a way it (the crisis) only strengthens the meaning of responsible investment...we aim to follow the responsible investment guidelines we have even better. (PF 010)

We understand responsible investment strategy gives a solid base to work with for these two pension funds. Stating 'responsible investment matters' and aiming to follow the responsible investment guidelines even better communicate about the role of governance and transparency. From governance, we identify two aspects: especially the first citation communicates about the importance of both internal and global governance. The interviewee is first referring to their responsible investment strategy, and then switches the focus to a more general level. In the second citation this double viewpoint is more difficult to spot directly. We find governance and transparency are linked to both financial crisis, and responsible investment literature.

These results suggest the financial crisis does not really impact the way the pension funds think about responsible investment, not at least in the negative sense. The second interview question, the way of doing responsible investment, is impacted at least in one pension fund which clearly states the homework from the crisis is transferred to their way of doing responsible investment – resulting in stronger internal governance:

> Now we are much more suspicious, and we will look even more carefully at a number of issues. Yes, so we will look at a lot of things much closer... (PF 001)

One interviewee, currently on the way of considering a more extensive responsible investment strategy answers:

> That is a possibly yes...socially responsible investment is always a decision by the board...and we see generally that there is a little more... discussion about when to (further) implement it...to a larger extent...following financial losses...meaning that however you look at it...the less those responsible investments you do...apparently most people still believe it allows you to...faster recover the losses. Let's say one might postpone further implementation a little longer to recover from incurred losses. (PF 002)

In the recent literature, we find no evidence that responsible investments would make the loss recovery process longer. If we relate this citation to the studies where responsible investment is related to lower financial performance, this citation is aligned with literature. The finding that investors are not ready to accept lower returns by prioritizing ethical objectives (Renneboog et al. 2008a), fits this citation well. This citation also reflects the commitment towards responsible investment, despite the estimated suboptimal financial performance.

Along the interviews, we also face the challenge in defining whether the crisis impacts the way of doing responsible investment or not – and what is responsible investing and what is not. We think this stems from the challenge of defining responsible investment:

> ...It is more a point of view whether it is responsible investment or does it come from another way that we have...or I can say that it is also responsible investment that we increase the weight of domestic companies... (PF 010)

> So one big thing is that now there has been interest in pension capital...as there are these recessions...and the employment issues are wanted to be promoted...and also in Finland there have been attempts to collect funds that would invest in companies that promote employment (PF 006)

Of course, the definition of responsible investment and its synonyms is awkward business. The most typical definition of socially responsible investment includes taking into account environmental, governmental and social issues (Eurosif 2008, Social Investment Forum 2009, Social Investment Organization 2009, UN PRI 2009). Often engagement is also considered to be a solid part of it (Vandekerckhove et al. 2008, UN PRI 2009). There is some indication that the financial crisis broadens up the concept of responsible investment even further, and that governance issues are taking a central place.

Impact on the Portfolio and the Liabilities

The pension funds experience a decrease of value especially in equities. Only one actively changes the allocation, the others 'naturally' experience a change through the decreased value. Five interviewees tell about the criteria they consider, like lower risk profile, real diversification and 'back to basics' thinking with more liquid investments. In general, we find the pension funds are moving towards a more careful approach:

> ...We did not actively switch our allocation, but we take...stands to wait the market a little bit before entering to certain investment types. (PF 002)

> ...So during the year 2008, we have progressively reduced our allocation on the risky assets...and (in) the...beginning of this year (2009)...we have maintained...a less risky profile for our pension funds...we don't plan to increase our risk profile in the future... (PF 004)

> Well...the risk level has needed to be put down like everyone else....is this permanent – probably not – it will be dragged upwards little by little until a crash puts it down again. And....perhaps it simplifies...this kind of back to basics thinking that...well the liquidity is appreciated at least for some time...and...this kind of simple investment instruments... (PF 007)

> So perhaps it is a little bit more conservative than what it was before...during the crisis we have invested more in index based products. (PF 008)

> What we are definitely doing because of the crisis...is to look for real diversification...and two...we're examining some sort of new asset classes which claim to be really diversified... (PF 001)

We think all these citations point at the importance of good governance and risk management that is strongly highlighted in the literature review. However, the interest in taking bigger risks along the development of the economic situation remains – until it starts all over again. We submit that all these comments relate to internal governance and risk management. The comment referring to back to basics thinking also addresses these themes from a more global aspect.

A decrease in the value of the funds raises the question of the value of the liabilities of a pension fund. In the third interview question, we examine whether the financial crisis impacts the way the pension funds see their liabilities towards a few stakeholder groups. As the pension funds have differences in these stakeholder groups, we receive answers accordingly. The comments regarding the liabilities are spread to concern one or several of the following stakeholders: the sponsor(s), members of the fund, employees paying a premium or employees receiving a pension.

Eight out of ten pension funds state there is no change in the liabilities. Two Belgian pension funds clearly state the value of the liabilities change towards at least one of the stakeholder groups. We find this originates from the country specific differences in the regulations of the pension systems in Belgium and in Finland. In the latter, the question of liabilities does not even come to the mind:

> So I don't see that our own liabilities would depend or change because of the financial crisis,
> or that we would somehow take these things more easily, or more relaxed. So in that sense
> the system is guaranteeing itself. . . .what is quite different compared to other countries. (PF
> 009)

Among the Belgian pension fund interviewees, the liability issues bring up a few comments:

> . . .Of course it has increased. . .because if everything is going fine, then there's no problems
> then. . .we could sort of give them confidence that don't worry about your pension, we have
> a lot of money here. . .that was a big responsibility for us. (PF 001)

> . . .The sponsors. . .simply have to sponsor in my point of view. . .and they didn't have
> problems. . .so we lost a lot of money last year, in the end of 2008, but this year it's going
> better. . .they were only concerned about the. . .financial situation of the fund. . .and there
> we had to communicate about the things we did. . .asking money from the sponsors. . .to
> guarantee. . .the possibility of the fund to be able to pay everyone in one go. . . (PF 005)

The change in the value of the liabilities in the Belgian pension funds is linked to the financial situation of the sponsor(s), or of the fund itself. The liability towards the pensioners and future pensioners increase in the situation where the sponsor(s), and/or the pension fund are not financially in a strong position due to the crisis. We think these two citations can be linked to each theme of the framework. In both citations, the pension funds bring up clearly the importance of communication. However, the situations in these two cases differ. In the first case, the pension fund is communicating about its financial solvency, and about the responsibility they take themselves. From the second, we understand the responsibility is transferred to the sponsor(s).

Therefore, it appears the composition of the pension fund portfolios have not been actively changed considerably, and investment decisions are taken with more caution. We find the value of the liabilities changes in two cases.

What If You Had Known?

We also asked whether the pension funds would have acted differently if they had known how the financial crisis turned out. We receive several stories that clearly relate to the factors of the financial crisis literature. However, one Belgian and four Finnish pension fund interviewees state they would not have done anything differently.

The global importance of governance, regulations and risk management is brought up in the literature. From the following citations we interpret too intensive obedience to the investment management tools may also cause blindness from the point of view of good internal governance and risk management – both in Belgium and in Finland.

> . . .We should have kept our long-term strategy. . .in which the risk level was kept somewhat
> lower than in this system in average. . . .but we lost our nerves, and the risk level was taken

to the system level...following up that system is the most important.....so we then followed that dogma and with damaging results...(PF 007)

...Our models...will tell you that in 95% of cases there is no problem. And we sort of assumed that 95 that's one hundred. We...never thought that in that 5% something could happen. And the impact, that was quite shocking to see...how much employee impact this could have had...with hindsight...not that much risk, not that much equities as we have... (PF 001)

The first case shows the fund relied on its system blindly: very low-risk alternatives are not an option, and it is not clear what to do in the financial turmoil. This is why it is too simple to rely on the information that is easily available. The second case presents the same kind of thinking: strong belief in the investment management models. Both examples match the thinking that a strong obedience of a governance tool can be contradictory from the point of view of risk management.

In general, the pension fund interviewees bring up comments that we integrate to better internal governance and more specifically, appropriate ways of working in the future. Especially the need to update ways of working and prioritize time usage arises:

...This traditional strategic asset allocation, fixed for the very long term, is probably no more the best solution, we need to work with a more dynamic strategic asset allocation... we don't really see so many interests to...spend a lot of time in the asset manager selection...but it's probably better to...spend much more time in having a good understanding of the global situation... to be able...to decide some significant tactical moves in the portfolio...We don't plan to apply an aggressive tactical asset allocation but to focus on main asymmetric risks on the financial markets in order to determine if it is possible to take profit from them (PF 004)

The financial crisis definitely gives a possibility to test risk management processes:

...We did a rebalancing of the portfolio towards bonds... they limited losses to a large extent with regard to equity... (PF 002)

Throughout the interviews, we also pick up comments that show the pension funds consider the financial crisis to be a good teacher:

...So this kind of a crisis it is a bad thing, but then again it can also provide fairly good possibilities for a long-term investor... (PF 008)

...We have clear targets regarding our financial soundness and also regarding the pension income payments, so this (crisis) only highlights that we have to stick to those targets... (PF 010)

The 'good teacher' aspect is brought up by the Finnish pension fund interviewees in particular. Solely based on the interview results, the Finnish pension funds seem to be less impacted by the financial crisis. However, on the basis of the annual reports the decrease in the value of the funds is roughly on the same level for Belgian and Finnish pension funds.

One of the responsible investment pension fund interviewees clearly communicates they strongly revise their ways of working due to the crisis. The other responsible investment pension fund interviewees are more underlining how the

Table 6.1 Classification of the interview results

	Result	Relation to the framework	Relation to responsible investment
Question 1	No change in the thoughts regarding RI.	–	Financial situation does not change how RI is perceived.
Question 2	Stricter ways of doing RI, several impacts.	All results relate to the framework. Especially governance, regulations and transparency are matching.	Responsible investment is not the focus point, and not considered as a solution in times of turmoil. It is postponed. Financial crisis strengthens the chosen responsible investment strategy.
Question 3	With one exception, the pension funds keep the same portfolio composition.	Pension funds bring up risk management and governance.	Pension funds which are engaged in responsible investment, are willing to keep their direction.
Question 4	No change in the liabilities in Finland. In Belgium, there is a change.	Belgian pension funds mention the changed value of the liabilities.	–
Question 5	Several pension funds wouldn't have done anything differently. Some pension funds bring up the importance of risk management, and the lessons they learned during the crises.	Clear relation especially to regulations.	–

'power' of responsible investment is revealed along the crisis. Based on these two citations and the comment where the revision of ways of working takes place, we understand the choice to make responsible investments is something which is held on to (Table 6.1).

In the remaining two sections, we reflect on these findings from the framework. We take into account the interview results from the spontaneous comments regarding the financial crisis. In this data seven out of ten mention or discuss the financial crisis. Two out of these seven have a clearly defined responsible investment strategy. In one case, the fund has a specific investment strategy, but it is unclear whether the pension fund considers it to be a responsible investment strategy or not at the time of the interview.

Transparency About the Value of the Funds and the Liabilities

We think the value of the funds can be understood in our context at least in two ways: it can mean a decrease or increase in the value of the funds' assets. It can also mean how the value of the funds is estimated in accounting, where it more clearly includes the transparency aspect too. The value of the funds come up only in the former meaning – the pension fund interviewees feel they have less money due to decreased value of the assets – but no one mentions the possible biased valuation in accounting. It is of course not a surprise that the decreased value of the funds is discussed in the spontaneous comments as well. In all cases, this theme pops up 'between the lines', or it is used as reasoning for something else.

> Size. . .around X M€, after a terrible year 2008. . .a general rule what we do is of course in investing the assets of X M€ is basically it's a liability driven investments, so we look at the liabilities, . . .(PF 001)

This comment describes well how the financial crisis is brought up regarding the value of the funds yet on the way of telling something else. When looking into the annual reports, we see the negative results mean approximately a 15–20% decrease in the portfolio value. Surprisingly, the pension fund which brings up the loss of the money the most in the interviews happens to lose the least value.

The decreased value of the funds and the contradictory results regarding the financial performance of responsible investment are reasons for one pension fund to continue with their 'conventional' strategy for the moment:

> . . .There are studies (regarding responsible investment) according to which you will lose money – and now we're in a situation where we cannot lose more money. We did –X% last year. . .we have to see that we have enough of money to pay the pensions and after. . .we can think about it. . .so, it (responsible investment) will for sure come to the agenda but today there are other things. . ..I think the other pension funds will say it as well. . .there are other priorities. . . (PF 003)

We do not find spontaneous comments in which a change in the value of the liabilities comes out clearly. The second and the third comment above mention the liabilities, but we find no change in the value of them. Both of them simply communicate the pension fund takes into account its normal liability of paying pensions. However, the direct questions regarding the financial crisis reveal the value of the liabilities towards the sponsor(s), employees paying a premium and pensioners have increased in three pension funds. The reason might be that especially in the Finnish pension system this question is not very relevant. Furthermore, the increased value of the liabilities in a difficult financial situation can easily be understood as being something not to be proud about. If the value of the funds drops considerably and the stakeholders are concerned about their pensions, the interpretation easily goes to a setting of 'who to blame'. However, the value of the liabilities can change – and can be unrelated with the value of the funds' assets.

As a conclusion, we find that the value of the funds is mentioned several times, but mainly as a 'side product' when the interviewee is telling about another topic. Based on these comments, we do not find indications towards the change in the value of the liabilities, even though there is a significant change (based on the data of autumn 2009). One pension fund interviewee states the challenging financial times and unclear research results regarding the financial performance of responsible investment are the reasons for not doing it.

Governance, Regulations, Risk Management and Transparency

Five annual reports describe the impacts of the financial crisis as unexpected or surprising, and seven disclose the year 2008 was difficult. The importance of good governance and regulations in a global setting are repeatedly suggested in the literature as a remedy to avoid financial crisis like this. Two annual reports mention the importance of risk management.

> I think this has also started from these corporate governance issues... one can think that without these really ...big bankruptcies...so would one has really started talking about corporate governance issues that much? That somehow created a basis that this (responsible investment) is not 'too green' or 'hugging the tree' or something similar, but this really has an influence...this really has a financial influence ...(PF 009)

> ...I think that if they (private equity funds and hedge funds) will ever be regulated, the motives of the regulators are totally elsewhere than in responsible investment...it is to make sure they cannot cause such a crisis we've experienced...and if one thinks about responsible investment, so in reality where investments or investors have caused harm is not at all the thing they have bought shares from oil or tobacco companies, but in the thing that they for example in this financial crisis drove certain big institutions down...I'm sure that these certain operations towards these financial institutions last autumn caused a lot of disaster in the world...that way I could even imagine that actually this kind of things could become criteria to some responsible investment programs. So...like short selling was prohibited. That well describes how harmful it was perceived. So why the funds that short sell to investors cannot then, be prohibited? (PF 007)

In both citations, the funds consider the financial crisis has an educational role in highlighting the global importance of governance, regulations and transparency. From the first citation, we find the financial crisis has given the pension fund encouragement regarding their responsible investment strategy. The interviewee also brings up the change from responsible investment being a too 'green' alternative into the mainstream. The second comment includes several viewpoints too. First, it includes considerations why good governance and transparency are important. Second, the interviewee is suggesting updates to 'responsible investment criteria', and to 'general' regulations in the financial market. Third, it also communicates how the interviewee ranks the power of screening versus good governance, regulations and transparency in the global level.

The global meaning of good governance, regulations and transparency brings the focus back to an organizational point of view:

> ...We are re-evaluating...the methodology...and drawing lessons from the financial crisis...how to...find solutions within SRI... (PF 001)

Despite the homework from the financial crisis – the fact of losing money – the interviewee is communicating the pension fund aims to find a solution from the responsible investment strategy. It seems the choice would not be easily changed. This same atmosphere is included in the first comment, in which the interviewee considers responsible investment to be more a mainstream phenomena than what it used to be. The same theme comes out with the data collected in autumn 2009 – we understand the responsible investment strategy is a real commitment.

The pension funds do not directly mention transparency. However, the meaning of it is brought up a few times, both on global and organizational level. The following comment encourages to stronger transparency in responsible investment:

> So some investors then again say that the bonds shouldn't belong (to responsible investment) because you don't have the same rights as shareholders. Shareholders have the possibility to influence. But I say this is. . .to make things look nicer. And especially in this market situation so one can say that the bond owners have even more weight in many cases versus shareholders. Companies need more financing, so they take good care of their investors. (PF 009)

The different definitions of responsible investment give a loose framework for doing and understanding it. This gives the possibility for looser moral considerations among responsible investors. What does it really mean in practice, having a responsible investment strategy? The comment reveals the possibility to 'ride' and promote a responsible investment profile *á la carte*.

The conventional pension funds and the pension funds with little engagement in responsible investment see responsible investment in times of turmoil in more than one way. Two pension fund interviewees are waiting for the financial situation to improve, and reconsider responsible investment later. One pension fund interviewee does not think responsible investment as a solution in challenging financial times, but has analyzed it earlier as an investment strategy alternative. Two other pension fund interviewees regard responsibility is, or should be, in the light of the themes of the framework, part of the financial market. These pension funds want to take responsibility into account in their conduct, and call for additional responsibility

Table 6.2 Classification of the results by using the data in which the pension funds tell about their approach to responsible investment

	Result	Relation to the framework	Relation to responsible investment
Value of the funds and value of the liabilities	Value of the funds is decreased. The pension funds mention this in several contexts.	Pension funds talk about the value of the funds in the sense of loosing money. Biased valuation of the funds does not come up. Governance and risk management fit well the results.	Conventional pension funds postpone the choice of responsible investment until later.
Governance, regulations, risk management and transparency	Pension funds mention the importance of good governance and regulations.	Results reflect well the framework.	Responsible investment can be applied to bond portfolio too – transparency is important also in responsible investment. Commitment to responsible investment.

in the financial market. However, the present crisis is not a reason for them to get engaged in responsible investment.

In the spontaneous comments regarding the financial crisis, the governance, regulations and transparency are brought up when telling about the pension funds' experiences regarding the financial crisis, both on organizational and global level. Risk management is not directly brought up in the spontaneous comments but we can argue its existence in the background. This is because in the first interview data several interviewees mentioned at several instances lower risk profiles and cautiousness in the current situation. When it comes to responsible investment, the pension funds engaged with it wanted to keep this approach with possible updates (Table 6.2).

Preliminary Conclusions and Further Considerations

The chapter presented exploratory research into how pension funds' responsible investment strategies are affected by the financial crisis. We interviewed representatives of, and analyze ten pension funds in Belgium and Finland in two consecutive rounds of questions. It appears that responsible investment is a deliberate choice of pension funds, also in the times of turmoil. In general, better governance, regulations and transparency in the financial market are called for by the pension funds. Furthermore, it seems that the financial crisis did not increase pension funds' interest in responsible investments so far. However, it appears they regard it as a more relevant issue than they did before the crisis.

We first set up a framework of the themes that repeatedly come up in literature. The themes are transparency about the value of the funds, liabilities, and risk management and governance and regulations. It turns out that the results from the interviews to some extent were congruent with the framework. However, we also find striking dissimilarities. More specifically, concerning the value of the funds, we find two aspects: the framework concentrates on the – biased – valuation of the funds, whereas the interviewees bring up the simple aspect of losing money. From the interviews, it appears that the Belgian pension funds are more impacted and concerned than the Finnish ones. However, from their annual reports it appears that this difference might result from the way the pension funds perceive the impact. Some pension funds seem to address the decreased value of the funds neutrally, whereas others appear to be rather concerned. Another reason for the dissimilarities can be differences in the pension systems in Belgium and in Finland. The latter ensures the employees and pensioners do not suffer from any failures with the pension funds. We find that the differences in the pension systems determine the way the pension funds regard their liabilities towards stakeholders: in Belgium, some respondents experience a change in the value of their liabilities, whereas in Finland this was not the case.

Another important topic is risk management, governance and regulations. We pay attention to these in the interview data in several ways: the pension funds are learning its meaning on an organizational level and considering its importance on a global level. In addition, we understand that in some cases, better risk management, governance and regulations may have been chosen if the *'what if I had known'* – option was present. The risk management aspect seems to touch several pension funds. Had they been hit by the financial crisis more or less, this kind of economic situations usually give a good reason to reconsider own organization's way of taking risk management into account. In general, the pension funds are moving towards a more careful approach – at least for the time being.

Transparency was another theme we took into account. Our interviewees did not directly mention transparency. However, it is referred to in the context of the liabilities, in which the stakeholder communication is mentioned. In this sense, we suggest several decisions in these pension funds, and also in the global setting, might have been taken differently if the transparency had been better. As good governance and transparency are characteristics of responsible investment, these should be appreciated by the responsible investors also. This point of view is particularly based on one Finnish pension fund's comment, which lets us better understand that the loose guidelines for responsible investors may also encourage window dressing: applying the responsible investment strategy solely to a minor part of the portfolio may mislead stakeholders and change the characteristics of responsible investment and responsible investors.

The pension funds which are investing responsibly are committed to the chosen strategy. They are either searching for updated solutions within the field or they consider the financial crisis has simply highlighted the importance of responsible investment. The conventional pension funds are either satisfied with their current strategy, or think of concentrating on responsible investment later due to the unclear financial performance. Both responsible and conventional pension funds bring up thoughts which call for better global transparency, liabilities and governance and regulations and risk management as characteristics for responsible investing. In no cases did the interviewees mention the need for more 'green' or more environmentally focused investments. We find these considerations bring forth a somewhat different aspect to responsible investing than what has been presented in the existing literature.

In all, we find the pension funds are impacted by the financial crisis in many ways. All the central themes from financial crisis literature – the value of the funds, the value of the liabilities, governance, regulations, risk management and transparency were found in our interview data. Nobody could escape the financial losses, or temporary decrease in the value of the assets. We find that governance, regulations and risk management were discussed the most, and the crisis gave possibilities to restructure or re-evaluate the importance of these factors. However, sometimes using lucidity and caution were forgotten due to the advanced systems and models. As a conclusion, some pension funds were confident with their approach, and would not have done anything differently. The meaning of the value of the liabilities was a more important theme in Belgium than in Finland due to the differences in the pension system. Transparency came up only in the discussion about the value of the liabilities, where communication towards important stakeholder groups was a way to ensure a calm mind. Finally, some pension fund interviewees also characterized the crisis a possibility, and an outcome that shows responsible investment matters.

In general, the impacts of the financial crisis have not much changed the way they approach responsible investment. The conventional pension funds had not thought about it or considered it as a possible future agenda item. One pension fund was in the process of building an approach to responsible investment, and the process was postponed due to financial performance analysis. Another one saw responsible investment relevant 'later'. An established responsible investment strategy in these times seemed to mean either a need to revise governance and risk management processes, or a strong guidance in difficult financial times.

Of course generalizing these conclusions must be done carefully. We interviewed only ten pension funds in two countries. The results and the conclusions might be very different if we had chosen another viewpoint, other countries and pension funds. Nevertheless, we feel this analysis brings additional insights from the financial crisis with respect to pension funds' position with respect responsible investments. As a conclusion, we find that the approach to responsible investment may have changed as a result of the crisis. However, in no case do they arrive at a negative attitude regarding responsible investment.

Acknowledgements I acknowledge Bert Scholtens, Wim Vandekerckhove and Jos Leys who have provided me with additional aspects to responsible investment. Especially I want to thank Bert Scholtens for his valuable and professional feedback on this article. I also gratefully acknowledge the financial support by Jenny and Anti Wihuri Foundation, Foundation for Economic Education and Niemi Foundation.

References

Abramson, Lome and Dan Chung. 2000. Socially responsible investing: Viable for value investors? Journal of Investing; 9: 73–80, In The Asset Management Working Group of the United Nations Environment Programme Finance Initiative and Mercer. 2007. Demystifying Responsible Investment Performance. A review of key academic and broker research on ESG factors.

Bengtsson, Elias. 2008. The history of Scandinavian SRI. Journal of Business Ethics 82: 969–983.

Benson, K.L., Brailsford T.J. and Humphrey J.E. 2006. Do socially responsible fund managers really invest differently? Journal of Business Ethics 65: 337–357.

Benson, Karen L. and Jacquelyn E. Humphrey. 2008. Socially responsible investment funds: Investor reaction to current and past returns. Journal of Banking and Finance 32(9): 1850–1859.

Crouhy Micael G., Robert A. Jarrow, and Stuart Turnbull. 2008. The subprime credit crisis of 2007. Journal of Derivatives 16: 81–111.

Cumming, Douglas and Sofia Johan. 2007. Regulatory harmonization and the development of private equity markets. Journal of Banking and Finance 31: 3218–3250.

Dăianu, Daniel and Laurian Lungu. 2008. Why is this financial crisis occurring? How to respond to it? Romanian Journal of Economic Forecasting 4: 59–87.

Derwall Jeroen, Nadja Guenster, Rob Bauer, and Kees Koedijk. 2005. Financial Analysts Journal 61: 51–63. In: The Asset Management Working Group of the United Nations Environment Programme Finance Initiative and Mercer. 2007. Demystifying Responsible Investment Performance. A review of key academic and broker research on ESG factors.

Eurosif. 2009. Transparency guidelines. Eurosif web-pages. http://www.eurosif.org/publications/european_sri_transparency_guidelines. Accessed 24 October 2009.

Eurosif. 2008. European SRI study 2008.

Fowler, Stephen J. and C. Hope. 2007. A critical review of sustainable business indices and their impact. Journal of Business Ethics 76: 243–252.

Galema Rients, Auke Plantinga, and Bert Scholtens. 2008. The stocks at stake: Return and risk in socially responsible investment. Journal of Banking and Finance 32: 2646–2654.

Hellwig, Martin F. 2009. Systemic risk in the financial sector: An analysis of the subprime-mortgage financial crisis. De Economist 157: 129–207.

Hockerts, Kai and Lance Moir. 2004. Communicating corporate responsibility to investors: The changing role of the investor relations function. Journal of Business Ethics 52: 85–98.

Kempf Alexander and Peer Osthoff. 2007. The effect of socially responsible investing on portfolio performance. European Financial Management 13: 908–922.

Keys Benjamin, Tanmoy Mukherjee, Amit Seru, and Vikrant Vig. 2009. Financial regulation and securitization: Evidence from subprime loans. Journal of Monetary Economics 56: 700–720.

Kleiner, Todd. 2007. In: Keys B.J., Mukherjee T., Seru A. and Vig V. Financial regulation and securitization: Evidence from subprime loans. 2009. Journal of Monetary Economics 56: 700–720.

Louche, Cèline. 2004. Ethical investment processes and mechanisms of institutionalisation in the Netherlands, 1990–2002. PhD dissertation. Erasmus University Rotterdam, The Netherlands.

McSweeney, Brendan. 2009. The roles of financial asset market failure denial and the economic crisis: Reflections on accounting and financial theories and practices. Accounting, Organizations and Society 34: 835–848.

Niinimäki, Juha-Pekka. 2009. Does collateral fuel moral hazard in banking? Journal of Banking and Finance 33: 514–521.

Orlitzky Marc, Frank Schmidt, and Sara L. Rynes. 2003. Corporate social and financial performance: A meta-analysis. Organization Studies 24: 403–441, in The Asset Management Working Group of the United Nations Environment Programme Finance Initiative and Mercer. 2007. Demystifying Responsible Investment Performance. A review of key academic and broker research on ESG factors.

Quarter Jack, Isla Carmichael, and Sherida Ryan (eds.) 2008. Pensions at Work: Socially Responsible Investment of Union-Based Pension Funds. University of Toronto Press. A book review. 2009, in Relations industrielles/Industrial relations 64: 2.

Renneboog Luc, Jenke Ter Horst, and Chedi Zhang. 2008a. Socially responsible investments: Institutional aspects, performance, and investor behaviour. Journal of Banking and Finance 32: 1723–1742.

Renneboog Luc, Jenke Ter Horst, and Chedi Zhang. 2008b. The price of ethics and stakeholder governance: The performance of socially responsible mutual funds. Journal of Corporate Finance 14: 302–322.

Social Investment Forum. 2009. http://www.socialinvest.org/resources/professionals.cfm. Accessed the 1 July 2009.

Social Investment Organization (Canada). 2009. http://www.socialinvestment.ca/documents/SIOpoint-of salepackage_factsheets_complete_English.pdf. Accessed July the 1July 2009.

Sparkes, Russel and Christopher Cowton. 2004. The maturing of socially responsible investment: A review of the developing link with corporate social responsibility. Journal of Business Ethics 52: 42–47.

United Nations Principles For Responsible Investment. Principles for Responsible Investment. http://www.unpri.org/principles. Accessed July the 1st July 2009.

Vandekerckhove Wim, Jos Leys, and Dirk Braekel. 2008. A speech-act model for talking to management. Building a framework for evaluating communication within the SRI engagement process. Journal of Business Ethics 82: 77–91.

Van den Heuvel, Skander. 2009. Comment on: Financial regulation and securitization: Evidence from subprime loans by Keys B.J., Mukherjee T., Seru A. and Vig V. Journal of Monetary Economics 56: 721–724.

Wen, Shuangge. 2009. Institutional investor activism on socially responsible investment: Effects and expectations. Business Ethics: A European Review 18: 308–333.

Yermo, Juan. 2008. Pension fund governance: Challenges and potential solutions. http://ssrn.com/abstract=1217266. Accessed October the 1st 2009.

Chapter 7
Private Equity as an Emerging Asset Class of Responsible Investment

Barbara Del Bosco and Nicola Misani

Introduction

One of the long-lasting consequences of the 2008 global financial crisis could be a pervasive public scepticism regarding financial instruments. Lord Turner, chairman of the UK's Financial Services Authority, expressed the prevailing sentiment when he stated that the financial industry had 'swollen beyond its useful social size' and must be cut down (The Economist 2009). This scepticism might be justified in respect of the financial innovations that have damaged the economy, such as collateralized debt obligations that inflated real estate prices and ultimately led homeowners to lose their houses and jobs. Nonetheless, this scepticism would create further damage if it were to turn into a lack of public support for financial innovations that could actually benefit society. This risk is particularly relevant to responsible investment (RI), which is a relatively young constituent of the financial industry and is still in need of growth.

Lydenberg and Sinclair (2009) recently argued that RI will definitively move into the mainstream only when investors start to perceive it 'as a continuum of varying initiatives across asset classes' and 'tailor responsible investments by asset class to be maximally effective in creating positive externalities' (Lydenberg and Sinclair: 60). Public equity (the stock of publicly traded firms) has traditionally been RI's dominant asset class and has inspired many of its characteristic instruments, such as screenings that look at the environmental, social, and governance (ESG) issues of firms or specialized indices of listed equities. Nevertheless, the last few years have witnessed the growing interest of responsible investors in other asset classes. In this paper, we focus on private equity, since the firms in the investor portfolios in this asset class face many of the same risks and opportunities from ESG issues as their listed counterparts (Unep PRI 2009a), and private equity investors are increasingly asked by society to answer to accountability issues (Young Foundation 2008).

B. Del Bosco (✉)
Entrepreneurial Lab, Centre for Research on Entrepreneurship, University of Bergamo, Bergamo, Italy
e-mail: barbara.del-bosco@unibg.it

W. Vandekerckhove et al. (eds.), *Responsible Investment in Times of Turmoil*, Issues in Business Ethics 31, DOI 10.1007/978-90-481-9319-6_7, © Springer Science+Business Media B.V. 2011

We define 'responsible private equity' (RPE) as the use of private equity deals to pursue RI objectives. We analyse the potentialities and criticalities of RPE in addressing some of the problems that have emerged during the global financial crisis. We refer especially to the widespread call for a cultural shift away from an ideological faith in the self-regulation of markets and towards greater management accountability and attention to societal and environmental problems. In this new business climate, RI will need to prove not only good intentions, but also effectiveness in the way it provides capital and support for socially responsible firms and for new initiatives that deal with social and environmental problems.

A particularity of RPE is that it can be used to finance new business initiatives in the broadly defined field of sustainable development: green products (e.g. organic agriculture), green services (recycling, brownfield remediation, waste reduction, pollution control, etc.), clean-tech (renewable energies, etc.), community investment (job creation and economic development in distressed communities), and bottom-of-the-pyramid initiatives (Vossman 2009, see also Agenda 21's definition of sustainable development in UN 2009). Some of these initiatives are non-profit and are financed by philanthropy, public grants, and other non-equity instruments, but others are able to generate revenue and are organized in a for-profit form (Townsend and Hart 2008). RPE investors targeting these ventures could thus improve their partners' opportunities to support society while achieving adequate financial returns.

RPE has shown resilience during the recent financial turmoil. The crisis has hit heavily all the asset classes, including private equity in general. In particular, in 2009, venture capital as a whole retreated to the levels of 2003 in terms of the number of deals and the volume of investment. The only sector that limited the losses was clean-tech, where the number of venture capital deals remained substantially unchanged with respect to the historical highs of 2008 and the volume of investments retreated only to the 2007 levels (Woody 2010).

While the potential role of private equity in RI is well understood by practitioners, existing literature on this theme is still scarce (Scholtens 2006, Cumming and Johan 2007). We add to this literature by analysing the conditions under which RPE could be financially and socially effective. We describe some of these conditions in an agency-theoretic framework, where private equity investors are seen as providers of incentives to portfolio firm managers, whilst different conditions require us to adopt a resource-based perspective. The literature on private equity has shown that portfolio performance is largely dependent on 'management effects' (Fitza et al. 2009), that is, on the investors' ability to coach portfolio firms and to transfer a variety of resources to them. While this is true of private equity in general, management effects are particularly critical for ventures with a social or environmental mission, which are often started by 'social entrepreneurs' without extensive business experience (Austin et al. 2006).

The paper is organized as follows. In Section 'Responsible Private Equity', we describe RPE in more detail by presenting its main categories. In Section 'Private Equity vs. Public Equity', we compare the similarities and differences of public equity RI and RPE, addressing the corporate governance implications. In Section 'A Resource-Based Perspective: Firm Resources and RPE Investor Resources', we explain the role of RPE investors as providers of financial and non-financial resources (knowledge, networks, and reputation). In Section 'Deployment and Accumulation of Resources by RPE Investors', we discuss how RPE investors deploy and accumulate resources, while in Section 'The Role of RPE in Financing CSOs: The Relationship with Other Investors', we address the interrelationships between RPE and the network of funders, co-investors, and financial markets in which they operate. In the conclusions, we summarize the conditions under which RPE could create real social value and help the RI movement to surmount the scepticism generated by the recent financial turmoil.

Responsible Private Equity

Viewed as the inclusion of ESG factors in investment decisions, RI allows investors to maintain a position in profitable firms that make positive contributions to society (SIF 2009). Public equity is historically the main target of RI. However, RI can be applied to other types of investments. Wood and Hoff (2007) list six asset classes, in addition to public equities, where opportunities for RI exist: cash or cash equivalents (e.g. deposits in responsible banks), fixed income (e.g. screening of bond issuers), private equity (which we will discuss imminently), real estate (e.g. 'green buildings'), hedge funds (e.g. long/short funds focused on renewable energy), and commodities (e.g. carbon trading). Each asset class may be more suited to different and particular social and environmental benefits (Lydenberg and Sinclair 2009).

RPE is the use of private equity deals to pursue RI objectives. A private equity deal usually involves a common or preferred equity investment in a privately held firm, although private equity firms can also negotiate large block investments in publicly listed firms. RPE investors target business initiatives that balance financial, social, and environmental considerations, but, as in traditional private equity, these investors want to pursue adequate rates of financial returns that compensate for the liquidity risk and other uncertainties typical of private investments.

RPE is currently a niche. According to Eurosif's (2007) study on 'venture capital for sustainability' (which also included later-stage financing), this segment represents 2% of the overall private equity market in Europe. However, RPE is a recent phenomenon and is rapidly growing. From 2000 to 2005, the number of investments in Europe (comprising initial and follow-on financing) more than quadrupled. The average amount per investment also increased significantly, even if the average size of deals in this segment remains limited when compared with traditional private equity/venture capital. Although all the stages of the firm's life cycle can be financed by RPE – start-up (through venture capital), growth or expansion, management buyouts, taking public companies private, etc. – currently RPE focuses primarily on the initial stages: half the amount invested corresponds to seed or early-stage

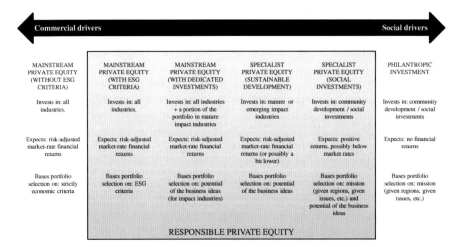

Fig. 7.1 Responsible private equity: types of investors

financing, while most traditional private equity capital is invested in the expansion stage (Eurosif 2007). This focus on the initial stages may be due to the relatively recent emergence of the financed industries (such as clean-tech or bottom-of-the-pyramid) and could evolve into a wide-spectrum approach involving all the stages once a sufficient number of firms mature. Funds specializing in the expansion stage have recently entered the market, and according to provisional estimates, more than $3 billion of non-venture private equity capital is already available in the US alone for the green industries (Sanati 2009).

RPE is identified by the type of financing (equity, or sometimes combinations of debt and equity) it makes available to firms and by the way in which the investments are decided. As illustrated in Fig. 7.1, RPE excludes both traditional private equity investors, who do not take ESG criteria into consideration, and philanthropists, who do not provide equity and generally do not expect a financial return from their investments. RPE investors can be classified between these two extremes according to the position they occupy in the continuum from commercial drivers to social drivers and the policies used in selecting their investment portfolios.

Mainstream private equity (with ESG criteria). The investors in this category can screen their portfolios on the basis of ESG risks and opportunities in the same way an RI fund does when investing in publicly listed stocks (Scholtens 2006). The motivation driving these investors may be risk mitigation, in order to avoid involvement in practices that could cause reputation damage, or value creation, when the investor believes that ESG improvements translate into operational efficiency or consumer attraction (Young Foundation 2008). In both cases, the investor can leverage large equity shares to push portfolio firms to improve their practices. ESG guidance and support can also be provided. Abraaj Capital is such an example (see Box 7.1).

Box 7.1 Abraaj Capital

Headquartered in Dubai, Abraaj Capital is a large investment firm specializing in private equity investments in the Middle East, North Africa, and South Asia (MENASA). Since its inception in 2002, the firm has raised US$7 billion and distributed almost US$3 billion to investors. Abraaj's investment strategy is to target firms that meet strict criteria addressed through rigorous due diligence and exhaustive screening processes.

Abraaj's dedication extends to the wider social responsibilities of portfolio firms. One of these is the Jordan Aircraft Maintenance Company (JorAMCo), an independent maintenance, repair, and overhaul (MRO) service provider offering a range of airframe maintenance services to Airbus, Boeing, and Lockheed fleets. Following the acquisition, Abraaj asked JorAMCo to conduct a sustainability benchmarking and assessment investigation, considering all the issues raised by stakeholders in the geographical and industry context. JorAMCo became one of the first companies in Jordan and the Arab region to produce a sustainability report (Unep PRI 2009b).

Mainstream private equity (with dedicated investments). A distinctive potential contribution of RPE is supporting new ventures or helping established firms to develop new lines of business that try to impact positively on society or the environment through a business approach. This set of initiatives is still in search of a definitive label, with various names being used by different sources, such as 'impact investing' (Monitor Institute 2009) or 'proactive social investments' (Kramer and Cooch 2006). The essential traits of these initiatives are:

- entrepreneurs actively seek a positive social and environmental impact (and do not simply accept the impact as a welcome by-product)
- they target what Grayson and Hodges (2004: 11) call 'corporate social opportunities' (CSOs), i.e., 'commercially viable activities that also advance environmental and social sustainability'
- funders expect to recoup their capital and achieve a financial return (possibly, but not necessarily, in line with risk-adjusted market rates).

This leads us to the mainstream private equity firms that dedicate a small portion of their portfolios to impact investing initiatives because they think they could be profitable. A defining trait of these investors is that they also invest most of their capital in traditional for-profit businesses, possibly without even considering ESG issues. This RPE category usually invests only in the most mature impact industries, e.g. renewable energy and environmental services, where well-structured funding ecosystems are already present. These RPE investors may be sensitive to both the idealistic content of the investment and the opportunity to invest in industries that are uncorrelated with other assets and therefore allow diversification and reduced risk. However, the diversification effects can be severely reduced in periods of global recession or financial turmoil, when all industries tend to be hit across the board. The Calvert Special Equities Program exemplifies this type of investor (see Box 7.2).

Box 7.2 Calvert Investments

Calvert Investments is a US asset management firm that serves institutional investors, workplace retirement plans, financial intermediaries, and their clients. The firm, founded in 1976, manages assets of over $12.5 billion and offers a variety of funds investing in equity, bonds, and cash using different asset allocation strategies, many of which feature environmental, social, and governance research (Kramer and Cooch 2006). As part of Calvert's RI programme, each of the funds managed by the firm can choose to allocate a small portion of assets to the Calvert Special Equities Program, a venture capital fund that directly invests in entrepreneurial firms that have identified profitable market-based ways of addressing the social, environmental, and health problems facing today's society. Examples of holdings include PowerZyme, a firm developing enzyme-based batteries that are more efficient and less environmentally harmful than lithium ion batteries; GRO Solar, a US-based manufacturer of solar systems and components; and AgraQuest, an international producer of bio-safe fungicides and pesticides (Calvert Investments 2009).

Specialist private equity (sustainable development). These are specialist private equity firms that focus on impact investing or on single areas of it. They can cover both mature and emergent impact industries (such as bottom-of-the-pyramid initiatives). These investors are defined by the fact that they do not invest capital outside the broadly defined sustainable development field and therefore provide an outlet for foundations or other partners who want to invest in areas that are close to their purposes but expect market returns. Examples abound of RPE specialists succeeding in performing in line with (or better than) private equity asset class benchmarks; one such example is Global Environmental Fund (see Box 7.3).

Box 7.3 Global Environment Fund

The Global Environment Fund (GEF) is a US private equity fund that was established in 1990 to invest in emerging firms whose business operations deliver measurable environmental improvements, cleaner energy, and the sustainable management of natural resources. The aggregate capital under

management is approximately $1 billion. GEF's investors include promi-
nent endowments, foundations, family offices, and pension funds. A flagship
investment was the REVA Electric Car, a firm based in Bangalore, India,
which was created in 1994 to manufacture environmentally friendly and cost-
effective electric vehicles. Following 7 years of research and development,
REVA, India's first zero-polluting electric vehicle for city mobility, was com-
mercialized in June 2001 (REVA 2009). The fund's gross internal rate of
return (IRR) on realized investments is over 36%.

Specialist private equity (social investment). These are private equity firms 'with
a mission' that go a step beyond, trading off social or environmental objectives with
financial returns. These firms, accepting below-market rates of return, are typically
involved in community development or in collaborations with third-sector partners.
Bridges Ventures is such an example (see Box 7.4). Private equity backing often
concurs with co-investors who exclusively have social drivers (i.e. new ventures
backed partly with private equity funds and partly with grants). This is a complex
area, where the funding models are mixed and varied, and where it is sometimes
difficult to distinguish equity funding from quasi-equity and philanthropic financing.
However, RPE does not extend to 'non-commercial' initiatives that do not generate
revenue or are structurally unable to turn a profit and must be kept separate from
venture philanthropy – that is, philanthropic grants given on the basis of strategies
and techniques that are typical of the venture capitalist approach (Letts et al. 1997) –
since RPE investors always expect to recoup the capital and to exit profitably from
the initiative once it has succeeded.

Box 7.4 Bridges Ventures

Bridges Ventures is a UK venture capital investor 'with a social mission'
endeavouring to achieve social or environmental aims as well as attractive returns for investors. Bridges Ventures was launched in 2002 by Apax
Partners and 3i (two leading UK private equity groups) together with the
entrepreneur Tom Singh. Two funds have been raised: Fund I (£40 m) and
Fund II (£75 m), which was oversubscribed. Invested firms must be located
in the most deprived 25% of the UK or must produce strong social benefits in sectors such as health care, education, and the environment (Young
Foundation 2008).

To date, Bridges Ventures has invested in 33 firms and Fund I has achieved
3 successful exits (Bridges Ventures 2009): Harlands (a firm that provides
self-adhesive labelling solutions, based in Hull, which is among the 2% most
deprived areas of England; IRR: 84%); SimplySwitch (a free online and

telephone-based price comparison and switching service that helps consumers find the most economical gas, electricity, broadband, and home or mobile phone suppliers; IRR: 165%), and HS Atec (a distributor of new spare parts for heavy goods vehicles and trailers, based in Sheffield, one of the most underinvested areas of the UK; IRR: 29%).

In summary, RPE extends the *scope* of RI, since it targets the large number of firms that are not listed. These firms are often agents of change, since many technological or market innovations historically originated from new ventures or from small- and medium-sized firms that are not stifled by legacy investments or by the conservative culture that characterizes many large organizations. This is even truer of ventures in impact industries, which are almost never listed and therefore remain out of the reach of public equity RI. In the following sections, we focus on the *instruments* that RPE investors can use to help portfolio firms pursue their economic, social, and environmental objectives.

Private Equity vs. Public Equity

Both RPE and public equity responsible investors want to provide firms addressing social and environmental issues with capital, in the hope of bringing about positive changes to modern society. Nevertheless, as Leys (2007) emphasized, the real-world consequences of an investment are usually difficult to observe. Firms can use 'whitewashing' or cosmetic changes to make themselves attractive to responsible investors. Even when firms change their actual behaviour, bringing it in line with stakeholder expectations, this change may fail to produce real results: for example, a firm can improve its supply chain by dismissing suppliers that do not enforce acceptable labour standards in their factories, but can do little to avoid these same suppliers starting to serve other clients.

Another common trait of RPE and public equity responsible investors is their expectation to obtain adequate rates of financial returns on their investment (different investors adopt varying definitions of what 'adequate' means). One of the underlying assumptions of RI is that firms that meet ESG criteria insure themselves against reputational damage, stabilizing returns in the short term and possibly creating value in the long term, thanks to the improved relationships with stakeholders. However, the empirical evidence on this 'insurance-like' benefit has always been varied (Godfrey et al. 2009) and the recent financial turmoil, which appeared to hit all the players of entire industries indiscriminately (banks, car makers, etc.), has raised doubts about the ability of RI to protect investors' money better than other investment policies.

The main differences between public equity RI and RPE pertain to the portfolio selection criteria, the size of the equity share, and the liquidity of the investment (see Table 7.1).

Table 7.1 Public equity RI vs. RPE: A comparison of governance mechanisms

	Public equity RI	RPE
Traits		
Selection of investments	Based on past and present performance	Based on future business and social opportunities
Equity share	Small	Large/control blocks
Liquidity of the investment	High	Low
Consequences		
ESG criteria	Central to portfolio selection	Used in due diligence
Influence on management	Weak	Strong
Information asymmetries between managers and shareholders	High	Low

(a) *Selection of firms.* Public equity responsible investors select their portfolios through positive, negative, or best-in-class screenings that look at the past and current ESG performance of a firm, as measured by standardized indicators. The idea is that screening must identify firms that have demonstrated their adherence to the business principles pursued by RI. Conversely, RPE cannot select portfolios on the basis of past and present firm performance, since the investment is made in ventures that are just starting their operations or in firms that are launching expansion and rejuvenating projects that need to be evaluated anew. Therefore, RPE investors (and especially venture capitalists) must base their decisions on the potentiality of the firms they invest in, taking into consideration factors such as entrepreneurial talent, the soundness of the business idea, the foreseeable impacts, and so forth (Randjelovic et al. 2003).

(b) *Equity share.* Public equity investors usually have small equity shares. This means that their contractual power in the invested firm is limited. On the contrary, RPE investors tend to hold substantial ownership positions, which amplify their ability to exert influence. Since RPE investors buy firms that are in the formative, growth, or turnaround stages, their scope for shaping their culture and policies in respect of social and environmental issues is larger; however, RPE investors will eventually exit the firm and there is no guarantee that the initial culture and policies will be preserved.

(c) *Liquidity*: investment in listed companies is liquid, while private equity investments are illiquid and riskier, since the firm usually cannot be sold when performance is unsatisfactory. The investment is illiquid not only concerning the RPE investor but also the funders, since they cannot normally sell their partnership without permission from the RPE investor. Disinvestments may become even more difficult in periods of bear markets, when the initial public offerings (IPOs) rarefy and private equity investors may have to postpone their exit. During 2009, the number of IPOs in the clean-tech sector declined in all the major stock markets with the only exception of China (Cleantech Group 2010).

These three differences have significant consequences for the way the investors try to fulfil their ideal and financial objectives.

(a) *ESG criteria.* Responsible investors who target public equity hope to orient firm behaviour by rationing the capital available to players who do not satisfy ESG criteria. On the contrary, RPE has no reason to ration capital against firms that do not currently respect ESG criteria. Even for mainstream RPE investors who do not make impact investments, the possibility exists to invest and improve firms with poorly managed ESG-related risks and opportunities, as exemplified by Abraaj Capital's interventions in JorAMCo (Box 7.1). While ESG criteria can be useful in the due diligence process, they are not usually a deal breaker (Unep PRI 2009a).

(b) *Influence on management.* That private equity deals have significant consequences for the governance of portfolio firms is well known. According to agency theory, managers must be incentivized and monitored to be efficient. Jensen (1989) described the firm controlled by private equity as an optimal organizational form where incentives are strong and managers are forced to align their behaviour with the interests of shareholders. Subsequent empirical studies on the performance of private equity funds obtained mixed results, but the literature agrees that private equity produces real performance gains and that these gains derive at least in part from improved firm efficiency and are not simply the result of wealth transfers from other stakeholders (Wright et al. 2009). In agency theory, the interests of shareholders are identified with the maximization of the financial performance of the firm, but this reasoning can easily be extended to cases where shareholders purse a complex objective function that includes social or environmental issues. Active ownership and engagement are the main instruments that responsible investors targeting public equity use to align managers with their objectives (Vandekerckhove et al. 2008). RPE investors can also use these instruments, but, thanks to their larger equity shares, they can also negotiate the right to appoint one or more directors to the board, call for board approval for certain actions, and obtain changes to the company's statute. This more extensive set of powers strengthens the RPE investor's ability to ensure the loyalty of portfolio firm managers to the objectives driving the investment.

(c) *Information asymmetries.* A limitation of public equity RI is that investors have no direct access to the internal workings of the invested firms. Investors who practice active ownership or engagement can have direct contact with firm managers, but this is usually focused on particular practices and policies (Leys 2007), without occasion to observe firm performance from within. This means that the pressured managers may adopt symbolic adjustments instead of real improvements. For example, David et al. (2007) found that shareholder activism may encourage the diversion of resources away from real CSR activities into political activities. When a firm is private, asymmetries may be even greater, at least in the initial stage of the relationship with investors, because there is not much information available on the firm and the private equity investors have to spend substantial time and resources on examining the operations of the firm before arriving at a decision. However, after the investment, RPE investors can almost act as insiders in portfolio firms, since they will have seats on the board, strict liaisons with managers, and the ability to monitor the practices actually taking place. Even though the firm managers will still have information advantages, RPE investors will have more opportunities to influence the way in which ESG issues are addressed than are usually available to public equity investors (UNEP Pri 2009b).

In summary, RPE investors can potentially leverage their large average equity share and their relatively better access to information to orient the firms in which they invest towards social and environmental goals (Vossman 2009). From this perspective, RPE may be an answer to one of the criticisms directed against RI: that it stimulates firms to create good appearances rather than actual good behaviour. Furthermore, the recent financial crisis has revealed gaps in the corporate governance systems of publicly traded firms that threaten investor trust. A debate is developing on how to change governance rules on a global basis in order to make managers more responsible to shareholders and orient firms towards the creation of sustainable value. RPE can at least partially evade this debate, in the measure in which it grants shareholders greater power of intervention in the invested firms.

A Resource-Based Perspective: Firm Resources and RPE Investor Resources

According to agency theory, private equity contributes to improving financed firm performance by monitoring and incentivizing managers (Jensen 1989). The resource-based perspective (Barney 1991) is complementary to agency theory in explaining the role of private equity, since it can help us to understand how the change in ownership related to a private equity investment can impact on firm resources (Meuleman et al. 2009). We apply this perspective in the context of firms assisted by RPE, to analyse whether RPE investors can contribute to improving both financial performance and social or environmental outcomes.

Our starting point in applying a resource-based perspective to RPE is the role of resources in firms financed by RPE investors. In this part of the paper we focus our attention mainly on the role of RPE in financing firms that integrate social issues into their strategies and value propositions (Grayson and Hodges 2004, Zadek 2004, Porter and Kramer 2006, Jenkins 2009), for two reasons. First, as previously mentioned, RPE often adopts investment selection criteria based on potentialities and expectations for future outcomes. Consequently, RPE represents a source of financing for start-ups and the new initiatives of existing firms aimed at exploiting CSOs. Second, the role of resources is crucial in explaining how RPE investors can support portfolio firms in realizing their potentialities.

The ability to identify and realize opportunities depends on the resources owned or controlled by the firm and the capacity to manage them effectively (Ireland et al.

2003). In particular, the ability to identify a CSO and the decision to exploit it are based on the resources and values of the firm and/or the entrepreneur. On one hand, the commitment to CSR and the capacity to face social issues and trends with an eye on potential opportunities (instead of focusing only on potential threats) are fundamental conditions for the identification of CSOs (Grayson and Hodges 2004). On the other, a firm's resources and competencies influence its actual capability to serve a societal issue and the possibility to create 'shared value', that is, a benefit for society that is also valuable to the business (Porter and Kramer 2006). The presence of resources that can be leveraged to realize an opportunity affects the opportunity evaluation and the decision to exploit it (Haynie et al. 2009).

The actual exploitation of CSOs, however, often requires resources and competencies that are not available to the entrepreneur or the firm. In some cases, these resources can be significant, since CSOs may concern new markets (i.e. bottom-of-the-pyramid initiatives), new technologies and industries (i.e. clean-tech and renewable energies), or new business models (i.e. combining competences and practices typical of the non-profit sector with for-profit logics and tools).

From this perspective, RPE investors can potentially access a wide range of financial, managerial, and relational resources and provide a variety of resources to the firms in which they invest. Private equity, in fact, typically combines financing and other services in order to contribute value to portfolio firms (Baum and Silverman 2004, Busenitz et al. 2004, Dimov and Shepherd 2005, Fitza et al. 2009, Meuleman et al. 2009).

An RPE investor can provide three different types of resources to portfolio firms:

- financial resources
- knowledge and competencies
- relational resources

Financial resources. From an evolutionary perspective, entrepreneurs generate variation by creating and managing firms aiming to exploit different opportunities that combine and deploy different sets of resources. External resource holders select firms by deciding how to allocate their resources among these firms, and financial intermediaries such as private equity firms are one of the dominant sources of selection (Baum and Silverman 2004). RPE investors differ from traditional private equity because they choose which firms to finance on the basis of both their potential financial performances and their social and environmental impacts. Therefore, they may decide to finance initiatives that otherwise could not be financed since they are not (or are not perceived to be) attractive to traditional investors. Some investments may not attract traditional operators because they offer below-market-rate financial returns. In other cases, there is a 'market gap', where a viable financial model to meet a social need is achievable but has not yet been developed (Kramer and Cooch 2006). RPE investors may try to fill this gap by investing in initiatives that have not been proven commercially and financially viable, but could be with the support of RPE investors, ultimately becoming attractive to traditional investors too. Moreover, RPE investors can help portfolio firms raise additional financial resources, thanks to their relationships with other potential investors and their reputation.

Knowledge and competencies. Private equity often plays an active role in helping to manage portfolio firms (Busenitz et al. 2004). Private equity firms combine two roles: they act as a 'scout', choosing firms to finance on the basis of their potential, and as a 'coach', helping them realize this potential and ensuring that they are well managed in the post-investment phase (Baum and Silverman 2004). This coaching activity requires private equity investors to apply their skills, knowledge, and competences to the management of the firms they finance.

From this perspective, RPE investors may add value to portfolio firms by using their resources and competencies to support a wide range of activities concerning both strategic and operational management (Fitza et al. 2009). First, RPE investors can contribute to shaping the portfolio firm's strategy, thanks to their direct and frequent contact with the firm's management, the information they gather, and their contractual power as shareholders and board members.

Second, the knowledge capital of the RPE investor can also be deployed to help portfolio firms in the execution of their strategy, providing specific technical expertise and facilitating the adoption of professional management systems. For example, RPE investors may provide assistance with management team recruitment, human resource policies, hiring marketing executives, or seeking and restructuring additional debt or equity capital (Wood and Hoff 2007, Fitza et al. 2009). In this regard, the empirical evidence shows that firms assisted by a private equity operator are more professionalized (Hellman and Puri 2002). This kind of support may be particularly important in the case of RPE, since many CSOs are realized by operators who have competences and experiences related to the non-profit sector or are specialists in social or environmental issues, but lack managerial expertise. In other cases, the RPE investor may help portfolio firms by providing them with advice on how to manage environmental and social aspects.

Relational resources. RPE investors can also provide relational resources (networks, reputation, social capital, trust), which may help portfolio firms collect additional complementary resources and competencies, as well as further financial funds. RPE investors belong to networks that include portfolio firms (present and past), other firms, and skilled people. Thanks to these networks, the RPE investors can facilitate contact between a portfolio firm and potential suppliers, partners, customers, or managers. Through these networks portfolio firms may obtain the complementary resources they need to exploit CSOs and this may occur due to private equity investors transferring their reputational resources (Fitza et al. 2009). Being financed by a reputable private equity investor tends to be a quality signal, since these investors are perceived as 'informed agents' (Baum and Silverman 2004) and contribute value to portfolio firms. The association with an RPE investor may represent a sort of guarantee – regarding both the economic potential of the firm and its social impact – related to the reputation and the investment policies of the investor. As we will see more clearly in Section 'The Role of RPE in Financing CSOs: The Relationship with Other Investors', this effect extends to financial resources that in the presence of an RPE investor facilitate portfolio firm fundraising. In this way, RPE investors may add value to portfolio firms by reducing the transaction costs related to the search for, and selection of, resources.

Deployment and Accumulation of Resources by RPE Investors

The resource-based perspective (Barney 1991) suggests that a firm's resources are the output of accumulation processes, which are also linked to how the firm deploys and combines its resources over time (Dierickx and Cool 1989). RPE investors differ in the sets of resources they control: knowledge, competencies, networks, and reputation. These differences may influence their capability both to scout and to coach portfolio firms. At the same time, by deploying their resources and competencies to select, support, and coach portfolio firms, RPE investors can develop their own resources and competencies. The activities developed by investing in a firm help the investor create new resources that may be deployed to select and manage future investments.

Figure 7.2 synthesizes the relationship between an RPE investor and a portfolio firm, showing the three categories of resources (financial, knowledge, and relational) deployed by the investor to support the firm and the subsequent accumulation effects.

By supporting and coaching portfolio firms, RPE investors may develop learning processes. Due diligence strategies used to select the firms to be financed are the output of past trial-and-error learning (Baum and Silverman 2004). Moreover, engagement in the portfolio firm's management allows the investors to improve their knowledge of the markets, industries, and managerial practices. In order to add value, the relationship between the RPE investor and a portfolio firm requires a mutual exchange of information, the sharing of knowledge, and the combination of that which the two operators have acquired separately (Busenitz et al. 2004).

These learning processes can positively impact on future investments, since relevant knowledge is important to evaluating risk, returns, opportunities, and

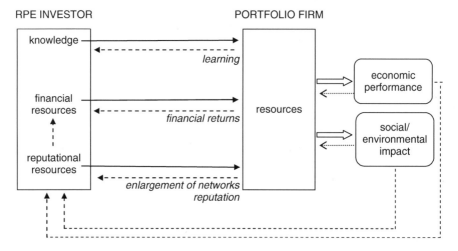

Fig. 7.2 Deployment and accumulation of an RPE investor's resources

threats adequately in pre- and post-investment activities. In particular, the ability to accumulate new knowledge can be critical when RPE invests in emerging markets (Dimov and Shepherd 2005). On the other hand, the ability to accumulate new knowledge is influenced by the existing stock of knowledge (Cohen and Levinthal 1990). The knowledge acquired in the relationship with a portfolio firm can be deployed to support a different portfolio firm, leading to potential knowledge brokering effects (Hargadon 1998, 2002, Hargadon and Sutton 2000). In this way, RPE investors can create 'new' knowledge and add value to portfolio firms by combining 'old' knowledge in new ways. There is cross-learning potential among the portfolio firms, and between these and the investor, in the case of both specialist RPE investors and mainstream private equity firms investing in impact industries alongside investments in traditional commercial sectors (Young Foundation, 2008).

Investments in portfolio firms and the active role in managing them may also allow the accumulation of relational resources over time. These activities can lead to an enlargement of the RPE investors' networks and thus create value for all those who are part of them, including the investors themselves, the portfolio firms, and other investors and resource holders. They may also contribute to accumulating reputational resources. The reputation of private equity firms and managers is traditionally related to their financial track records; in RPE, the reputation of investors is also related to the social and environmental impact of portfolio firms. In turn, the reputation of the RPE investor may influence both the capability to help firms access resources and the RPE investor's fundraising.

Moreover, when portfolio firms obtain positive economic performances and increase their value, RPE investors can divest, obtaining an adequate financial return and increasing their financial resources.

In summary, RPE investors may help firms achieve their objectives thanks to the integration of their competences and networking resources with those of the firm. At the same time, through the relationship with the firm, the investors develop their resources and create new resources that can be shared and leveraged in the selection and management of future new investments. This sort of virtuous circle allows RPE investors potentially to play a crucial role in fostering sustainable initiatives and in helping RI to overcome the financial turmoil, since the accumulation of RPE investor resources can improve their capability to evaluate the firm's potential and help realize it. The actual exploitation of this potential is related to how RPE investors manage their relationships with portfolio firms and the extent to which they are effective in providing knowledge and relational resources.

The Role of RPE in Financing CSOs: The Relationship with Other Investors

It is interesting to analyse the relationships between RPE and other investors (traditional and socially responsible) in order to understand better the potential role of RPE and the features that may help this form of RI overcome the current financial turmoil. RPE does not only represent a possible form of financing for CSOs, but can also create opportunities for other operators to carry out socially responsible investments. However, the relationship with other operators is critical for the development and the efficacy of RPE. We analyse the interrelations between RPE and other investors with reference to three aspects:

- the presence of co-investors financing portfolio firms
- the fundraising of the private equity investor
- the exit or way out.

Co-investors. Generally, RPE finances portfolio firms alongside other investors. A Eurosif (2007) study demonstrates that only 21% of investments are without some sort of co-investor. In all other cases, RPE investors share the risks with other investors: traditional venture capitalists (34%), business angels (18%), other RPE investors (16%), and public funding (11%).

As previously mentioned, reputable private equity investors may be perceived as informed agents. In particular, the presence of an RPE investor may represent a certification of economic and sustainability aspects, contributing to the reduction of problems related to information asymmetry. Moreover, co-investors may expect to benefit from the potential value-added effect of the RPE investor's coaching activity. Recent case studies analysed by the Young Foundation (2008) illustrate that in some cases the RPE investor confers credibility to the portfolio firm and helps it raise funds from other sources, merely by making the first funds available with a cornerstone investment. In other cases, the capability to raise additional financial resources emerges once the RPE has guided the development of the portfolio firm.

Fundraising. RPE investors are intermediary funding organizations. They collect money from other investors and then use it to finance portfolio firms. From this perspective, RPE represents an alternative opportunity of RI. Instead of directly financing firms aiming at realizing CSOs, operators can invest in a private equity fund. This solution has several potential advantages. First of all, funders can benefit from the selection, monitoring, incentivizing, and coaching activities of RPE. Some investors are interested in finance initiatives aimed at realizing CSOs but lack adequate resources and competencies to select and support these initiatives. Moreover, by investing through intermediaries, funders lower the transaction costs thanks to economies of scale and higher levels of efficiency.

Investing in an RPE fund may also allow a higher level of portfolio diversification compared with direct investment or public equity RI. It can also contribute to increasing the diversification of mainstream investors (such as pension funds) by allowing them to extend the range of business activities and markets in which they invest, including emerging industries and firms serving new markets, even if the recent crisis has shown that all the asset classes suffer in periods of turmoil, and this may reduce the importance of the diversification benefits.

Acting as intermediaries, RPE investors can also increase the capital available by pooling funds from different categories of investors. RPE, in fact, is financed by operators seeking to make investments that generate social and environmental value as well as financial returns, but the expectations regarding the mix of social and financial results differ according to the category of investors. According to Eurosif (2007), the most prominent funders of European venture capital for sustainability are family offices (18%), domestic public institutions (15%), high net worth individuals (13%), public pension funds (12%), corporations (11%), and banks (9%). Intermediaries, such as RPE investors, can combine different forms of financing (grants, market-rate, and below-market-rate investments, as well as tax credits) and provide different combinations of financial returns to differently motivated investors. Philanthropic capital, below-the-market-rate investments, and tax credits permit RPE to insulate other investors from the first tier of risk or provide them with market-rate returns, thus becoming attractive to traditional investors (Cooch and Kramer 2007).

The effective capability to raise funds, even from traditional investors, is a critical aspect, since the growth of RPE and its effective role are related to the funds that it will be able to collect. In this regard, Eurosif (2007) maintains that one of the key factors restraining the growth of European RPE is the dearth of capital being allocated to this sector and in particular the relatively limited role currently played by pension funds and foundations.

The current state of financial markets can render fundraising particularly difficult, since the recent scandals and the economic crisis have generated scepticism and exposed the importance of problems related to information asymmetry. As we have already mentioned, RPE has some advantages related to the close relationship between the investor and the portfolio firms. On the other hand, RPE is characterized by information asymmetry between the fund managers and the partners who invest in it.

Exit. RPE investors may also facilitate the RI of other operators when the former divest portfolio firms. When firms that combine positive economic results with social or environmental aims are divested, they may prove to be an attractive investment for socially responsible investors. Moreover, if offering adequate financial returns, these firms can also be acquired by mainstream investors or firms sensitive to CSR issues. Even when these investors adopt a risk management perspective on CSR, they may prefer to invest in a firm divested by an RPE investor due to the low costs and liabilities related to social and environmental issues that are expected to characterize these firms (Randjelovic et al. 2003).

In summary, RPE investors can create opportunities for RI, facilitating co-investment in portfolio firms by other traditional and socially responsible investors, acting as intermediary funding organizations, and divesting the portfolio firms that have obtained positive results (selling them to the market or to other investors). In all these cases, the role of RPE investors can represent a certification for other investors, thanks to their position as informed agents, their role in corporate governance, their engagement in the portfolio firm's management, and their focus on the social and/or environmental dimension. Following the turmoil and mistrust generated by the financial scandals, these certified investments represent an opportunity for investors interested in the social impact of the firms in which they invest.

Moreover, RPE investors can play a role in the process through which a sector moves from being non-commercial to being commercially proven and thus attractive to traditional investors (Young Foundation 2008). Cornerstone investments and the investor's engagement can contribute to creating a market where one did not previously exist and pave the road to traditional investment models. Portfolio management criteria aimed at value creation can contribute to ensuring the sustainable commercial viability of initiatives in emerging markets, creating opportunities for subsequent traditional investments. Clean-tech and renewable energies are examples of industries that, thanks also to the crucial role of public intervention, have become attractive to mainstream investors (after being developed by specialized private equity operators). Other sectors could be helped to develop in this direction.

However, in cases in which it is not possible to reach market-rate returns, the exit may become problematic and the range of potential buyers may be limited to investors who trade off financial returns for social ends. Another criticality in the exit stage is that buyers may not share the original business principles and the ideal values of the firm and consequently reorient it towards strictly commercial purposes.

Conclusions

The main objective of this paper was to investigate the prospects of private equity as an asset class of RI, taking into account the recent developments in capital markets. We analysed how RPE may mobilize capital and other resources in order to improve portfolio firm management of ESG issues and support new business initiatives with positive social and environmental impacts. Finance has had a crucial role in the recent economic and financial crisis, raising criticism against financial innovation and creating a shortage of capital for both traditional and responsible investors. The economic scandals and the pervasiveness of the crisis, which also hit 'best-in-class' firms, led to disillusionment in CSR and RI due to their alleged failure to produce real changes and the whitewashing policies that some firms adopted in response to calls for responsibility. In this paper, we focused on the particularities of RPE that could allow it to overcome the current difficulties and respond to some of the limits of RI that emerged with the crisis.

We analysed the potential role of RPE by adopting the complementary perspectives of agency theory and the resource-based view. In an agency-theory perspective, the large equity share that RPE investors usually have in portfolio firms gives them the structural power potentially to orient managers to maximizing a complex objective function including both financial returns and social and environmental outcomes. The resource-based perspective helps us to understand another particularity and strength of RPE, that is, its role in coaching portfolio firms. RPE investors can access a wide range of resources, ranging from experienced managers to network relationships, and can provide a combination of financial, managerial, and relational assets to the firms in which they participate. In this way, RPE investors may help portfolio firms realize their potential by improving the management of ESG issues and, in many cases, exploiting business opportunities that also lead to a positive social or environmental impact. By deploying their resources in the relationship with portfolio firms, investors may develop them and create new resources that improve their scouting and coaching capabilities. Moreover, RPE investors may create positive externalities in the financial community thanks to their reputational resources. They are informed agents, powerful shareholders, and resource providers, and thus play a certification role for portfolio firms. In this way, they may facilitate the RI of funders, co-investors, and buyers of divested portfolio firms.

Even though it is still an emerging asset class, RPE extends the funds available to entrepreneurs engaging in 'impact investing' and is especially suited to supporting sectors where the social and environmental impact must be obtained through a business approach. The fact that capital is recouped and can be recycled into new investments adds to the financing pool available to these entrepreneurs. In comparison, grant makers may be relatively disadvantaged in these areas since they may lack the managerial approach that is required to invest in initiatives based on a business approach.

The capability to foster initiatives aimed at exploiting business opportunities with a positive social or environmental impact is a strength of RPE and a potential response to criticism and scepticism regarding the real-world consequences of RI and CSR policies. A strategic approach to CSR, à la Porter and Kramer (2006), where social and environmental issues are integrated into the value proposition of firms, could be a better way to improve both the firm's economic performance and its contribution to society. RPE is in line with this perspective, even though the growth potential of RPE is still to be confirmed and some criticalities exist.

First, an important concern regards the future capability of RPE to raise sizeable funds, involve co-investors, and find an adequate way out of the investments, which is an essential condition for the growth of this asset class.

Second, RPE may reduce information asymmetries between the managers of the firms and the investors, but asymmetries remain between the RPE investors and their funders, who do not have access to the internal dealings of the portfolio firms. In contrast, investors in RI public equity funds are exposed to comparatively lower information asymmetries because they can avail themselves with the ESG ratings made available by independent agencies.

Third, the actual impact of RPE depends on how and to what extent RPE investors provide non-financial resources to the portfolio firms. For example, cultural conflicts between firms engaged in social and environmental issues and investors with a financial background may be an obstacle to positive collaboration and the effective transfer of knowledge.

Further research is needed to reach a better understanding of the workings of this emerging asset class. The literature on this topic is at its beginning; the available data are very limited and mainly focused on green industries and venture capital, due to the recent origin of this phenomenon. Our general framework has to be further developed, taking into consideration the different approaches that characterize the different types of RPE investors that we have defined and the variety of national institutional and social contexts in which RPE investors have to operate around the world. In order to test this developed framework empirically, it will be necessary to collect data on the types of businesses financed by the RPE investors, the practices used in different contexts and in different investment stages, the business and financing network, the financial performance, and the actual social and environmental outcomes.

References

Austin, James E., Howard Stevenson, and Jane Wei-Skillern. 2006. Social and commercial entrepreneurship: Same, different, or both? Entrepreneurship Theory and Practice 30: 1–22.

Barney, Jay B. 1991. Firm resources and sustained competitive advantage. Journal of Management 17: 99–120.

Baum, Joel A.C. and Brian S. Silverman. 2004. Picking winners or building them? Alliance, intellectual, and human capital as selection criteria in venture financing and performance of biotechnology start-ups. Journal of Business Venturing 19: 411–436.

Bridges Ventures. 2009. A selection of our exits. http://www.bridgesventures.com/node/177/. Accessed 15 July 2009.

Busenitz, Lowell W., James O. Fiet, and Douglas D. Moesel. 2004. Reconsidering the venture capitalists' 'value added' proposition: An interorganizational learning perspective. Journal of Business Venturing 19: 787–807.

Calvert Investments. 2009. Sustainable and responsible investing special equities. http://www.calvertgroup.com/sri-special-equities.html/. Accessed 15 July 2009.

Cleantech Group. 2010. Press release. 6 January. http://cleantech.com/about/pressreleases/20090106.cfm. Accessed 4 February 2010.

Cohen, Wesley M. and Daniel A. Levinthal. 1990. Absorptive capacity: A new perspective on learning and innovation. Administrative Science Quarterly 35: 128–152.

Cooch, Sarah and Mark Kramer. 2007. Aggregating impact: A funder's guide to mission investment intermediaries. http://www.fsg-impact.org/ideas/item/545. Accessed 15 July 2009.

Cumming, Douglas and Sofia Johan. 2007. Socially responsible institutional investment in private equity. Journal of Business Ethics 75: 395–415.

David, Parthiban, Matt Bloom, and Amy J. Hillman. 2007. Investor activism, managerial responsiveness, and corporate social performance. Strategic Management Journal 28: 91–100.

Dierickx, Ingemar and Karel Cool. 1989. Asset stock accumulation and sustainability of competitive advantage. Management Science 35: 1504–1511.

Dimov, Dimo P. and Dean A. Shepherd. 2005. Human capital theory and venture capital firms: Exploring 'home runs' and 'strike outs'. Journal of Business Venturing 20: 1–21.

Eurosif. 2007. Venture capital for sustainability report 2007. http://www.eurosif.org/content/download/715/4214/version/1/file/VC4S_final_web_22022007.pdf/. Accessed 15 July 2009.

Fitza, Markus, Sharon F. Matusik, and Elaine Mosakowski. 2009. Do VCs matter? The importance of owners on performance variance in start-up firms. Strategic Management Journal 30: 387–404.

Godfrey, Paul C., Craig B. Merrill, and Jared M. Hansen. 2009. The relationship between corporate social responsibility and shareholder value: An empirical test of the risk management hypothesis. Strategic Management Journal 30: 425–445.

Grayson, David and Adrian Hodges. 2004. Corporate social opportunity! Seven steps to make corporate social responsibility work for your business. Sheffield (UK): Greenleaf.

Hargadon, Andrew B. 1998. Firms as knowledge brokers: Lessons in pursuing continuous innovation. California Management Review 40: 209–227.

Hargadon, Andrew B. 2002. Brokering knowledge: Linking learning and innovation. Research in Organizational Behavior 24: 41–85.

Hargadon, Andrew and Robert I. Sutton. 2000. Building the innovation factory. Harvard Business Review 78: 157–166.

Haynie, J. Michael, Dean A. Shepherd, and Jeffery S. McMullen. 2009. An opportunity for me? The role of resources in opportunity evaluation decisions. Journal of Management Studies 46: 337–361.

Hellman, Thomas and Manju Puri 2002. Venture capital and the professionalization of start-up firms: Empirical evidence. Journal of Finance 57: 169–197.

Ireland, R. Duane, Michael A. Hitt, and David G. Sirmon. 2003. A model of strategic entrepreneurship: The construct and its dimensions. Journal of Management 29: 963–989.

Jenkins, Heledd. 2009. A 'business opportunity' model of corporate social responsibility for small- and medium-sized enterprises. Business Ethics: A European Review 18: 21 36.

Jensen, Michael C. 1989. The eclipse of the public corporation. Harvard Business Review 67: 61–74.

Kramer, Mark and Sarah Cooch. 2006. Investing for impact. Managing and measuring proactive social investments. http://www.fsg-impact.org/ideas/item/287. Accessed 15 July 2009.

Letts, Christine W., William Ryan, and Allen Grossman. 1997. Virtuous capital: What foundations can learn from venture capitalists. Harvard Business Review 75: 36–44.

Leys, Jos. 2007. Having a look at the effectiveness of SRI-endeavours. Philosophica 80: 121–130.

Lydenberg, Steve and Graham Sinclair. 2009. Mainstream or daydream? The future for responsible investing. Journal of Corporate Citizenship 33: 47–67.

Meuleman, Miguel, Kevin Amess, Mike Wright, and Louise Scholes. 2009. Agency, strategic entrepreneurship and the performance of private equity-backed buyouts. Entrepreneurship: Theory and Practice 33: 213–239.

Monitor Institute. 2009. Investing for social and environmental impact. A design for catalyzing an emerging industry. http://www.monitorinstitute.com/impactinvesting/. Accessed 15 July 2009.

Porter, Michael E. and Mark R. Kramer. 2006. Strategy and society: The link between competitive advantage and corporate social responsibility. Harvard Business Review 84: 78–92.

Randjelovic, Jelena, Anastasia R. O'Rourke, and Renato J. Orsato. 2003. The emergence of green venture capital. Business Strategy and the Environment 12: 240–253.

REVA. 2009. Born green. http://www.revaglobal.com/Visitor/VisitorDefault.aspx?fid=bornGreen. Accessed 8 April 2010.

Sanati, Cyrus (2009). New private equity firm focuses on 'green tech'. New York Times. 26 October. http://dealbook.blogs.nytimes.com/2009/10/26/new-private-equity-firm-focuses-on-green-tech/. Accessed 4 February 2010.

Scholtens, Bert. 2006. Finance as a driver of corporate social responsibility. Journal of Business Ethics 68: 19–33.

Social Investment Forum (SIF). 2009. Socially responsible investing facts. Errore. Riferimento a collegamento ipertestuale non valido/. Accessed 15 July 2009.

The Economist. 2009. Financial innovation and the poor. September 25. http://www.economist.com/displaystory.cfm?story_id=E1_TQQJPDJR. Accessed 8 April 2010.

Townsend, David M. and Timothy A. Hart. 2008. Perceived institutional ambiguity and the choice of organizational form in social entrepreneurial ventures. Entrepreneurship Theory and Practice 32(4): 685–700.

UN. 2009. Agenda 21. http://www.un.org/esa/dsd/agenda21/res_agenda21_00.shtml. Accessed 9 October 2009.

Unep PRI. 2009a. Responsible investment in private equity. A guide to limited partners. http://www.unpri.org/privateequity/LPGuide. Accessed 29 September 2009.

Unep PRI. 2009b. Responsible investment in private equity. Case studies. http://www.unpri.org/privateequity/PEcasestudies. Accessed 29 September 2009.

Vandekerckhove, Wim, Jos Leys, and Dirk Van Braeckel. 2008. A speech-act model for talking to management. Building a framework for evaluating communication within the SRI engagement process. Journal of Business Ethics 82: 77–91.

Vossman, Laura A. 2009. Private equity advantages for socially responsible investors. SageCap Research, http://www.sagecap.us/advantag.htm. Accessed 15 July 2009.

Wood, David and Belinda Hoff. 2007. Handbook on responsible investment across asset classes. Boston, MA: Boston College Center for Corporate Citizenship.

Woody, Todd. 2010. Clean technology investing slips, but could be worse, report finds. New York Times. 6 January. http://greeninc.blogs.nytimes.com/2010/01/06/clean-technology-investing-slips-but-could-be-worse-report-finds/. Accessed 4 February 2010.

Wright, Mike, Kevin Amess, Charlie Weir, and Sourafel Girma. 2009. Private equity and corporate governance: Retrospect and prospect. Corporate Governance: An International Review 17: 353–375.

Young Foundation. 2008. The role of private equity in social and sustainable development. http://www.youngfoundation.org.uk/files/images/publications/Equity_in_Social_and_Sustainable_Development.pdf. Accessed 15 July 2009.

Zadek, Simon. 2004. The path to corporate responsibility. Harvard Business Review 82(12): 125–132.

Chapter 8
Responsible Investment and Exclusion Criteria: A Case Study from a Catholic Private Bank

Michael S. Aßländer and Markus Schenkel

Introduction

During the last years, numerous cases of corporate misconduct have undermined public confidence in financial institutions. Especially during the recent economic crisis, the way financial institutes have handled their legal and ethical responsibilities came to be questioned. Dubious customer relation management and inadequate customer information have eroded banks' reputation. The involvement of large financial institutions in various cases of business fraud during the last years, like insider trading, stock manipulation etc. (see Boatright 2008), has jeopardized the capability of banks for self-limitation and the self-regulation mechanism of markets (Aßländer 2005, Aßländer and Roloff 2004, Thielemann 2005, Thielemann and Ulrich 2003).

Notwithstanding the legitimate criticism of corporate behavior in these cases, this critique does not address the fact that the responsibilities of financial institutions go beyond their internal organisational practices, as Crane et al. (2008: 343) point out: 'as a service provider to other organisations, the financial service industry has an important role to play in taking responsibility for its support and facilitation of responsible (or irresponsible) practices on the part of its customers'. Banks, as financial intermediaries, at least indirectly influence the refinancing options of stock companies with their buy and sell recommendations and hence define corporations' business policy and the ecological and social issues those companies stand for (Scherer 2003). This influence of the financial sector is increasingly being recognized in literature: No project can be realized, no company can produce, and no private or governmental organization can operate without capital. Thus, every investment has environmental as well as social consequences.

RI funds are offered as an investment opportunity that 'combines investors' financial objectives with their concerns about environmental, social and governance (ESG) issues' (Eurosif 2008, see also Sparkes 2002). Although this definition

M.S. Aßländer (✉)
University of Kassel, Kassel, Germany
e-mail: michael.asslaender@gmx.de

W. Vandekerckhove et al. (eds.), *Responsible Investment in Times of Turmoil*, Issues in Business Ethics 31, DOI 10.1007/978-90-481-9319-6_8, © Springer Science+Business Media B.V. 2011

remains vague and customers' connotations and national shaping of CSR and RI might differ regarding the question of what 'environmental' and 'social' means in a certain context (see De George 2008, Marquis et al. 2007, Matten and Moon 2008, Muñoz-Torres et al. 2004, Schäfer 2004, Signori 2009, Sandberg et al. 2008), the finance sector presents RI as a solution for ethical investment.

In this chapter we attempt to question the 'taken-for-grantedness' of RI funds as ethical investment. We will illustrate this by the example of 'SUPERIOR', one of the first and market-leading ethical funds in Austria that is issued by the Austrian Catholic bank Schelhammer & Schattera. More precisely, using document analyses, we will be testing to what extent this fund delivers on what we can expect from funds that claim to be ethical funds.

In the next section we distinguish market driven from deliberative funds, where the latter have a higher moral pitch. In terms of ethicality we would expect these funds to (1) be well founded in terms of investment policy rationale, (2) have a complete and unambiguous set of screening criteria, (3) be strong in monitoring investee corporations. Section three introduces the case 'SUPERIOR'. Sections four, five, and six analyse the three dimensions we would expect these funds to be strong at. The outcome of our analysis is however that the justification of the specified criteria, the delimitation of companies and the monitoring of the application of criteria pose serious problems. Section seven finally draws some conclusions. While we cannot generalize from one case, our analysis suggests we cannot take for granted the ethical high ground of even deliberative funds. We formulate some tentative ways out of what is looming as a delusion risk for RI.

Deliberative Funds' High Moral Ground

Mackenzie (1998: 85) notes:

> Market led-funds choose their criteria from EIRIS [or other rating agencies] on the basis of their perception of market demand. (. . .) Deliberative funds, on the other hand choose their criteria on the base of reasoning about the ethics of corporate practice.

In contrast to market-led funds, deliberative funds are based on ex ante defined, ethical selection criteria by the funds management. In other words: while market-led funds just provide a list of companies regarded as ethical by the market, deliberative funds use differentiated criteria assessing companies for investment decision (Crane and Matten 2007). However, this differentiation of approaches to choosing ethical criteria respectively RI funds should be seen as an Ideal type. As Mackenzie already stated, funds could not clearly be separated to one type that easily. Nevertheless, this differentiation serves as a good starting point to clarify basic requirements or characteristics of RI funds if they should be called 'ethical'. As Thielemann and Ulrich (2003) point out, those who truly care about ethics do not have merely personal preferences but principles. Thus, ethics is something that 'conveys certain principles of altruism, of self-sacrifice, of a normative and systematic code of conduct' (Sparkes 2001: 198). Accordingly, we can expect funds choosing their criteria on the base of reasoning rather than only by picking criteria out of given lists according to potential ethical investors' preferences respectively perceived market demands to have a sound moral base to clarify and justify their criteria. Particularly funds that refer to religious norms and values – respectively where religious institutions set the moral case – can be seen as ideal-typical form of this. Such funds commonly use, like other funds, an ethical advisory board to clarify the ethical base of the criteria and to monitor whether or not they are applied correctly. Accordingly, we expect such funds to have a good, well-founded ethical base for clarifying and justifying their criteria, to be clear about them and have a 'clean' funds universe in terms of ethicality. However, this does not inevitably mean that the selected criteria of market-led funds could not have an ethical base.

Furthermore, deliberative funds should have a complete and unambiguous set of screening criteria due to their reasoning and ethical base. Because they ground on principles they should aim to foster social and ecological change in corporations as active stakeholders and to be anxious to monitor investee corporations to be able to divest, if their criteria are violated. However, it has to be noted that many RI funds (currently) hold small proportion of shares in corporations. Accordingly, their possibilities to influence companies seem to be limited on investing and divesting. Benjamin Richardson (2009: 558) notes in this context:

> The Eurosif research tallied the value of shareholder engagement and proxy voting practices, yet there is no extensive research on the actual extent and quality of such practices. Because the SRI market is likely to be much smaller than these surveys suggest, its capacity to leverage change by raising the financing costs of polluters or pressuring for change through shareholder activism is probably rather limited.

In this chapter, we use a case study to examine to what extent the expectations towards a deliberative fund hold with regard to the well founded investment rationale, the complete and unambiguous set of screening criteria, and the strong monitoring process.

Introducing the Case Study 'SUPERIOR'

Schelhammer & Schattera is an Austrian Catholic private bank founded in 1832 in Vienna. Their market share for SRI is over 20% (the whole SRI market in Austria is €1.17 billion). Their public funds have a volume of €300 million, but the bank also does asset management for private investors (church linked). Since the beginning of the twentieth century the bank started with the administration of charity estates and foundation's assets beside its regular business and became known for serious business policy. One of the core business principles of Schelhammer & Schattera, laid down in an early 'code of conduct' in 1908, became the maxim not to invest in speculative business, which is one of the leading rules till nowadays. (Schelhammer & Schattera 2009a). Thus, in the annual report 2008 of Schelhammer & Schattera abbot Ambros Ebhart, president of the supervisory board, reminds this ethical principle and warns of irresponsible investment practices (Schelhammer & Schattera 2009i: 4–5). Accordingly, the bank was (and is) pursuing a conservative investment strategy before as well as during the financial crisis of 2008 and 2009. Nevertheless, also the SUPERIOR funds issued by Schellhammer & Schattera have been affected negatively but the bank did not take this as an opportunity to change its policy. Due to the fact that the Roman Catholic church of Austria holds 85% stake in Schellhammer & Schattera the bank is in the unique situation not to be forced to sacrifice its ethical principles.

The bank provides investment funds since 1988. One of the reasons to engage in this new business was the request of the Austrian monastic communities to have suitable investment opportunities for the retirement programs of their members (Schelhammer & Schattera 2009a). Actually Schelhammer & Schattera offer 12 different ethical funds under the umbrella 'SUPERIOR' including two bond funds, four mixed funds, four stock funds and two money market funds (Schelhammer & Schattera 2009b). In the following we will focus on the equity funds issued by the bank.

Schelhammer & Schattera uses a two-stage evaluation process to include companies in its RI funds 'SUPERIOR'. First, potential investments are examined according to various negative criteria and, second, a 'best-in-class' methodology is used for the final investment decisions. The bank thereby is taking into account the 'Corporate Citizenship Rating' of Oekom Research that assesses companies' corporate responsibility towards the social, cultural, and environmental sustainability according to the 'Frankfurt-Hohenheimer guidelines' (Hassler 2003, Oekom Research, Werther 2007). Thus, although RI funds' list of criteria vary the negative exclusion criteria used by Schellhammer & Schattera are commonly used, in the one or the other way, by conventional RI funds like Pioneer Funds-Global Ecology, Allianz RCM Global Sustainability or F&C Stewardship Fund etc. Furthermore, like other institutional investors the bank not only tries to invest according to social, ecological or governmental issues but to actively influence their portfolio companies (Schelhammer & Schattera 2009c). In this respect the RI fund SUPERIOR can serve as example for conventional RI funds. However, in contrast to other RI funds the bank's investment policy and strategy is based on a strong normative or religious basis. Referring to the distinction mode in section two, the fund can be considered to be a 'deliberative fund'.

Regarding our topic we consider the fund SUPERIOR to be a good example due to the strong normative base, respectively the investment policy, and the use of an ethical advisory board by Schellhammer & Schattera.

The exclusion criteria for Schelhammer & Schattera's 'SUPERIOR' fund are as follows (Schelhammer & Schattera 2009d, Werther 2007):

Controversial business fields:

– no support of nuclear power
– no support of abortion or euthanasia
– no drugs
– no pornography
– no armaments
– no tobacco

Controversial business practices:

– no serious human rights violations
– no serious labor law violations
– no conflicting ecological activities/behavior

Exclusion criteria for countries:

– no countries with serious human rights violations
– no countries with nuclear energy accounting for more than 10% of the total energy mix
– no countries that did not ratify the Kyoto protocol
– no countries that spend more than 3% of GDP on arms
– no countries that still execute capital punishment

Taken the above characterisation of our case – the SUPERIOR fund – into regard, it leans towards the deliberative fund type on MacKenzie's continuum (MacKenzie 1998). In what follows, we will use this example to see how well a deliberative fund delivers on the high moral ground which the RI discourse tends to endow itself with. At appropriate times throughout the remainder of this text we will tap other examples to connect our analysis with broader connecting issues.

Well Founded Rationale

At first glance, the specified criteria all seem to be ethically relevant and do not need any further explanation. However, on closer examination, it becomes apparent that the ethical normative basis for justifying the specified criteria has to be clarified. In the case of Schelhammer & Schattera, it seems to be obvious that the bank refers to its Christian background and Christian values for justifying and formulating every single criterion (Werther 2007). Thus, the bank states on its homepage (Schelhammer & Schattera 2009e):

> As an independent Austrian private banking institution, our commitment is only to our values and the objectives of our clients. Our banking business follows a value-oriented approach. As the bank of the Catholic Church of Austria, Christian ethics guide our behaviour. People are at the focus of our activity. [...] In line with the trend of the times, our investment activity is supportive of business concepts based on ethical standards and the principle of sustainability...

Nevertheless, other religious communities may choose differing exclusion criteria for the same reason. For example, an 'Islamic' fund might choose criteria like: no investment in pork-related products, no investment in financial institutions lending money at interest or no investment in alcohol producing or selling companies (Kurtz 2009). Thus, it becomes obvious that a commonly accepted ethical rationale of several exclusion criteria depends on the personal view of the fund provider.

However, in terms of transparency RI-fund suppliers should clarify the normative ethical base of their funds decisions. As Mark Schwartz (2003: 202) states:

> Without proper justification or rationale, investors may be prevented from making an informed investment decision. In addition, if the screens do not contain any ethical justification, then it may be misleading or deceptive to investors to label them as ethical screens.

Thus, RI-funds providers have to formulate and specify a code of conduct to obtain their exclusion criteria in a similar manner. Otherwise, individual criteria may seem to be arbitrarily selected (Anderson 1996). It may occur in this case that the specified criteria are based only on investors' preferences and thus are formulated only according to what potential investors (may) demand. Accordingly, it is debatable whether such a product can be called an ethical fund (Schwartz 2003). In the end, a fund policy that is not grounded on an ethical base and only economically motivated may turn out to be a customized concept of more or less arbitrarily selected customer preferences that are claimed to be ethical (Voigt and Kratochwil 2004). But preferences (as criteria) are interchangeable and do not have a sound ethical base that would allow deciding what behaviour should be considered to be morally acceptable. Accordingly, Craig Mackenzie (1998: 84) referring to deliberative funds states that 'one of the biggest challenges facing deliberative ethical funds at present is to ensure that their criteria are chosen on the basis of good, well-grounded ethical reasons which stand the test of critical scrutiny.'

However, regarding the ethical base of ethical screens Mark Schwartz (2003: 211–212) critically notes:

> It is not even clear that at least two of the currently predominant ethical screens, such as those related to gambling and the military, are ethically justified. If the ethical investing movement were to be honest and forthright, they would not label their screens as 'ethical' at all. They are simply screens developed with the intention of reflecting intended investor's social, religious, or political attitudes or beliefs, and nothing more.

Complete and Unambiguous Screening Criteria

Another problem arises when the catalogue of criteria is checked for completeness. In the case of Schelhammer & Schattera, the catalogue of controversial business fields might be extended without any problem. The bank would have reason to do so: genetic engineering, alcohol, and gambling are issues that are not specified as exclusion criteria even though they might be justified by the Christian values of the investors. Interestingly (or quite the opposite), this Catholic bank holds shares of the Casinos Austria AG respectively the Austrian Lotteries (Austrian Lotteries 2010). However, it has to be noted that these shares are not part of SUPERIOR funds investment universe and Casions Austria AG is engaged, although critically evaluated on several occasions, in CSR, among other things to foster Responsible gaming.

The same as for controversial business fields applies to the categories of business practices and country criteria that have to be avoided. The former can be extended, among other things, to animal experiments, corruption, and white collar criminality and the latter to apartheid or sexual discrimination. However, it is debatable whether country criteria do make sense at all because companies only have limited possibilities to influence national policy. Furthermore, they do not depend on governmental policy to engage in social and ecological issues. Thus, for example, companies can meet or adapt to international ecological standards even in countries that did not ratify the Kyoto protocol. If RI funds claim to encourage and ensure that business is carried out ecologically and socially responsibly, it should be the aim of RI funds to support such desirable organizational behaviour.

Whereas the problem of criteria selection is mainly a normative problem, the decision on a company's exclusion from or inclusion in an RI fund's portfolio poses a serious problems of delimitation.

First, this is related to problems in interpreting the individual criteria. (a) The less precise the product group to be avoided is specified, the more problematic distinguishing among companies becomes. The exclusion criterion 'drugs,' for example, offers various possibilities for interpretation: if the criterion is interpreted broadly, it also includes 'alcohol' and other 'legal' drugs, but it only defines 'illegal' drugs if a very strict interpretation is adopted. However, because the interpretation of the term 'illegal' differs from country to country, a precise specification of the criterion is obviously not at hand. (b) Furthermore, a set of imprecise criteria complicates companies' classification. In this respect, serious difficulties arise when we talk, for example, about serious human rights violations. What action is considered to be a serious human rights violation and justifies a company's exclusion from the investment portfolio? The question of the possibility of fund managers gaining knowledge and insight in this field notwithstanding, it remains unspecified whether human rights violations will be sanctioned in any case or not until in case of recurrence, whether companies are excluded in any case where they violate a single person's individual rights or not until several employees are affected by the violation, or whether the fund managers have to react in the case of faint suspicion or not until there is strong evidence that a company is violating human rights. (c) Finally, the various possibilities of ethical interpretation of the used terms leads to further problems of delimitation. Abortion or euthanasia, for example, are rather vague and ambiguous terms even within the field of ethics.

Second, using a 'best-in-class' approach to identify the top performers of single industries does not provide a sufficient basis to distinguish 'good' from 'bad' companies. In the case of Schelhammer & Schattera for the ethical assessment a multistage selection process is used which combines a negative criteria list with best in class approach. Criteria for the best in class selection are, among others: Social Responsibility engagement, diversity management, management compensation practices and business ethic principles as social indicators and application of environment management systems, ecological efficiency of production or ecological design as environmental criteria (Schelhammer & Schattera 2004). One problem here is that solely companies and not the entire sector and its social and ecological performance are screened and rated. As a consequence, the top performers are very difficult to compare, especially since the 'best-in-class' rating provides not an absolute but a relative criterion: there is no information on whether a company behaves objectively in an ethical manner; it just states that a company turns out to be better than others (Hassler 2003). Such a relative assessment bears the risk that the bad prevails over the ugly or, as a saying states: 'Unter den Blinden ist der Einäugige König' (Among the blind a one-eyed man is king).

Third, regarding the fact that companies are widely linked through capital interlocking, that they are internationally operating, and that they often have a multinational structure, further problems and uncertainties occur. The question arises of how to deal with investments held by international holdings or companies' international investments. Even though Schelhammer & Schattera note that any subsidiary and associated company also has to meet the negative criteria (Tometschek 2007), it remains difficult to assess the effects mergers and acquisitions will have on the rating and valuation of a company. What effect did the DaimlerChrysler merger have on Schelhamer & Schattera's rating concerning the explicit criterion for exclusion 'no companies based in countries that still execute capital punishment'? Although there may be a well-defined solution to the mentioned problem other mergers and acquisitions in highly diversified companies pose a far more serious problem. In 2007, the tobacco company Philip Morris – renamed as Altria in 2001 – for example, announced that it would merge with the food maker Kraft. As a result of the announcement, Philip Morris's stock price gained 10% (Banerjee 2007). Despite the strong price performance, however, this poses a crucial question to the fund management: do they now have to deal with a food maker that also produces cigarettes or with a tobacco company that has acquired a majority interest in a food company? In 2005 Pax World Funds had to deal with a similar problem when its portfolio company Starbucks Coffee made the deal with the whiskey maker Jim Beam to sell a coffee-based alcoholic beverage. In accordance with the fund's criteria 'no alcohol' it divested itself of the company shares (Carroll and Buchholz 2008: 73).

Fourth, a similar problem, as with classifying conglomerates on the basis of an obviously simple criteria list, arises with regard to multifunctional artefacts. Various products coming from aerospace, telecommunication, or information technology industries – which make nearly 30% of the funds universe of 'SUPERIOR 6' and about 15% of 'SUPERIOR 4' (Schelhammer & Schattera 2009f) – can be used for civil as well as military purposes. In most cases, the use of artefacts cannot simply be classified as 'armaments industry' or 'non-armaments industry' anymore (Michelson et al. 2004). Thus for example, SAP, a company making 8.36% of 'SUPERIOR 6' (Schelhammer & Schattera 2009f), also develops specific solutions for the armament industry with the 'SAP for aerospace and defence' program (SAP 2010).

As in the case of SAP, most producers are engaged both in armament and civil production: what percentage of 'armament supply' does it take to be considered to be a company belonging to the armament industry? Which industrial sectors can be considered part of the armament industry and which sectors cannot despite casual orders for military purposes? As Berthold Brecht (1979) had already noted in his play 'Fear and Misery of the Third Reich,' the boundaries between the armament industry and any other industry are not clear-cut: in the case of war, even the production of light bulbs is a vital part of the armament industry. In view of the lack of clarity in the classification, fund providers have to deal with the problem of how to meet their negative criteria entirely. Obviously, grey areas in this context have to be tolerated, but in terms of transparency it would be helpful for investors to specify ex ante which range has to be accepted by them as system-dependent.

Thereby, the fund managers are navigating between Scylla and Charybdis regarding their communication policy and the disclosure of investment criteria: the more they engage in transparent communication, the more vulnerable the organization becomes in a crisis situation. The less they communicate and the more generally the criteria are defined, the less reliable and credible the label 'RI' becomes.

Strong Monitoring Process

Despite the launch of the European SRI Transparency Guidelines by the European Social Investment Forum in November 2004, in practice things did not change very much. Under the guidelines, the undersigned are obliged not only to reveal common basic information but also to disclose, among other things, what criteria and evaluation methods are used and how many times the criteria are checked (Tometschek 2008). Nevertheless, these procedures are unable to solve a fundamental problem of all ethical funds: how to evaluate and validate the relevant company data.

For this Schelhammer & Schattera like other fund providers base their decisions on the assessment of professional rating agencies. Such RI rating agencies, for example GermanWatch, ökoinvest, Oekom Research, RiskMetrics Group or Innovest, help to verify negative criteria and (the efficiency of) the investment decision or investment risk. However, Henry Schäfer (2009) points out that RI ratings currently not work perfectly and are unable to reveal investment risks. Analysing the sustainability indices FTSE4Good and Dow Jones Sustainability Growth before the recent crises, Schäfer reveals that they, for a long time, contained many financial institutions that get into economic difficulties during the recent crisis like Hypo Real Estate or Dexia. Even when Moodys downgraded the ratings of first shares containing Subprime credits and the ABX-index for Mortage Backed Securities lost over 80% in 2007, rating agencies did not seem to consider this as fundamental governance problems of the involved actors (Schäfer 2009).

For their company assessments Schelhammer and Schattera use the Corporate Responsibility Rating of oekom research, which is based on the 'Frankfurt Hohenheim guidelines' and combines social and ethical criteria. Even though, such ratings make possible a comparison of the social and ecological performance of different companies due to standardized criteria the evaluation of such data reveals general problems. In practice the data used for the reports are mainly drawn, in addition to readily assessable and general market data, from surveys based on self-reports, evaluations of business and company figures, internet and database research, and consultation with experts, if necessary (Hassler 2003). Hence, many RI rating agencies do basically and mainly evaluate reports according to formal criteria (GR3, EMAS) and the information that companies disclose voluntarily. For fund managers the asymmetric distribution of information makes it difficult to screen companies efficiently according to the selected criteria. As long as binding rules for third party evaluation for ecological and social data are missing, rating agencies or shareholders trying to evaluate companies' policy and behaviour remain dependent on the self assessment and the information provided by the companies. To avoid these informational asymmetries Thomas W. Dunfee (2003: 250) proposes to extend financial auditing practices:

> Social reports generated by the firms themselves would be more reliable and thus of greater use to social screeners if they were audited by professional, independent auditors. The highly developed profession of financial auditors is critical to the functioning of capital markets. An initial question is whether financial auditors would be capable of effectively auditing social reports. If so, the need for social auditors is essentially solved because the established profession of financial auditors could step forward to provide this service.

Without such independent evaluation, ratings only indicate that a company has in place a code of conduct or social and ecological standards and is reporting about the ecological and social issues it engages in but cannot provide any information about the implementation of these issues in day-to-day business. Regarding the informative value of such CSR reports, Subhabrata Banerjee (2007: 43) arrives, at least for US-American companies, at the conclusion that: 'Glossy corporate social responsibility reports are forms of green-washing that often do not reveal the grim realities that lie behind them.' The validity of data and findings leading to a company's exclusion from or inclusion in an RI fund's portfolio has therefore to be considered carefully.

A further problem is posed by the 'level of exclusion' because various fund providers do not exclude companies until they conduct 5% or more of their business in an ecologically, socially, and ethically irresponsible manner. Especially, when companies do have a high financial performance, fund managers tend to interpret the criteria broadly.

This room for maneuver has to be considered a serious problem because it principally offers, within certain limits, fund managers the opportunity to play a company's financial performance off against a possibly weak corporate social performance. In the long run, those fund providers that interpret their criteria softly may gain competitive advantage over those that are adopting a stricter interpretation. A survey by the Austrian Association for Consumer Information reveals that, although fund providers may not intentionally create room for maneuver, they are aware of it and are exploiting the existing opportunities to strengthen the funds' financial performance (Neugebauer and Greutter 2007).

Schelhammer & Schattera comparatively follow a strict funds policy. So for example in 2008 Unilever was excluded from the funds universe of 'SUPERIOR 4' because of labour right violations at Hindustan Unilever and human rights violations at a company owned tea plantation in Kenya reported by human rights organization SOMO (Schelhammer & Schattera 2009g: 5). Similar reasons lead to the exclusion of Michelin from SUPERIOR 6 in September 2009: The company was accused by NGOs of human rights violations in its rubber plantations in Nigeria (Schelhammer & Schattera 2009h: 6). Although in most cases human and worker rights violations lead to exclusion from SUPERIOR funds universe also mergers and company restructurings can cause exclusion. Thus, in 2007 the bank excluded StatoilHydro derived from restructuring NorskHydro because of controversial environmental policy (Schelhammer & Schattera 2008: 4).

Although Schelhammer & Schattera regularly report company exclusions for ethical reasons it remains difficult to decide to what extend violations of the funds criteria have to be tolerated. Thus, some fund providers do not exclude companies from their investment portfolio until more than 10% of their turnover is generated through irresponsible operations and a company's listing cannot therefore be justified any longer (Neugebauer and Greutter 2007, Schwartz 2003). In the long run, this may lead to a decline of morality in markets because investors do not only seek a quiet conscience but also a financial return of investment (McLachlan and Gardner 2004). Thus, Britain's first ethical fund, the F&C Stewardship, has been criticised for poor performance and investing in 2009 in banks that were originally excluded from its portfolio (Telegraph 2009). Hence, while RI and its market share may grow, it may become less distinctive from conventional or non-socially responsible investment (see Michelson et al. 2004). Fund providers may increasingly need to adjust to their competitors with lower ethical standards because the more broadly the criteria are interpreted and the better the financial performance of the fund, the more it will attract investors. If other fund providers want to stay in competition, they will have to loosen their moral standards (Nell-Breuning 1975). RI funds therefore may contain shares and shared certificates that meet the criteria as well as some that do not (Finanztest 2004, Signori 2009). It therefore seems to be debatable to investors whether or not the fund management consistently applies the selected criteria and any selected company complies with them. An example of this is the Climate Change fund offered by Virgin as ethical investment opportunity that came in for criticism because it strongly invested in such companies that should have been excluded from the fund universe (Guardian 2009, Telegraph 2009). Referring to a US American study on RI funds, Benjamin Richardson (2009: 558) highlights that '25% of nominal SRI funds screen only on the basis of *one* of these criteria [tobacco, alcohol, gambling etc.].'

To limit this problem, Schelhammer & Schattera, like other European RI funds, use an 'ethical' advisory board that ensures that the selected criteria are interpreted according to the chosen standards. Despite some bank officials the advisory board of Schelhammer & Schattera mainly consists of practitioners and experts in the field of ethics and representatives from monastic communities which underpins the banks self understanding as Catholic bank. Additionally, an independent accountant monitors compliance with the selection criteria and the established selection procedures (see Muñoz-Torres et al. 2004, Signori 2009, Tometschek 2007). Even so, the validity of the obtained data remains questionable. Although several prominent representatives of society and the church are now morally liable for their compliance with the selected criteria, the problem with the available data basis remains due to the fact that this might not solve the problem of informational asymmetries as discussed above. Establishing an ethical advisory board, at best, may give credibility to the fund management's effort to comply with ethical standards but cannot reduce the difficulties in conducting single-case evaluations.

Conclusion and Prospect

In this chapter, we critically examined to what extent our expectations towards RI funds with regard to well founded rationale, complete and unambiguous screening criteria, and strong monitoring process hold. We used the example of SUPERIOR, a deliberative fund, for this purpose. We found that even though SUPERIOR showed great endeavour on most aspects, none of our expectations was met beyond doubt. This raises serious questions with regard to the high moral ground with which RI tends to endow itself. Even though we cannot generalize from this case study, it should warn us not to take for granted the panacea RI seems to offer. If even a deliberative fund fails to cut away the arbitrariness of its rationale, is unable to define a complete and unambiguous set of screening criteria, and cannot guarantee an appropriately strong monitoring process, then what is it we are repelling mainstream investment for?

But, does that mean that RI is just a moral gimmick only responding to consumers' interests? We feel that would be an exaggeration as well. Especially in the case of Schelhammer & Schattera it becomes obvious that we have to differ between systematic problems of RI-funds and the more or less serious efforts banks undertake to secure 'ethical standards' of their products. But the point we need to take from this is that as RI grows there is also a growing need to safeguard it from becoming a moral gimmick. On that line, we make two final comments.

First, it can be assumed that the financial return of investment will remain investors' first or at least second priority. 'These individuals are neither cranks nor saints: they are commonly middle-income professionals mixing ethical investments with not so ethical ones' (Lewis and Mackenzie 2000, Lewis and Webley 1994, Michelson et al. 2004, see also Syse in this book). Only few socially responsible investors are willing to commit their entire portfolio to socially and ecologically orientated investment (Mackenzie and Lewis 1999). Therefore, RI funds will only remain in the market if they (can) achieve a competitive rate of return. Studies thereby confirm that RI funds neither out-perform nor under-perform compared with conventional or non-ethical funds (Kreander et al. 2005, Schröder 2005) but '[as] long as the mainstream finance community believes that incorporating ESG [environmental, social, and governance] criteria into investment decisions comes at the cost of portfolio performance, mainstreaming of SRI is uncertain' (Juravle and Lewis 2008). Referring to the theories of Frederick Herzberg (1968), ethics can be considered to be a 'dissatisfier' or 'hygiene factor' in this context: deliberative funds (or what we have taken to be ethical funds) run a delusion risk because they fail to deliver on their claims – at least for those investors that choose them because of these claims.

Second, if the label 'ethical' or 'socially responsible' should be established in capital markets, binding rules for the selection procedures, including unified specifications of the range of tolerance that is allowed, have to be developed to decide whether or not a fund can be labeled 'RI.' Here, policy makers and particularly the banking industry are called to support, initiate, and establish standardization. As Thomas Dunfee (2003: 252) points out:

The availability of accurate, relevant information is key. The development of generally accepted social accounting principles and generally accepted social auditing principles is necessary in order to insure that useful, comparable information is available to investors and investment managers.

However, in view of the heterogeneity within the RI movement the question arises whether a standardization of RI is possible and desirable (Sandberg et al. 2008). Especially (parts of) the financial industry may show no interest in this issue. Sandberg et al. (2008: 527) presume that this is grounded in

the market setting in which the SRI movement operates, and the fact that it would seem to give fund companies incentives to develop their own conception of SRI. (...) As long as they are rewarded for conceptualising and implementing SRI somewhat differently, market actors are not incentivised to collaborate with each other to reach unification or compromise.

Due to this respectively the heterogeneity and vagueness of RI products have been created that are making non-sense of the label like specific certificates or hedge funds. In many cases costumers are offered socially responsible investment opportunities that are not 'ethical' but rather conventional investment and nothing more than 'Style Investings' (Schäfer 2009). Thus, transparency and comparability are a fundamental prerequisite if investors and the credibility of the label should be protected. Accordingly, governmental or other accepted binding standards are needed and demanded. This does not mean that RI funds must be absolutely homogenous. But, like in comparable fields (green products, organic products etc.) a minimum standard should be specified to ensure consumer protection in the field of RI.

References

Anderson, Digby C. 1996. What Has Ethical Investment to Do with Ethics? London: Social Affaire Unit.
Aßländer, Michael S. 2005. Governance can't make it all – das Versagen der Governance-Strukturen am Beispiel Enron. In Zwischen Gewissen und Gewinn – Beiträge zur wertorientierten Personalführung, eds. Uto Meier and Bernhard Still, 249–266. Regensburg: Pustet.
Aßländer, Michael S. and Julia Roloff. 2004. Sozialstandards als Beispiel für soziale Verantwortung von Unternehmen. Journal für politische Bildung 3: 26–36.
Austrian Lotteries. 2010. http://www.lotterien.at/olg/CS_struktur_unternehmen.html?sessionID=ad33af59-1401-583d148-99b0-7700d89f6d9c/. Accessed 1 February 2010.
Banerjee, Subhabrata B. 2007. Corporate Social Responsibility – The Good, the Bad, and the Ugly. Northampton: Edward Elgar Publishing Ltd.
Boatright, John R. 2008. Ethics in Finance (2nd ed). Malden and Oxford: Blackwell.
Brecht, Berthold. 1979. Furcht und Elend des Dritten Reiches. Frankfurt am Main: Suhrkamp.
Carroll, Archie B. and Ann K. Buchholz. 2008. Business and Society: Ethics and Stakeholder Management. Mason: South-Western.
Crane, Andrew and Dirk Matten. 2007. Business Ethics. 2nd ed. Oxford: Oxford University Press.
Crane, Andrew, Dirk Matten, and Laura Spence. 2008. Corporate Social Responsibility – Readings and Cases in a Global Context. New York, NY: Routledge.
De George, Richard T. 2008. An American perspective on corporate social responsibility and the tenuous relevance of Jacques Derrida. Business Ethics: A European Review 17: 74–86.

Dunfee, Thomas W. 2003. Social investing: Mainstream or backwater. Journal of Business Ethics 43: 247–252.

Eurosif. 2008. European SRI Study 2008. http://www.eurosif.org/publications/sri_studies/. Accessed 13 June 2009.

Finanztest. 2004. Gewissenhaft anlagen. http://www.test.de/themen/geldanlage-banken/test/-Ethisch-oekologische-Fonds/1204233/1204233/1204340/. Accessed 17 March 2008.

Guardian. 2009. Vrigin Money's climate change ISA gets Richard Branson in a pickle. http://www.guardian.co.uk/environment/blog/2009/oct/15/greenwash-virgin-money-climate-change-isa/. Accessed 29 October 2009.

Hassler, Robert. 2003. Nachhaltigkeits-Rating: Ein innovatives Konzept zur Förderung der nachhaltigen Entwicklung bei Unternehmen und auf den Finanzmärkten. Eine Chance für Stiftungen. In Ethik für den Kapitalmarkt? Orientierung zwischen Regulierung und Laissez-faire, eds. Andreas G. Scherer, Gerhard Hütter, and Lothar Maßmann, 205–213. München: Rainer Hampp Verlag.

Herzberg, Frederick. 1968. Work and the Nature of Man. London: Staples Press.

Juravle, Carmen and Alan Lewis. 2008. Identifying impediments to SRI in Europe: A review of the practitioner and academic literature. Business Ethics: A European Review 17: 285–310.

Kreander, Niklas, Rob. H. Gray, David. M. Power, and C. Donald Sinclair. 2005. Evaluating the performance of ethical and non-ethical funds: A matched pair analysis. Journal of Business Finance and Accounting 32: 1465–1493.

Kurtz, Lloyd. 2009. Socially responsible investment and shareholder activism. In The Oxford Handbook of Corporate Social Responsibility, eds. Andrew Crane, McWilliams Abagail, Dirk Matten, Jeremy Moon, and Donald S. Siegel, 249–280. Oxford: Oxford University Press.

Lewis, Alan and Craig Mackenzie. 2000. Morals, money, ethical investing and economic psychology. Human Relations 53: 179–191.

Lewis, Alan and Paul Webley. 1994. Social and ethical investing, beliefs, preferences and the willingness to sacrifice financial return. Ethics and Economics Affairs 8: 171–183.

Mackenzie, Craig. 1998. The choice of criteria in ethical investment. Business Ethics: A European Review 7: 81–86.

Mackenzie, Craig and Alan Lewis. 1999. Morals and markets: The case of ethical investing. Business Ethics Quarterly 9: 439–452.

Marquis, Christopher Ann Mary, and Davis F. Gerald. 2007. Isomorphism and corporate social action. Academy of Management Review 32: 925–945.

Matten, Dirk and Jeremy Moon. 2008. 'Implicit' and 'explicit' CSR: A conceptual framework for a comparative understanding of corporate social responsibility. Academy of Management Review 33: 404–424.

McLachlan, Jonathan and John Gardner. 2004. A comparison of socially responsible and conventional investors. Journal of Business Ethics 52: 11–25.

Michelson, Grant, Nick Wailes, Sandra van der Laan, and Geoff Frost. 2004. Ethical investment processes and outcomes. Journal of Business Ethics 52: 1–10.

Muñoz-Torres, María J., María Á. Fernández-Izquierdo, and María R. Balaguer-Franch. 2004. The social responsibility performance of ethical and solidarity funds: An approach to the case of Spain. Business Ethics: A European Review 13: 200–218.

Nell-Breuning, Oswald von. 1975. Der Mensch in der heutigen Wirtschaftsgesellschaft. München: Olzog.

Neugebauer, Christian and Georg Greutter. 2007. Ethikfonds in Österreich – Ein kommentierender Streifzug. Forum Wirtschaftsethik 15: 22–25.

Oekom Research. http://www.oekom-research.com.

Richardson, Benjamin J. 2009. Keeping ethical investment ethical: Regulatory issues for investing for sustainability. Journal of Business Ethics 87: 555–572.

SAP. 2010. http://www.sap.com/industries/aero-defense/businessprocesses/manufacturers/index.epx/. Accessed 23 January 2010.

Sandberg, Joakim, Carmen Juravle, Ted Martin Hedesström, and Ian Hamilton. 2008. The heterogeneity of socially responsible investment. Journal for Business Ethics 87: 519–533.

Schäfer, Henry. 2004. Ethical investment of German non-profit organizations – conceptual outline and empirical results. Business Ethics: A European Review 23: 269–287.

Schäfer, Henry. 2009. Nachhaltiges Bankgeschäft als Heilsbringer in der Bankenkrise? Forum Wirtschaftsethik 17: 28–37.

Schelhammer & Schattera. 2004. http://www.schelhammer.at/m045/internet/downloads/kag/tls4$\delimiter"026E30F$_aktien.pdf/. Accessed 22 January 2010.

Schelhammer & Schattera. 2008. Superior 4. Ethik Aktien. Halbjahresbericht 1.8.2007 – 31.1.2008. Wien: Schelhammer & Schattera.

Schelhammer & Schattera. 2009a. http://www.schelhammer.at/m045/internet/de/individuelle_seite/geschichte.jsp$\delimiter"026E30F$#002/. Accessed 22 January 2010.

Schelhammer & Schattera. 2009b. http://www.schelhammer.at/m045/internet/de/kag/kag_individuelle_seite/superiorfonds.jsp/. Accessed 22 January 2010.

Schelhammer & Schattera. 2009c. http://www.schelhammer.at/m045/internet/de/kag/kag_individuelle_seite/engagement.jsp/. Accessed 22 January 2010.

Schelhammer & Schattera. 2009d. http://www.schelhammer.at/m045/internet/de/kag/kag_individuelle_seite/kriterien.jsp/. Accessed 22 January 2010.

Schelhammer & Schattera. 2009e. http://www.schelhammer.at/m045/internet/de/individuelle_seite/aboutus.jsp/. Accessed 22 January 2010.

Schelhammer & Schattera. 2009f. http://coop.sparinvest.com/fondsdaten/fondsblatt_schelhammer.asp/. Accessed 23 January 2010.

Schelhammer & Schattera. 2009g. Superior 4. Ethik Aktien. Halbjahresbericht 1.8.2008 – 31.1.2009. http://coop.sparinvest.com/fondsdaten/rechenschaftbericht.asp?fid=509%cid=6455/. Accessed 23 January 2010.

Schelhammer & Schattera. 2009h. Superior 6. Ethik Aktien. Rechenschaftsbericht – 1. Rechnungsjahr. http://coop.sparinvest.com/fondsdaten/rechenschaftbericht.asp?fid=3609%cid=6455/. Accessed 23 January 2010.

Schelhammer & Schattera. 2009i. Geschäfts- und Nachhaltigkeitsbericht 2008. http://www.schelhammer.at/bankhaus/nachhaltigkeit/. Accessed 23 January 2010.

Scherer, Andreas G. 2003. Braucht der Kapitalmarkt eine (Unternehmens-) Ethik? In Ethik für den Kapitalmarkt? Orientierung zwischen Regulierung und Laissez-faire, eds. Andreas G. Scherer, Gerhard Hütter, and Lothar Maßmann, 15–33. München: Rainer Hampp Verlag.

Schröder, Michael. 2005. Is there a difference? The Performance Characteristics of SRI Equity Indexes. ZEW Discussion Paper No. 05–50. http://madoc.bib.uni-mannheim.de/madoc/volltexte/2005/1124/pdf/dp0550.pdf/. Accessed 29 June 2009.

Schwartz, Mark S. 2003. The 'ethics' of ethical investing. Journal of Business Ethics 43: 195–213.

Signori, Silvana. 2009. Ethical (SRI) funds in Italy: A review. Business Ethics: A European Review 18: 145–164.

Sparkes, Russel. 2001. Ethical investment: whose ethics, which investment? Business Ethics: A European Review 10: 194–205.

Sparkes, Russel. 2002. Socially Responsible Investment. A Global Revolution. Chichester: Wiley.

Telegraph. 2009. F&C Stewardship fund under fire for poor performance and investing in banks. http://www.telegraph.co.uk/finance/personalfinance/investing/5418646/FandC-Stewardship-fund-under-fire-for-poor-performance-and-investing-in-banks.html/. Accessed 30 October 2009.

Thielemann, Ulrich. 2005. Compliance und Integrity – Zwei Seiten ethisch integrierter Unternehmensteuerung. ZFWU 6: 31–45.

Thielemann, Ulrich and Ulrich Peter. 2003. Brennpunkt Bankenethik. St. Galler Beiträge zur Wirtschaftsethik, Vol. 33. Bern: Haupt Verlag.

Tometschek, Gerhard. 2007. Zukunftsfähiges investment: Aus der Praxis des ethischen Fondsmanagements. Glocalist 22: 20f.

Tometschek, Gerhard. 2008. Mehr Transparenz an den Kapitalmärkten. Glocalist 23: 31.

Voigt, Matthias and Martin Kratochwil. 2004. Wie ethisch sind Ethikfonds? – Sozial verantwortbare Geldanlagen. In Ethik im Management – Ethik und Erfolg verbinden sich, eds. Hans Ruh, Klaus M. Leisinger, and Joseph E. Stiglitz, 309–319. Zürich: Orell Fuessli.

Werther, Alexander. 2007. Doppelte Dividende – Die Praxis nachhaltiger Kapitalanlagen am Beispiel des Bankhauses Schelhammer & Schattera. Forum Wirtschaftsethik 15: 34–37.

Chapter 9
Islamic Banking and Responsible Investment: Is a Fusion Possible?

Reza Zain Jaufeerally

Introduction

The biggest financial crisis since 1929 is forcing the world to look for more sustainable financial models that would combine value-creation, stability and morality. Amid the chaos, two financial sectors are thriving: Ethical banking/Socially Responsible Investment (hereafter 'SRI') and Islamic Banking and Finance (hereafter 'Islamic Banking'). The Islamic Banking sector is growing at about 10–15% per year. In contrast with conventional financial institutions the sector has been, so far, mostly insulated from the global financial turmoil. With approximately 1.5 billion Muslims worldwide, including numerous oil and gas producing nations, growth potential is tremendous. Thus, the sector is attracting increasing attention from all the usual contenders. Amongst Western Nations, the UK has established a strong lead and aims to be, in the words of Prime Minister Gordon Brown (2006), a 'gateway to Islamic finance and trade'. France (with the largest European Muslim population), Luxembourg and Germany have also entered the race to become the global Islamic Banking centre. As Mrs Christine Lagarde, the French Finance Minister stated in November 2008: 'Nous sommes déterminés à faire de Paris une grande place d'accueil de la finance islamique (We are determined to make Paris a great haven for Islamic Finance)' (Le Parisien 2008). There is even positive interest from unexpected places. The Vatican stated banks should look at the rules of Islamic finance to restore confidence amongst their clients at a time of global economic crisis. On 4 March 2009 an article in the Osservatore Romano, the Vatican's official newspaper stated: 'The ethical principles on which Islamic finance is based may bring banks closer to their clients and to the true spirit which should mark every financial service.' (Bloomberg 2009)

At its core Islam preaches a morally responsible social economy sharing a significant conceptual overlap with SRI objectives. The fusion of the two sectors is the latest buzzword in the Islamic Banking press. We endeavour to investigate whether

R.Z. Jaufeerally (✉)
Centre for Economics & Ethics, Catholic University of Leuven, Brussel, Belgium
e-mail: rjaufeerally@gmail.com

W. Vandekerckhove et al. (eds.), *Responsible Investment in Times of Turmoil*,
Issues in Business Ethics 31, DOI 10.1007/978-90-481-9319-6_9,
© Springer Science+Business Media B.V. 2011

a fusion is feasible and if so, under what conditions. The implication is that if the real focus of Islamic Banking becomes Shari'ah-based SRI, then we should expect exponential growth in the SRI sector. Moreover, even conventional consumers are increasingly attracted to Islamic Banking, especially when compared with conventional banking alternatives.

While modern Islamic Banking is still in its infancy (in existence for about 35 years), the sector is constantly evolving due to its transformation from a niche sector to an industry in about 6 years. The sector is now facing many challenges mostly stemming from its youth; plenty of basic research work has yet to be conducted. Islamic Banking is too often described as banking without the use of interest. Behind this over-simplification is a banking and financial system that aims to be consistent with Islamic law (Shari'ah) which prohibits usury, investing in activities contrary to ethical principles and outright speculation. Moreover, in Islam there is no separation between commercial life and religious life; religion applies to every facet of a Muslim's life. Islam requires Muslims to be ethical in their commercial and business transactions just as they would be in their family circles.

While Shari'ah has negative connotations in the popular mind, it actually advocates an entrepreneurial and trade-based ('real') sustainable economy with the aim of elimination of poverty. Islamic Banking institutions have so far been mostly spared from the financial turmoil as Shari'ah prohibits from dealing in CDOs. Thus, Islamic Banks did not accumulate toxic assets as compared to conventional banks because from the start they were forbidden, by the Koran, from actually dealing in instruments such as CDOs.

Despite its explicit religious roots and grounds, Islamic Banking is open to everyone regardless of faith and is proving increasingly popular amongst both Muslims and non-Muslims. There is no single predominant cause which makes Muslims worldwide very receptive to the idea of an alternative financial system, rather it is a combination of factors. These include the global political context, greater prosperity and increased religiosity. Given that Islamic Banking is derived from Koranic principles, this gives the sector great credibility amongst many Muslims. Additionally, numerous Muslims are satisfied to bear a faith discount: a willingness to accept a lower return on investment from the moment that return is *halal* i.e. religiously acceptable. It is common knowledge that many Muslims (in Western nations) simply waive the right to any interest on their conventional bank accounts to avoid the sin of *riba*.

Generally, non-Muslims are attracted to Islamic Banking because they consider it a moral alternative to conventional finance. The latter is increasingly assimilated to casino capitalism due to the excesses that lead to the present crisis. Islamic Banking with its insistence on avoidance of interest and limited leverage is considered far safer than conventional finance. This is further strengthened by the general belief (as conveyed by the media) that Islamic Banks are immune from the current financial crisis. Equally important, Islamic Banking addresses the *moral issue* of interest and usury. The rejection thereof is *not* limited to the Islamic faith; it is also present in Plato and Aristotle and in early Christianity.[1]

---

[1] Plato, Laws, Book V; Aristotle, Politics, I, 10; Luke 6:35.

Islamic Banking is also viewed *as a viable alternative* in a world dominated by a cynical global financial system. Within the Islamic Banking sector, there exist outstanding financial institutions providing excellent financial products that genuinely satisfy consumer needs. For instance, Chinese Malaysians buy Takaful (Islamic Mutual Insurance) from Etiqa[2] because the latter is a reliable insurance company with transparent financial products. Etiqa's products are not merely Shari'ah compliant, they are also fair and straight-forward. In effect, this approach is a welcome breath of fresh air for consumers growing confused and weary from conventional finance. When properly executed with the right mind-set, Islamic Banking can prove attractive to consumers regardless of faith.

In this chapter we consider to what extent Islamic Banking is ready for the growth we can expect based on the increased attention it receives in the aftermath of the crisis. Also, to what extent does Islamic Banking meet RI investor expectations with regard to both moral standards as well as transparency standards. The chapter is structured as follows. The next section sketches modern Islamic Banking. The third section deals with Shari'ah boards. These currently guarantee the quality of Shari'ah based finance but at the same time constitute its barrier to growth. Section four examines the potential of Shari'ah based investment becoming a subform of what is called SRI or RI. Finally, section five builds on the previous sections to draw some conclusions and recommendations for what might become Shari'ah based SRI.

Modern Islamic Banking

There was substantial trade, commerce and finance in the Islamic world for hundreds of years. Nonetheless, as Vogel and Hayes (1998: 4) put it:

> the centuries-old practice of finance in Islamic form was largely eclipsed during the period of the European colonial empires, when almost the entire Islamic world came under the rule of Western powers. Under European Influence, most countries adopted Western–inspired banking systems and business models and abandoned Islamic commercial practices. Thus the modern period of Islamic finance traces its beginnings to the independence of Muslim countries after World War II.

Islamic Banking is re-born, or rather modern Islamic Banking is born, in the early 1960s with the creation of MitGhamr Savings Bank (in Egypt) and the Tabung Haji (in Malaysia). These early experiences occurred for different reasons in countries with a Muslim majority but with different socio-politico-economic circumstances and also led to different outcomes. The Mit Ghamr was eventually taken over by the Nasser Government for political reasons whereas the Tabung Haji was the first step into making Malaysia the leading Islamic Finance jurisdiction (Tripp 2010: 136–137). While it could be assumed that the beating heart of Islamic Banking would be the Middle East, in fact the most advanced country is Malaysia that has produced such Islamic finance innovations as the Sukuk (Islamic bonds). Additionally, the most promising Islamic Banking market is not Middle Eastern

---

[2] http://www.etiqa.com.my

Table 9.1 Summary of key facts about Islamic Banking (source: Moody's)

Origin	Beginning of the 1960s in Egypt (MitGhamr Savings Bank) and in Malaysia (Tabung Haji)
First Islamic Commercial Bank	Dubai Islamic Bank, created in 1975 in Dubai
Market Size as at end of 2007	500 Billion USD in Islamic Banks and in Islamic Insurance Companies; 700 Billion USD, including off-balance sheet items and Shari'ah-compliant funds
Average annual growth rate for the last 10 years	Between 10 and 30%, depending on asset class
Geographical spread	60% in the Persian gulf region; 20% in South Asia; 20% in the rest of the world.
Size of the *sukuk* market as at 31st December 2007	97 Billion USD (+50% in 2007), two thirds of which from Malaysia alone
Eurosukuk quoted on world markets as at 31st December 2007	Around 35 Billion USD

but South East Asia's Indonesia; the country with the largest Muslim population in the world. Table 9.1 summarises some key facts.

Moreover, according to the CFA institute, it is estimated that there are over 300 Islamic financial institutions worldwide and over 325 Islamic mutual funds and Exchange-Traded Funds. These figures are constantly evolving. Many commentators are predicting spectacular growth in Islamic Finance in the coming decade reflecting previous growth levels. In 2000, the sector was estimated at 140 Billion USD and currently stands at around a trillion USD. The future looks very promising. Luxembourg Finance Minister Frieden estimated in May 2009 that Islamic Banking would reach four trillion USD within 5 years. (La Voix du Luxembourg 2009) Such growth rate and prospects have certainly caught the interest of banks and financial institutions especially given the global financial downturn.

There are 5 fundamental principles to Modern Islamic Finance. This consists of 3 interdictions and 2 positive obligations:

(a) No *riba* (interest, usury)[3]
(b) No *gharar* or *mayssir* (uncertainty and speculation)
(c) No *haram* (Sinful) sectors
(d) Sharing of profit and losses
(e) Asset-backed Financing

Typically, a Shari'ah board validates whether a financial product and/or transaction is *halal* or not. While Shari'ah boards might have provided adequate

---

[3]The subtilities involved in expanding upon different conceptions of interest (as a financial concept, i.e. a predetermined cash flow) and usury (as a despised or forbidden social practice of extracting money) according to different strands in religious and wordly ideologies, largely surpasses the scope of this contribution and even the book

supervision when Islamic finance was an unsophisticated niche sector, it is very unclear whether this supervision system is viable now that Islamic Banking is an industry. Shari'ah boards are coming under increasing criticism.

Islamic Banking is too often presented as *Shari'ah compliant finance*. In fact, Islamic Banking also includes *Shari'ah based finance*. The distinction is as follows: Shari'ah compliant finance consists in taking conventional financial products and tweaking them to avoid the presence of interest. This is criticised by some as window-dressing. An illustration is *murabaha*; a sale of goods with an agreed profit mark-up on the cost price. While extremely popular, murabaha has often been criticised as complying with the letter but *not* the spirit of the Koran. In contrast, Shari'ah based finance is about creating new financial products based on Koranic principles and the hadith.[4] A good example is Takaful (Islamic mutual insurance) which is used to alleviate pain and suffering.

In contrast to conventional finance, excessive leverage is banned in Islamic Banking. Leverage in Islamic Banking is measured by the debt-equity ratio and should not exceed a third. This specific ratio does not vary depending on the industry or the specificities of the companies involved; it was set by Shari'ah scholars via consensus. This ratio could be considered as completely artificial and detached from commercial realities. However, it is the ratio applied by Shari'ah scholars sitting on *Shari'ah Supervisory Boards*.

Shari'ah Supervisory Boards

A standard definition is: The Shari'ah Supervisory Board (SSB) is an independent body of specialized jurists in *fiqh al-mua'malat*, Islamic Commercial Law; it may include a non-jurist (who nonetheless needs to be an expert in Islamic Banking). It is the body entrusted with the duty of directing, reviewing and supervising the activities of the Islamic Financial Institution (IFI). Their *fatwas* or decrees and rulings on specific Shari'ah problems are binding for the IFI. Their appointment must be done at the Annual General Meeting by the shareholders with the recommendation from the Board of Directors who would also recommend the remuneration and the terms of engagement. The standard mentions that the SSB must consist of at least three members (Sultan 2007).

The Accounting and Auditing Organisation for Islamic Financial Institutions (AAOIFI) has issued the Governance Standard No. 1 on the 'Shari'ah Supervisory Board: appointment, composition and report'. According to this standard every IFI will have an SSB which (Nienhaus 2007):

(a) 'is an independent body of specialized jurists in fiqh almua'malat (Islamic commercial jurisprudence)',

(b) 'is entrusted with the duty of directing, reviewing and supervising the activities of the Islamic financial institution in order to ensure that they are in compliance with Islamic Shari'ah rules and principles',

---

[4] Reports of the sayings and activities of Muhammad and his companions.

(c) can issue fatwas and rulings which 'shall be binding on the Islamic financial institution',

(d) 'shall consist of at least three members' who are 'appointed by the shareholders ... upon the recommendation of the board of directors (not including 'directors or significant shareholders of the Islamic financial institution'),

(e) shall prepare a report on the compliance of all contracts, transactions and dealings with the shari'ah rules and principles,

(f) shall state that 'the allocation of profit and charging of losses related to investment accounts conform to the basis that has been approved' by the SSB; finally,

(g) 'shareholders may authorize the board of directors to fix the remuneration of the Shari'ah Supervisory Board.'

The management of an IFI is responsible for ensuring that the actual business complies with Shari'ah. Comparatively, the SSB's duty is 'to form an independent opinion' on Shari'ah compliance.

Unfortunately, AAOIFI standards say nothing about the appointment, reappointment, dismissal and duration of tenure of SSB members. There are currently no global specific criteria regarding the selection and appointment of SSB members. Such issues as their education (in Islamic law or any other subject), their necessary reputation as scholars, their goodwill amongst public, their Islamic school of thought, doctrinal strictness flexibility or inflexibility, compatibility with other professions and sources of income, SSB membership duration, reappointment and dismissal and crucially their remuneration terms and conditions are left completely on an ad-hoc basis. Moreover, this information is rarely if ever made available to the general public. There is a dearth of empirical research on SSB members' selection process and their professional paths prior, after and during SSB membership. Also, there is very limited data on the effects of multiple memberships of individual scholars in different SSBs. As per AAOIFI guidelines, the board of directors proposes candidates for the SSB and determines their remuneration. Nonetheless, board of directors may be influenced by the management. Thus, top management may exert an important say in the choice of their company's SSB and the conditions, monetary and non-monetary, of membership. Prima facie, it could be argued that there is a blatant conflict of interest in that SSB members are asked to review (for the benefit of the public) the actions of those who are remunerating them.

The main counter-argument is the fact that there is a dearth of scholars capable of serving on SSBs. Very few Islamic scholars combine expertise of *fiqh mua'malat* (Islamic Commercial law) with a good understanding of conventional finance making them apt to perform as SSB members. According to the Financial Times 'there are only about 60 Islamic scholars with expert knowledge of finance, while an even smaller group of around 12 are highly sought after by western institutions.' (FT 2008) Due to penury of qualified scholars, most respected SSB members sit on the boards of numerous IFIs at the same time. A recent survey (FAW 2008) revealed that the Top 20 scholars occupied amongst them 339 board positions, equal to an average of 17 SSB positions per scholar. None of them sat on less than 6 different SSBs. Moreover, the Top 10 scholars worldwide share 253 positions, leading to an average of 25.3 positions per scholar. None of the Top 10 scholars sits on less than 15 different SSBs. The members of this Shari'ah scholars' elite are extremely well paid; some earning up to fifty thousand USD per position, that is more than a million dollars annually. Following this reasoning one might argue that none of the established Shari'ah scholars would risk compromising their professional reputation (and recurrent income) simply to accommodate one client. This is unfortunately an argument *à la* Andersen/ENRON. Ultimately this reasoning is purely wishful-thinking rather than actually constituting reliable protection against abuses and fraud.

Beyond the financial aspect, what is more remarkable is the degree of influence exerted by the Top 20 scholars on the whole of the Islamic Banking industry. In the eyes of the general public, the prestige and standing of any IFI is proportional to the recognition and reputation of its SSB members. Thus, there is strong competition amongst IFIs to hire and retain the services of the most well-known Shari'ah scholars to act as their SSB members. This has an interlocking and compounding effect; the SSBs of major IFIs are consistently staffed with the same Shari'ah scholars. Moreover, the most well known Shari'ah scholars very often sit together on the same boards. For instance, Sheikh Nizam Yaquby (accurately described as a 'major financial powerbroker' in Reuters 2008) has 16 SSBs in common with Dr. Abu Ghuddah and 10 SSBs with M.Daud Bakar (Oummatv 2008: 79).

The Top 6 Shari'ah scholars worldwide are arguably: N. Yaquby, A.S. Abu Ghuddah, M.A. El Ghari, Y. DeLorenzo, M. Daud Bakar and M.T. Usmani. They are referred to as the 'Sheikhs of Wall Street' as they all sit on the SSB of the Dow Jones Islamic Index. Between them, they control the SSBs of more than 106 IFIs (Oummatv 2008: 80). By being able to rule on what IFIs transactions are *halal* and which ones are *haram*, such scholars are able to steer the overall direction of the Islamic Banking industry. They can make or break new financial instruments and concepts. An illustration is the global impact on the sukuk (Islamic Bonds) market of Usmani's comments from November 2007 regarding the unacceptable structure of certain sukuk. The power and influence of Top Shari'ah scholars cannot be understated; not only do they sit on major SSBs but they are also members of advisory boards and committees of regulatory authorities and standard-setting organisations (such as AAOIFI or IFSB). Nienhaus (2007: 140) suggests 'this raises several governance issues at the macro or policy level. For example, if prominent members of SSBs determine the Islamic framework of Islamic banks, set the tone of public opinion and give advice to regulatory agencies, how will the independence of regulators be assured?'

In order to solve this problem, countries such as Malaysia and Sudan have installed a National Shari'ah Board; in the case of Malaysia under the control of the Central Bank. The role of the National Shari'ah Board is to issue religious rulings which are then applied by the SSB of the IFI. Whether this will become a standard set-up is unclear. What is nonetheless certain is that in the short and medium term the existing elite of Shari'ah scholars will continue to wield great power and influence in the Islamic Banking industry. Given that the number of internationally accepted scholars is stagnant while the industry is steadily growing, there is lack of competent scholars. A pipeline of people have started training but it will be some time before they reach the market; it takes about 15 years to train in Islamic jurisprudence and become an expert in finance (FT 2008). Meanwhile as the industry expands, internationally recognised Shari'ah scholars will retain individual and unchecked power over a whole industry.

SRI and Islamic Banking

According to Eurosif, 'socially responsible investing' (SRI) 'a generic term covering ethical investments, responsible investments, sustainable investments, and any other investment process that combines investors' financial objectives with their concerns about environmental, social and governance (ESG) issues' (Eurosif 2008: 6). Hereafter, we shall be using the term SRI as defined by the Social Investment Forum.

In numerous recent articles, a number of authors have represented a whole range of views on a possible joint future of Islamic Banking and SRI. According to some, it is a no-brainer and there will be a de facto fusion between the 2 sectors (Barkatulla 2009). For others, there is strong conceptual fit between what Islam preaches and SRI (Novethic 2009). Moreover, while there is a religious duty for Muslims to act in a more socially responsible manner (including regarding the environment) not enough is actually being done (Brugnoni 2009). One even submits that 'SRI currently seems incompatible' with Islamic Asset Management and the 'continued growth of investors in its home markets, paired with dissimilarities in investment philosophies, makes widening the Islamic prospective investor base into SRI appear both unnecessary and inappropriate' (Stanley and Jaffery 2009: 257). Another set of authors describes Islamic Finance as one 'extremely popular' from of SRI (Zahari and Shanmugam 2009: 244). Hence, a gamut of opinions exists regarding compatibility of Islamic Banking and SRI.

If we consider the relevant Koranic verses, we find that Islam preaches ecology, kindness, labour rights, social justice and sustainability.[5] Thus, there is a significant

---

[5] English translation from Haleem 2004. '**It was He who created all that is on the earth for you,** then turned to the sky and made the seven heavens; it is He who has knowledge of all things.' [2:29]

[Prophet], when your Lord told the angels, '**I am putting a *khalifa* on earth,**' they said, 'How can you put someone there who will cause damage and bloodshed, when we celebrate Your praise and proclaim Your Holiness?' but He said , 'I know things you do not.' [2:30]

The concept of ***Khalifa*** defines our position in the cosmos as 'trustees' of God. As trustees, we have the responsibility to safeguard nature and resources of the planet, and will be accountable for their abuse both in this world and the Hereafter. The Islamic principle of ***Akharah*** ('the Hereafter') is the concept that we are all accountable for our actions in the Hereafter where depending on our actions we shall be rewarded or punished. The central concept of Islam is ***Tawheed***, it literally means 'unity of God' but also implies the *unity and equality of all humanity* in the eyes of God.

Islam also imposes on the Muslims the concept of ***Adl,*** or to do justice but in the most wide-ranging sense of the word. This means that to justice in every aspect of individual and social life is a primary obligation for all Muslims. Very close to the concept of Adl is ***Istislah,*** or public interest which a fundamental source of Islamic law. This Islamic principle makes it a responsibility of individuals, communities and the state to consider the common good and welfare of the society and the planet as a whole. Istislah is a far more extensive concept as compared to SRI. All these

overlap between original Islamic principles and SRI aims. Arguably, 'traditionalists' might claim that using SRI's sophisticated screening methods is incompatible with the spirit of Islam. Nonetheless, that would be negating the Islamic Principle of *Ilm* (meaning knowledge) which makes the pursuit of knowledge a duty for all Muslims, male and female, and the following authentic hadith: *The search for knowledge is a sacred duty imposed upon every Muslim.*

Research was conducted as to whether the tenets of Islam are consistent with the 'Ten Principles' of responsible business outlined in the UN Global Compact (OWW 2006, Williams and Zinkin 2010). It argues that there is no fundamental divergence between the tenets of Islam and the principles of the UN Global Compact. While Islam's focus on personal responsibility and the non-recognition of the corporation as a legal person could undermine the concept of corporate responsibility, Islam often goes beyond what the Global Compact asks for and has the advantage of a clearer codification of ethical standards as well as a set of explicit enforcement mechanisms. A further elaboration of Islamic teaching in today's business that focuses on this convergence of values could be lead to the development of a new understanding of CSR in a global context and help avert the threatened 'clash of civilizations'.

Islamic Banking (as opposed to Islam and Muslims) has goodwill as IFIs did not invest in CDOs. The sector thus acquired overnight an aura of respectability as it was viewed as safe finance compared to the excesses of casino capitalism. This could not last. IFIs have historically over-invested in real property and there will be vast losses as real estate values collapse (Synovitz 2009). It is unclear what will be the reaction of Islamic Banks depositors when they start facing the liability for losses; accounts in Islamic Banks are technically profit-and-loss sharing accounts. Additionally, even the fabled *sukuk* (Islamic Bonds) are under pressure. In May 2009, Investment Dar Co., the owner of half of Aston Martin Lagonda Ltd., missed a payment on $100 million of debt, becoming the first Persian Gulf company to default on Islamic bonds. Ironically, in 2007 Investment Dar had won

---

are fundamental Islamic Principles.

Let me refer to the following hadith:

- *The world is green and beautiful and God has appointed you his trustee over it.* Clearly, this is undeniably a command to act in an ecological and environmentally-friendly manner.
- *God is gentle and loves gentleness in all things.* This is in sharp contrast with the calls for blind violence advocated by some self-proclaimed clerics.
- *Pay the worker before his sweat dries.* From this hadith, we can certainly deduce a recommendation for labour rights. Most unfortunately, this recommendation is often ignored; for instance, the appalling treatment of migrant workers in the UAE is well documented.
- *He is not a believer who eats his fill while his neighbour remains hungry by his side.* A command to fight famine or malnutrition whether amongst Muslims or non-Muslims. More generally, a call to promote social justice.
- *Little but sufficient is better than the abundant and the alluring.* This need for sustainability.
- *The special character of Islam is modesty.* Clearly a recommendation against living materialistic lives.

the award for 'most innovative financing transaction' for its acquisition of the Aston Martin Car Company at the inaugural Islamic Finance Awards. However, these defaults were nothing compared to the 'Dubai Debacle'. The latter is a complex case which revealed many fault lines in Islamic Finance. While we do not have enough space to explain the case fully, suffice to say that Islam bans *riba* as well as *gharar* and *maisir*. This raises the question as to how certain financial instruments that were highly speculative in nature could have been declared Shari'ah compliant.

The real threat is that Islamic Banking gets dismissed as a gimmick once the novelty of Shari'ah-compliant instruments has worn off by neither achieving what Islam recommends nor by offering adequate returns to its users. Jaded users would then revert to conventional finance, compromising the future of Islamic Banking. This threat is immediate, bearing in mind the lack of adequate supervision in many jurisdictions and the forthcoming problems caused by snake oil salesmen. As recently pointed out by Prof. Mahmoud El-Gamal of Rice University in a blog insightfully titled 'Crooks in the name of Islam' (El-Gamal 2009), all kinds of dubious investment schemes are being marketed by some very unscrupulous promoters under the banner of Islamic Banking. Thus, a unique window of opportunity (i.e. Islamic Banking becoming an attractive alternative to conventional finance) risks being lost forever especially with the forthcoming squander of its current halo of sanctity.

Can there be Shari'ah Based SRI?

For Islamic Banking to survive this forthcoming crisis of confidence and ultimately fulfil its full potential, it needs to be superior to conventional finance, not merely equal to. In effect on Islamic Finance instruments must follow the true spirit of the Koran and the Sunna while also providing financial returns comparable to conventional financial instruments. To become perennial, Islamic Finance needs to be optimised; however, the challenge is ensuring *both* financial returns and ethical quality. Therefore, Islamic Banking must upgrade from mere Shari'ah-compliance to becoming Shari'ah-based SRI; thus empowering itself to become epoch changing. Similarly in the 1980s, SRI moved from mere political-correctness (e.g. Avoiding investments in Apartheid South Africa) to positively changing the life of its users. As Zahari and Shanmugam (2009: 244) put it:

> As mentioned by Good Money, Inc., a social investing firm that conducts and advocates for socially responsible investing: 'Until the mid 1980s, SRI was considered to be nothing more than what Fortune magazine sarcastically called 'feel-good investing' or what would be labelled today as 'politically correct' behaviour. The movement needed to get over two credibility hurdles – one social/political and the other economic. In addition, years of accumulating research began to demonstrate that corporations with good social records on the whole outperformed corporations with bad social records. In turn, socially screened portfolios, no matter what the social issue, rewarded investors better than unscreened portfolios. As a result, SRI took off in the U.S. in the 1980s.

The application of SRI principles in Islamic Banking would *not* be a wasted effort; there would be value-added as companies satisfying SRI principles produce (on average) better long-term returns as compared to their counter-parts. Incorporating SRI principles in Islamic Banking Instruments would help ensure better financial returns making the sector more sustainable. Nonetheless, the *main challenge* would be ensuring *not only* the financial returns but *also* the ethical quality of financial products supplied to the public under a Shari'ah-based SRI label. Therefore, incorporation of SRI screening methods in the Shari'ah audit process is a *Sine Qua Non*. The caveat is that transparency is a non-negotiable in SRI. This transparency contrasts with the usual workings of Shari'ah Boards; their structures, functions and decisions are far too often opaque.

In the event that Shari'ah Based/Compliant SRI financial instruments would be offered to the public, vetting such financial instruments would certainly demand a different audit process than the one currently used in the Islamic Banking industry. Shari'ah SRI audits would have to be transparent and made available, especially to the end consumer. Such audits would have to explain in detail why a financial product satisfies the requirements of SRI and Shari'ah. Disclosure of these audits could ideally lead to creation of a 'case law' databank which might be used for audits of such financial instruments. Through the sharing of insights and experience, Shari'ah boards would not have to 're-invent the wheel' every time they come across a situation which has already been documented. This will also greatly help in the necessary standardisation of Islamic Finance products.

Islamic Banking would certainly greatly benefit as an industry if it were to shift to Shari'ah-based SRI; it would become a value-added finance that could genuinely appeal to the mainstream consumer. The industry would not need to be only reliant on Muslims willing to pay a premium to avoid *riba*. While the industry would gain, the power of Shari'ah scholars might be eroded as the greater transparency (brought by SRI) would lead to increased standardisation of financial instruments. This standardisation would enable Islamic Banking to become truly global in nature rather than purely regional and subject to the susceptibilities of SSBs. It would also enable the successful creation and distribution of more specialized financial instruments worldwide. Shari'ah scholars would no longer be needed for run-of-the-mill questions but only for genuinely complicated issues.

Shari'ah aims for social justice just like SRI. However, prima facie, Islamic Banking is obsessed with the idea of *riba* and (conveniently?) ignores the social objectives of Shari'ah. Bizarrely, Shari'ah scholars have not opted to be more vocal of the social justice endeavours of Islamic law. So far, they have certainly benefitted financially from the *status quo*. The question is whether as a group they will amend their stance considering that the sector might be endangered if they do not. The dilemma is whether Shari'ah scholars will foresake their own position in order to benefit the industry as a whole; will they prefer to be the gate-keepers of a threatened financial sector or the spearhead of a sustainable industry?

However, the current hype about Islamic Finance should not obscure the fact that Islamic Banking is still very much in its infancy and there are numerous fundamental issues that still need to be settled. For SRI principles to be successfully implanted into Islamic Banking, fundamental research on the synergies between Islamic Banking and Ethical/SRI must be conducted. To enable the reaping of such synergies we must start by the creation of a research framework. Moreover, the research must be conducted by neutral organisation(s) and *not* by any entity subject to a conflict of interest. In effect, fusion between Islamic Banking and SRI without serious groundwork is wishful thinking. However, pragmatically, in the short and medium term there are definite synergies that can be achieved but crucial research work needs to be performed before this can be envisaged.

In the very insightful words of Willem Buiter in the FT:

> What we need is the application of Islamic finance principles, in particular a strong preference for profit-, loss-and risk-sharing arrangements and a rejection of 'riba' or interest-bearing debt instruments. I am not talking here about the sham Shari'ah-compliant instruments that flooded the market in the decade before the crisis; these were window-dressing pseudo-Islamic financial instruments that were mathematically equivalent to conventional debt and mortgage contracts, but met the letter if not the spirit of Shari'ah law, in the view of some tame, pliable and quite possibly corrupt Shari'ah scholar. I am talking about financial innovations that replace debt-type instruments with true profit-, loss-and risk-sharing arrangements. (Buiter 2009)

References

Barkatulla, M. 2009. Ethical fusion. Islamic Banking and Finance 7: 23.

Bloomberg. 2009. Vatican Says Islamic Finance May Help Western Banks In Crisis. Bloomberg News Service 4th March 2009, http://www.bloomberg.com/apps/news?pid=20601092%26sid=aOsOLE8uiNOg%26refer=italy Accessed April 2010.

Brown, Gordon. 2006. UK's Brown backs Islamic Finance. BBC News, 13th June 2006. http://news.bbc.co.uk/2/hi/business/5074068.stm Accessed April 2010.

Brugnoni, Alberto. 2009. Smoke signals. Islamic Banking and Finance 14: 22.

Buiter 2009. Maverecon: Willem Buiter. Islamic finance principles to restore policy effectiveness. Financial Times, 22 July 2009.

El-Gamal, Mahmoud. 2009. Crooks in the name of Islam. Available at http://elgamal.blogspot.com/search?q=snake+oil Accessed May 2010.

Eurosif. 2008. European SRI Study. Paris: Eurosif.

FAW 2008. Shariah Scholars in the GCC. 2008. A Network Analytic Perspective. Funds at work. Available at http://www.funds-at-work.com. Accessed May 2010.

FT 2008. Scholars and harmony in short supply. Financial Times, 19 June 2008.

Haleem, Muhammed A. S. A. 2004. The Qur'an: A New Translation. Oxford: Oxford University Press.

La Voix du Luxembourg. 2009 Une attirance réciproque. La Voix du Luxembourg, 6 May 2009.

Le Parisien. 2008. Les Banques Islamiques arrivent en France, Le Parisien, 27 November 2008.

Nienhaus, Volker. 2007. Governance of islamic banks. In Handbook of Islamic Banking, eds. M. Kabir Hassan, and Mervyn K. Lewis. Cheltenham: Edward Elgar Publishing. Available at http://www.google.com/books?hl=en%lr=%id=jvTtDzD5uFQC%oi=fnd%pg=PA128%dq=nienhaus+2007+%E2%80%98is+an+independent+body+of+specialized+jurists+in+fiqh+almua%E2%80%99malat+(Islamic+commercial+jurisprudence)%E2%80%99,%ots=72kNbiTZpy%sig=98bW6hRvPf7OwBgcB3d9MmCE0AM#v=onepage%q%f=false Accessed 25 May 2010.

Novethic. 2009. Finance Islamique et ISR. 2009. Convergence Possible. Novethic working paper. Available at http://ribh.files.wordpress.com/2009/06/novethic-finance-islamique-et-isr.pdf Accessed May 2010.

Oummatv. 2008. La finance islamique à la française: un moteur pour l'économie, une alternative éthique SECURE Finance. http://oummatv.tv/La-finance-islamique-un-moteur Accessed April 2010.

OWW. 2006. Islam and CSR: The compatibility between the tenets of Islam and the UN Global Compact, Research Report December 2006, OWW Consulting. Available at http://www.oww-consulting.com/downloads/research/islam-and-csr/download.html Accessed May 2010.

Reuters. 2008. Holy man joins jet set as Islamic finance booms. 5 February 2008. Available at   http://www.reuters.com/article/IslamicBankingandFinance08/idUSL059423620080205 Accessed April 2010.

Stanley, Mark and Salmaan Jaffery. 2009. Can Islamic asset management aim a little higher? Achieving maturity and the impact of socially responsible investment. In Islamic Wealth Management: A Catalyst for Global Change and Innovation, London: Euromoney Books, ed. Jaffer, S., 247–260.

Sultan, S A M. 2007. Sharia'ah Audit for Islamic Financial Institutions   A Primer. Kuala Lumpur: CERT publications.

Synovitz, Ron. 2009. Islamic Banks Unhurt By Toxic Assets, But Could Suffer As Crisis Evolves, Radio Free Europe, 3 March 2009. Available at http://www.rferl.org/content/Islamic_Banks_Unhurt_By_Toxic_Assets_But_Could_Suffer_As_Crisis_Evolves/1503409.html   Accessed May 2010

Tripp, Charles. 2010. Islam and the Moral Economy. Cambridge: Cambridge University Press.

Vogel, Frank E., and S.L. Hayes III. 1998. Islamic Law and Finance: Religion, Risk and Return. Boston, MA: Kluwer Law International.

Williams, Geoffrey and John Zinkin. 2010. Islam and CSR: A Study of the compatibility between the tenets of Islam and the UN Global Compact. Journal of Business Ethics 91(4): 519–533.

Zahari, Zaha Rina and Bala Shanmugam. 2009. Socially responsible investing. In Islamic Wealth Management: A Catalyst for Global Change and Innovation, ed. Sohail Jaffer. Euromoney Books, 234–246.

Chapter 10
What are Your Investments Doing Right Now?

Joakim Sandberg

Introduction

In the present times of financial crisis and economic turmoil, many people are worried about their investments. A rather straightforward and understandable worry concerns what will happen to the particular investments one currently holds, or those held before the onset of the turmoil, and whether there will be anything left of these once the crisis is over. A more strategic worry, however, is how to invest so to avoid the kind of ethical problems in the future (e.g., the taking of unreasonable financial risks) which generally are thought to, at least partly, have given rise to the crisis. One possibility some investors may be looking at here is the kind of investing which is the topic of this book – so-called 'ethical', 'responsible' or 'socially responsible' investment (SRI). Over the last decade or so, an increasing number of banks and fund companies have launched investment vehicles with an explicit 'ethical', 'social' or 'environmental' profile and these vehicles have indeed attracted a vast amount of investment capital. According to some recent (although probably exaggerated) estimates, the total amount of assets under management with this kind of profile was as much as \$2.29 trillion in the US (Social Investment Forum 2006) and €1.03 trillion in Europe (Eurosif 2006) at the end of 2005.

But is this a good idea? Does so-called ethical investing really constitute a more ethical way of investing? One would think that this interest in a kind of investing which explicitly incorporates ethical or social considerations should have triggered an intense debate about ethics and social responsibility in the investment sector. That is, a debate about what really characterises a (genuinely) ethical fund. Unfortunately, while the SRI movement has received quite a lot of attention from both academics and journalists, the aims of these authors have most often been to simply describe it, explain it or compare it to mainstream investments. Financial comparisons between

J. Sandberg (✉)
University of Gothenburg, Gothenburg, Sweden
e-mail: joakim.sandberg@filosofi.gu.se

W. Vandekerckhove et al. (eds.), *Responsible Investment in Times of Turmoil*,
Issues in Business Ethics 31, DOI 10.1007/978-90-481-9319-6_10,
© Springer Science+Business Media B.V. 2011

'socially responsible' and conventional portfolios, it may be noted, is the topic of an overwhelming part of this literature.[1]

This article tries to fill this gap by critically engaging with a very popular idea about what makes ethical investing ethical, or what makes socially responsible investing socially responsible. In a series of adverts from the Swedish fund company KPA Pension, the Swedish public has been shown pictures of, e.g., environmental pollution, dirty missiles, and children working in factories, together with the question 'What are your investments doing right now?' (or perhaps more adequately 'What is your pension money doing right now?'). The idea behind these ads seems to be that many investors unknowingly support companies with morally questionable business activities – e.g., armament production or child labour – and that this is morally problematic in some way. By redirecting one's investments to ethical funds and thereby avoiding investments in this kind of companies, it is implicitly suggested investors can stay clear of this kind of moral controversy. What makes an ethical fund ethical in this view then, is that it does not support companies with morally questionable business activities (or of morally questionable character) – and to this list of questionable business activities may then be added the taking of unreasonable financial risks.

But is this view philosophically sound? I will here focus on the more general idea that it is wrong to support companies with morally questionable business activities and, while this idea probably can be understood in many ways, I will concentrate on a *causal*, or *factual*, understanding of its appeal to support.[2] Thus, I suggest that a central question when evaluating the idea above is: Can individual investors really 'make a difference' – can they influence the companies they find morally disagreeable to any extent – by simply refraining from investing in certain companies on the stock market? I will present a number of moral principles that proponents of the SRI movement could appeal to (and have appealed to) in order to try to justify the investment strategy of the ethical funds, and discuss which is the most plausible one in the present context. My conclusion, however, is that none of the suggested principles can lend satisfactory support to this kind of 'ethical' investment strategy. Individual investors simply cannot make much of a difference, at least not by simply refraining from investing in 'disagreeable' companies on the stock market.

While my main conclusion is negative in one sense, it may be noted that it leaves a certain opening for investors genuinely interested in ethics. Perhaps there is something to the idea that genuinely ethical investing is the kind that makes the world a better place. My point is simply that this idea, when taken seriously, demands a lot more of the ethical investor than what today's so-called ethical funds can offer.

---

[1] For an overview of some of these studies, see UNEP FI and Mercer 2007.

[2] For a critical discussion of other possible interpretations of this idea, see Sandberg 2008.

The No-Harm Principle

Let us start with a fairly straightforward understanding of the idea that it is morally problematic, or wrong, to support certain kinds of (morally problematic) companies. The slogan that KPA Pension has chosen to use seems to suggest, if read literally, that there is a very direct and tangible relation between an investment decision and its consequences – either your money 'does' something good, or it 'does' something evil. A similar relation seems implicit in certain academic accounts of the basic principles of the socially responsible investment (SRI) movement. According to Miller (1991), for instance, the principle that rationalises the strategy of ethical funds to refrain from investing in certain companies is 'First, Do No Harm'. While it may be possible to understand this principle in other ways, I take it as saying that the most basic responsibility of investors is to refrain from directly harming others.[3] We may call this *the no-harm principle* in what follows.

The no-harm principle is often regarded as a central part of 'common sense morality', and it has been suggested as one of the basic principles of, e.g., biomedical ethics (Beauchamp and Childress 2001). Perhaps, then, it can also be seen as one of the basic principles of the ethics of investing. In an article on SRI in the *Encyclopedia of Applied Ethics*, Christopher Cowton appeals exactly to the intuitive nature, or public acceptance, of the no-harm principle when he suggests that this principle can explain why ethical investors ought to avoid investing in certain kinds of companies:

> If a duty not to impose damage or harm on other people is regarded as a minimum responsibility which runs through all morality, then it might be concluded that the avoidance of certain investments is appropriate, as under [the standard account of socially responsible investment]. (Cowton 1998: 188)

We need perhaps not devote too much time to the no-harm principle in this context. The fundamental issue here, I believe, is whether an appeal to the no-harm principle is enough to justify the strategy of avoiding investments in morally problematic companies, or if some more general consequentialist principle is needed. What speaks in favour of the no-harm principle in the present context is that it seems to capture very straightforwardly the idea that it is wrong to support certain companies' activities through investing in them. If you invest in companies that engage in harmful activities or sell harmful products, it seems possible to say that you in some sense harm people. But is this really plausible?[4]

A number of things could be taken to distinguish the no-harm principle from a more general consequentialist ethics like, e.g., utilitarianism. Most obviously, the

---

[3] For a discussion of other possible interpretations of this idea, see Sandberg 2008.

[4] I will in this context not address the issue of whether the kinds of companies that ethical funds normally refrain from investing in (e.g., weapon and tobacco companies) really are harmful in (any of) the sense(s) outlined above. All of the principles discussed here are intentionally a bit vague on the issue of exactly what companies they recommend that investors should refrain from investing in. An in-depth discussion of this issue would simply take us too far from the main subject, which is the plausibility of the principles and the avoidance strategy as such.

no-harm principle focuses only on avoiding harm, or not causing pain and suffering (negative utility), and gives no moral weight to how happy or content people are made (positive utility). Furthermore, the no-harm principle is often underpinned by the view that the distinction between *action* and *inaction* is morally important – that is, while it may be morally wrong to harm others *yourself*, it is not necessarily wrong to *allow others* to harm someone (or *not* to help someone *escape* harm) (Simon et al. 1972). But what is really the difference between harming someone *yourself* and allowing *others* to harm someone? Well, connected to this is often the idea that the *directness* of the causal relation between action and effect has moral significance. While it is wrong to harm others *directly*, then, it is not necessarily wrong to give *indirect* support to the harmful activities of others (Mackenzie 1997).

It seems obvious to me that the no-harm principle, at least if it is understood along the lines above, is less applicable in the investment context than in the biomedical context. Surely, investors never harm anyone – at least not in their role as investors – *as directly as doctors may harm their patients* and, therefore, as directly as the no-harm principle forbids? In the investment context, it should be noted, it is the activities or products of the relevant *companies* that may harm people directly, not the investment decisions of some remote investors. Of course, individual investors may *invest resources* in companies that have harmed or will harm people, but this hardly constitutes investors *themselves* harming people. How should we understand Miller's and Cowton's ideas here? Well, perhaps we may allow at least *some* involvement of other agents and say that as long as companies use money they have gotten *directly from investors* to harm people, investors harm people themselves at least *fairly* directly.

The problem is however, that the relation between investment decisions and their possible consequences most often is even more indirect. Most investments take place on the stock market, where investors buy and sell shares from and to each other. When I buy, say, five hundred shares of Microsoft on the stock market, the money I pay does not go to the Microsoft corporation but to the seller on the stock market, i.e. to another individual investor (Irvin 1987, Mackenzie 1997). Only when Microsoft itself *issues* shares, either during a new share issue or a bonus issue, Microsoft actually sells the shares and gets the money. But even during such issues some large bank or financial intermediary normally acts as an *underwriter* of the share issue. What this means is that the bank 'guarantees' the sale and basically buys the shares from the company and sells them further to individual investors (Irvin 1987). Thus, not even in this case do individual investors really give money directly to the underlying companies.

One could of course argue at this stage that individual investors, even though they seldom finance companies *directly*, still play an important part in the overall financial scheme. If no individual investors were interested in buying a certain company's shares, for instance, it is rather unlikely that a big bank or financial intermediary would be prepared to act as an underwriter of the company's new share issue (Irvin 1987). It should be noted, however, that we now are moving beyond the scope of the no-harm principle outlined above. To say that investors have moral reasons to act so that certain types of companies are not financed by *others*, some more general principle is needed – it is not enough to say that it is wrong of investors to harm others *directly themselves*. The causal role that investors play in the financial scheme is simply too far removed from the actual harming, or, which amounts to the same, the causal chain from investor to harm passes too many other agents on the way.

The Appeal to Consequences

Perhaps the no-harm principle is not the best interpretation of the general idea of many SRI proponents outlined at the outset. A formulation which suggests a more general consequentialist interpretation of this idea, and which is very common among proponents of the SRI movement, is that of investors being able to 'make a difference' by investing in ethical funds. According to Pietra Rivoli, this formulation is very common in marketing campaigns for SRI in the US, and it could be seen as an idea central to the very notion of socially responsible investment:

> Perhaps the most striking claim of the SRI [socially responsible investment] industry – and certainly the most appealing to many socially conscious investors and perhaps the most dubious to critics – is the claim that SRI 'makes a difference' to society. Advertisements for Domini Social Investments state that 'social investors are shaping tomorrow's world by investing responsibly.' Material from the Friends Ivory Funds tells prospective investors that 'you could help create a better world.' A recent conference for the SRI industry was titled 'Making a Profit while Making a Difference. (Rivoli 2003: 273)

As always, it may not be obvious how the claims or formulations above should be understood more exactly – that is, how to go from marketing formulations to moral principles. Interesting questions here are: Just how much of a difference are investors morally required to make – should I go on caring for 'tomorrow's world' to the point of exhaustion, or have I done enough as long as I make *some* or *a* difference? Exactly what kind of difference should I make – is reducing harm or alleviating suffering (negative utility) still more important or should I also strive to make people happy? We can disregard these complications in what follows, and speak of *the appeal to consequences* as the simple idea that investors have moral reasons to invest in a certain manner to the extent that doing so at least to *some* degree and in *some* sense makes the world a better place.[5]

Does the appeal to consequences imply that investors have moral reasons to refrain from investing in certain kinds of companies? I mentioned above that individual investors seem to play a central role in the overall financial scheme – even though they do not finance companies *directly* themselves, they may be able to influence the willingness of banks and other actors to finance companies and, thus, they

---

[5] Fortunately, little in my arguments below depends on whether negative utility is given extra weight or not. I will in what follows discuss the appeal to consequences without a specific axiological theory (theory about value) in mind – the reader may fill in the one he or she finds most attractive.

may be able to influence these companies *indirectly*. It seems likely that the demand for a certain companies' shares at least would influence the ability of the company to raise money through new share issues. I will elaborate on this kind of reasoning below. Unfortunately, I think the chances of investors influencing companies, even in this very indirect manner, are very slim – at least with regards to individual investors.

According to standard financial theory, the relevant factor when banks assess the creditworthiness of a certain company is primarily the general valuation of the company on the market, i.e. the value of the company's stock (Mackenzie 1997). The value of the company's stock obviously depends on the price of its shares on the stock market and this, in turn, is decided by the balance of buyers and sellers on the stock market. If many investors, say, want to sell Microsoft's shares, but only a few want to buy them, this will create a downward pressure on the price of Microsoft's shares – since sellers will have to lower their compensation demands to attract enough buyers. Now, a similar scenario is probably what ethical investors will have to hope for if the idea is that an avoidance of a certain company's shares could influence its ability to raise money through the market – if they can control the demand for the company's shares they control the share price.

I see two major problems with this line of reasoning though. First of all, the liquidity in the market for most quoted companies' shares is very high, i.e. the amount of investors buying and selling these companies' shares on the stock market every day is gigantic (Mackenzie 1997). This means that ethical investors will have a hard time trying to influence the price of a given company's shares – for (almost) each seller and price there will be a lot of buyers interested in buying the shares at that price. Perhaps it could be possible to influence the price of certain shares for which the market is less liquid – given a high number of ethical investors who controlled sufficiently much capital on the market. The thing is, however, that most individual investors obviously have very limited resources and so control a very limited part of the stock market. The difference in demand for a certain company's shares that a single individual investor can make is very small and, therefore, so are the chances of a single individual investor influencing the price of a certain company's shares (Irvine 1987, Simon et al. 1972).

As if this was not enough, it seems likely that the motivational structure of non-ethical investors actually will counterbalance any attempts of ethical investors to influence the price of a certain company's shares. According to fairly standard financial theory the so-called equilibrium price of a certain company's shares, i.e. the price a certain share will tend towards at a given time, depends mainly on the 'fundamentals' of the company, i.e. factors relevant for the economic situation of the firm – for instance, demand for the firm's products, the effectiveness of managers and the general economic climate (Haigh and Hazelton 2004, Mackenzie 1997). These fundamentals are not likely to change just because some ethical investors decide to boycott the firm's shares. If the ethical investors then, against all odds manage to create a downward pressure on the company's shares, the company will (in theory) be underpriced and its shares available at a discount. This means that other, non-ethical investors will be motivated to buy more of the company's shares until the price returns to equilibrium. The slight dent that the ethical investors had done to the share price will only be temporary (Haigh and Hazelton 2004, Miller 1991).

All in all it seems very hard for individual investors to influence a given company's ability to raise capital and, thus, very hard to actually 'make a difference' – at least in economic terms – by simply refraining from investing in a certain company. Perhaps other kinds of consequences are relevant here – perhaps a boycott of certain companies can influence these companies or society in other ways? I will return to this issue below. First however, we may ponder whether I have been asking the wrong kind of questions above. I just said that it could be possible to influence the price of certain shares for which the market is less liquid, given a high number of ethical investors who controlled sufficiently much capital on the market. Perhaps what is most important is not the consequences of a *single* investor's choice of investing in this or that way but what would happen if *many* or *all* investors acted similarly?

The Generalisation Principle

In her book on 'making a difference' as an investor (*Socially Responsible Investing – Making a Difference and Making Money*), Amy Domini, CEO of one of the largest ethical fund companies in the US, does not seem to require that she *herself* makes any significant difference. The important point is that many investors, *taken together*, can make a difference and – of course – that she is a part of this. Don't we all want to be a part of something greater than ourselves?

> Most people care and want to do what they can. Most of us are grateful for a chance to have so much impact for so little effort. We can invest and achieve results as good as those achieved by ordinary investors, yet we can be a part of something greater than we could give ourselves. We can be a part of shaping a world of justice and of environmental sustainability and one in which simple pleasures can be enjoyed by all. (Domini 2001: 17)

This certainly sounds inviting. Perhaps I was mistaken when I understood the references to 'making a difference' along the lines of the appeal to consequences above. Well, so says philosopher William Irvine at least. He admits that the fact that each individual investor him/herself controls such a little part of the investment universe can be seen as problematic in this context. But from a moral point of view, he thinks that we should not give too much weight to such considerations:

> I agree that small purchases of stock do not, in and of themselves, affect the ability of a company to do its business; nevertheless, I don't think this gets the average investor off the hook, morally speaking. The real question, from a moral point of view, is not whether his one purchase affects the ability of the company to conduct its business, but rather whether his purchase, if imitated by many other investors, would affect the ability of the company to conduct its business. (Irvine 1987: 239)

In what follows we may refer to Irvine's suggestion as *the generalisation*. According to the generalisation principle then, the exact consequences of *my* investing in this and that way are not so important – what is important is what the consequences would be if *everyone*, or at least *many others*, acted in a similar way.[6] Irvine supports his principle with a familiar kind of philosophical example. Even if one person's walking across newly-seeded grass does not actually harm the grass, we are still inclined to say that it is wrong to do so. This is, he suggests, because we care about what would happen if others did the same – if everyone walked across the newly-seeded grass it would obviously be destroyed (Irvine 1987). In conclusion then, the consequences of a certain *collective* action is what is morally important, not the consequences of just this individual act.

I do not wish to deny that the generalisation principle has interesting results in the present context and that it could be used to rationalise an investment strategy similar to the one employed by today's ethical funds. According to the line of reasoning introduced in the previous section, the market price would certainly plummet swiftly if a certain company's shares were shunned like the plague. In such a scenario, it would be impossible for the company to raise capital for new ventures and it would probably stagnate or go bankrupt. Perhaps this could be a desirable scenario with regards to certain (already *morally* bankrupt) enterprises. However, what should we say about the generalisation principle as such?

First of all, it seems less plausible to say that the important question is 'What would happen if everyone did X?' when in fact only very few are doing X. Say for example, that I would refrain from investing in weapon companies but that no one else or only very few others would do so. What is really the point of saying that I 'could be part of something greater', or that 'we together' can change the way in which weapon companies do their business, if nobody else is doing their part in this? According to the Mackenzie (1997) today's ethical investors are actually in a situation quite similar to this. In order to have any non-negligible influence on quoted companies, he estimates that the SRI movement would need to control at least 5% of the total stock market value. However, the total capital invested according to ethical or social criteria is considerably lower than this, and it does not seem reasonable to assume that it will reach 5% any time in the foreseeable future. It should be noted on top of this, that the SRI movement is extremely heterogeneous when it comes to concrete exclusion criteria – whereas some only exclude e.g. weapons and pornography, others only exclude companies that pollute the environment or something else. After having seen Mackenzie's figures – a stark contrast to the high estimates referred to at the outset of this article – Domini's invitation may feel a bit less inviting and a bit more fantastic.

---

[6] It may be noted that Irvine never gives the generalisation principle any more detailed formulation. As it stands, it seems possible to understand it in many, rather different, ways. One possibility, for example, would be to understand it along the lines of rule consequentialism, i.e. the idea that one ought to follow the rules which, if everyone followed similar rules, would yield the best consequences. Another possibility would be to understand it along the lines of Kant's categorical imperative. For my present purposes however, I believe no more detailed understanding of the generalisation principle is needed.

A second comment is that arguably, what the alternatives are must be relevant here, i.e. what investors could do instead of a boycott or, more specifically what they could bring about by actually investing in certain types of harmful or morally problematic business activities. It may seem plausible to say that it is wrong to walk across newly-seeded grass as long as the only relevant consequence is what happens to the grass. It does not seem plausible however, to say that it is wrong to walk across newly-seeded grass if this is the only way in which one could, say, save a child in need. Now I actually think there are great opportunities for the less scrupled ethical investor to really do some good here. One suggestion is that one actually should invest in weapons companies when their shares are on the rise and then use the profits to help people in need – one could donate the money to charitable organisations that help poor people in the third world or, why not, the victims of war (Zweig 1996). If what I said in the previous section is true, i.e. that what an individual investor does on the market is unlikely to affect the underlying companies, it seems rather probable that what a single investor *can* influence is only what profit he or she makes for him/herself. Accordingly, the best thing an individual investor could do might just as well be to invest for maximum profit and then donate the proceeds to some socially worthwhile cause.[7]

I will return to this suggestion below. All in all, the considerations above seem to speak against the moral plausibility of the generalisation principle, at least in the present context. There is certainly much more that could be said about this, and other ideas similar to the generalisation principle, but we will have to leave this discussion here.

Social Consequences

Is it really impossible to justify the investment strategy of the ethical funds from an appeal to consequences? Before closing, we may return to this interpretation of the SRI proponents' idea, and the issue of what influence individual investors can have. Perhaps the interesting consequences are not ones of direct or indirect *economic* nature as I assumed above, but rather ones of (indirect) *social* nature?

When looking closer, the SRI literature actually abounds in suggestions of relevant social consequences and there are probably countless ways in which the present kind of argument can be formulated. Some suggest, for example, that managers often are hypersensitive to *all* attempts of influencing share prices – irrespective of

---

[7] A similar strategy which an increasing number of ethical funds focus on is that of investing in companies with morally questionable business activities in order to (try to) influence them from within. Either they initiate informal dialogues with managers in order to try to make them change the companies' ways, or they can use their power to vote at shareholder meetings for similar goals. However, there is little evidence that suggests that the possibilities for individual investors of making a difference are greater with regards to this kind of investment strategy. For further discussion of this strategy, see Sandberg 2008, chapter VI.

whether they actually stand a chance of succeeding (Brill et al. 1999). A rather different suggestion from Amy Domini (2001) is that the existence of ethical funds creates a demand for information about social responsibility in general, that is, information about the social and environmental impact of different companies' business activities. Perhaps, she suggests, this information in itself can make a certain difference.

One of the most interesting arguments in this context comes from Alan Miller. According to Miller, the most potent aspect of the investment strategy of ethical funds is not the direct financial impact it is likely to have on the underlying companies. Rather it is the social impact it may have on other investors and the media:

> Indeed, if [...] investors' decisions to sell stocks or not to buy them in the first place were secret, those decisions probably would have virtually no effect at all. [...] The fact is, however, that once these decisions are made, they are generally not kept secret, at least not by institutional investors, but are disclosed in ways intended to create maximum adverse publicity for the affected company or companies. [...] Thus, just as the main negative effect of a consumer boycott is seldom the actual direct revenues loss but rather is the publicity surrounding the boycott, so too, the principal impact of an avoidance strategy on companies subjected to it is often the negative publicity that accompanies it. (Miller 1991: 34–35)

While I cannot discuss all of the above suggestions in detail here, one way of formulating what they have in common is to follow Miller in cultivating the social aspect of investing. My line of reasoning above, it could be argued, built on the idea of a strict separation of the consequences of a *single* investor's actions on the one hand, and the consequences of actions of larger *groups* or the *totality* of investors on the other. But perhaps such a strict separation is impossible to make, as some may suggest 'no man is an island'. If I choose to refrain from investing in weapon companies for moral reasons, this may very well influence other investors to refrain from investing in weapon companies. Furthermore, it may very well influence corporate managers – many of which are keen on portraying their companies as socially responsible – and it may influence the greater society. For instance it may lead to an extended debate in society on business ethics and corporate responsibility. Taken together, then, it may not be too unreasonable to think that a single investor can make an important difference after all. In any case, how do I know that this is not so?

Well, issues about possible social consequences are hard to settle empirically. It is certainly not impossible for a single individual's behaviour to create a kind of snowball effect and influence how many other investors act, or even how a whole society frames or discusses a certain issue. Thus, a single individual may give rise to a kind of collective behaviour similar to that which was discussed above. But how common is this? We certainly *want* our actions to mean something in this way. If we felt that how we acted was totally insignificant to how people around us acted, even to our closest friends' and family members' behaviour, life would feel meaningless for many of us. But perhaps life is less meaningful in this sense than we think?

Without having empirical evidence for either standpoint, I would think that our belief in the social consequences of our actions often is exaggerated. A famous quote attributed to Olin Miller goes: 'We probably wouldn't worry about what people think of us if we could know how seldom they do'. Perhaps there actually is more to this than we commonly think – at least, it seems difficult for an individual investor to influence how other people live their lives. Concerning their possibility to influence corporate managers and the societal debate in general, I think there is reason to be just as pessimistic. While many people may follow the examples of certain famous or especially charismatic people, the vast majority of individual investors is certainly not opinion makers in this sense – rather, they most probably feel that very few are interested in hearing their side on things.

Furthermore, even if there is *some* social dimension to most investment decisions and so they have *some* kind of social consequences, the moral importance of these has to be compared to the possible consequences of alternative actions. As indicated above, I believe the possibility of actually making a difference probably is greater for the less scrupled ethical investor in this context. Even if my avoidance of investments in, say, weapon companies would be able to influence three to four other investors to become ethical investors, and even if the word got out to one or two of the managers of these companies, these effects do not seem comparable to the very tangible and life-and-death-decisive kind of influence I could have on people in the third world. If I, for instance, invest in weapon companies when their shares are on the rise, following the suggestion above, I would probably make a lot of money which I then could use to help many people with very desperate needs. Perhaps it is not so strange after all to think that this may have better consequences than simply refraining from investing in certain companies on the stock market?

The idea that investors ought to maximise their profit in order to donate it to charitable causes is of course in many ways more *demanding* on investors than the suggestion that ethical investing is just about staying clear of weapon and tobacco companies. Some people may be put off by this – haven't I done enough as long as I make *some* or *a* difference, along the lines of the suggestion above? But this sudden temperance in the call for making the world a better place, I believe, seems rather ad hoc. If the appeal to consequences really should be taken seriously, this could hardly be enough. If we really care about making the world a better place, why not *really* make the world a better place?[8]

Concluding Remarks

In this article, I have criticised the idea of many proponents of the SRI movement that one reason for investing in ethical funds is that it is wrong to support certain kinds of companies (for instance, weapon or tobacco companies) in the way one

---

[8] For a more detailed discussion of the demandingness of the ethical responsibilities of investors, see Sandberg 2008, chapter VII.

normally does when one invests in them. I have argued that individual investors simply cannot make much of a difference by simply refraining from investing in certain kinds of companies. If the appeal to consequences is a plausible interpretation of the general idea of SRI proponents, I have suggested, this appeal actually seems to demand a lot more of individual investors than what today's ethical funds can offer. One (perhaps extreme) suggestion is that they could invest in whatever currently gives the most profit – even if this turns out to be weapon companies – and then donate the proceeds to charity.

There are certainly other ways of understanding the idea that it is wrong to support certain kinds of companies than how I have understood this idea here. In light of my arguments above, proponents of ethical funds may want to appeal to some completely different set of moral principles in order to justify their strategy of refraining from investing in certain kinds of companies. What to think about these principles or about ethical funds in general however, is not the topic of this article. As always, we are left with more questions than we had when we started.

Acknowledgements This article is an adapted version of a paper in Swedish, 'Vad gör dina pensionspengar just nu?' 2007. Published in *Filosofisk tidskrift* 28: 45–56. For comments on earlier drafts, I once again wish to thank the participants in the higher seminar in practical philosophy at Stockholm University, the philosophy research seminar at the Royal Institute of Technology (Stockholm) and a seminar in industrial and financial economics at the School of Business, Economics and Law, University of Gothenburg.

References

Beauchamp, Tom L. and J. F. Childress. 2001. Principles of Biomedical Ethics (5th ed.). Oxford: Oxford University Press.

Brill, Hal, Jack. A. Brill, and Cliff Feigenbaum. 1999. Investing with Your Values: Making Money and Making a Difference. Princeton, NJ: Bloomberg Press.

Cowton, Christopher. J. 1998. Socially responsible investment. In Encyclopedia of Applied Ethics, ed. R. Chadwick. San Diego, CA: Academic.

Domini, Amy L. 2001. Socially Responsible Investing – Making a Difference and Making Money. Chicago, IL: Dearborn Trade.

Eurosif. 2006. European SRI Study 2006. Paris: Eurosif.

Haigh Matthew and James Hazelton. 2004. Financial markets: A tool for social responsibility? Journal of Business Ethics 52: 59–71.

Irvine, William B. 1987. The ethics of investing. Journal of Business Ethics 6: 233–242.

Mackenzie, Craig. 1997. Ethical investment and the challenge of corporate reform. Ph.D. dissertation, University of Bath.

Miller, Alan. J. 1991. Socially Responsible Investing – How to Invest with your Conscience. New York, NY: NYIF.

Rivoli, Pietra. 2003. Making a difference of making a statement? Finance research and socially responsible investment. Business Ethics Quarterly 13: 271–287.

Sandberg, Joakim. 2008. The Ethics of Investing. Making Money or Making a Difference? Gothenburg: Acta Universitatis Gothoburgensis.

Simon, John G., Charls W. Powers, and Jon P. Gunnemann. 1972. The Ethical Investor: Universities and Corporate Responsibility. London: Yale University Press.

Social Investment Forum. 2006. 2005 Report on Socially Responsible Investing Trends in the United States. Washington, DC: SIF Industry Research Program.

UNEP FI (United Nations Environment Programme's Finance Initiative) and Mercer. 2007. Demystifying Responsible Investment Performance: A Review of Key Academic and Broker Research on ESG Factors. Paris: UNEP FI.

Zweig, Jason. 1996. Why 'socially responsible investment' isn't quite as heavenly as it might sound. Money 25: 64.

Chapter 11
Sustainability and Social Justice

Johann A. Klaassen

Introduction

Every fall, my company First Affirmative Financial Network (in collaboration with the non-profit Social Investment Forum) produces a major conference for financial professionals interested in learning more about 'sustainable and responsible' or 'socially responsible investing' (SRI). The conference is called 'SRI in the Rockies' because of this focus, and because it has usually been held somewhere in the Mountain West of North America. For the last several years, the official conference themes have had something to do with 'sustainability' – for example, in 2009 the theme was *From Crisis to Opportunity: Investing for a Sustainable Economy.* Since sustainability as it is usually understood has broadly positive connotations and is generally seen as a good encapsulation of a wide variety of environmental issues, this has seemed like a good thing to most attendees. The SRI industry in general certainly should pay attention to environmental sustainability.

In the last few years, though, I have heard rumblings of dissent. During the Q&A periods following presentations, someone will ask the speakers something like this: 'We are glad to hear about environmental sustainability here, but what about *social justice*? Is it possible that we could be losing sight of human suffering in our attempts to save the natural environment? Are we sure that we want to neglect the very important set of goals set by considerations of social justice in favor of a single-minded pursuit of sustainability?' For the most part, the speakers and large parts of the audience respond to such questions with bewilderment: Surely any notion of sustainability worth pursuing would contain the seeds for, if not require as a fundamental condition, some kind of basically just social structure! Some are additionally puzzled at the 'directionality' of the question: that is, while we seldom pause to consider whether environmental sustainability implies social

J.A. Klaassen (✉)
First Affirmative Investment Committee, Colorado Springs, CO, USA
e-mail: johann@firstaffirmative.com

W. Vandekerckhove et al. (eds.), *Responsible Investment in Times of Turmoil*, Issues in Business Ethics 31, DOI 10.1007/978-90-481-9319-6_11,
© Springer Science+Business Media B.V. 2011

justice, there seems to be broad consensus that social justice implies environmental sustainability.[1]

Others are confused, it seems, by this use of 'sustainability' to mean 'merely' environmental sustainability. In the context of the current worldwide financial crisis, the word 'sustainable' seems to be most frequently used by politicians, business leaders, and the media to describe any system that is strong enough that it will probably survive. Regulating (or re-regulating) the financial system in order to make it more *stable*, for example, is discussed as a lynch-pin to making the system *sustainable* – so, as Stephen Green, the Group Chairman of HSBC Holdings plc, said in a conference speech recently,

> The litmus test for sustainable regulation is not just whether it makes individual firms more stable, but: does it contribute to a sustainable financial system, will it support economic growth, and can it be applied internationally? In particular, we must consider the impact of regulation on the wider economy. (Green 2009)

In this speech, Mr. Green was clearly not concerned with the potential long-term environmental impacts of new regulation of the financial industry (whatever those environmental impacts might be), but 'merely' on the economic impacts. Had he given this speech to a group of SRI-oriented fund managers or financial planners, this usage of the word 'sustainable' would have caused great confusion.

But even if we can agree to limit the use of the word 'sustainability' to the environmental sense, I believe that the various participants in this dispute have two fundamental disagreements: one over the meaning and scope of the word 'sustainability', and one over the time frame to be considered. Those with broader and stronger definitions of environmental sustainability and longer time frames tend to see a connection between sustainability and social justice; those with narrow or weak definitions, and those with shorter time frames, tend to be skeptical of that connection. This difference is more than merely semantic, though – it has clear implications for policy and politics.

In this essay, I want to bring my dual roles as (a) an SRI-focused investment adviser and (b) an academic philosopher to shed some light on these differences, by discussing the concepts in question and in dispute – 'social justice', 'sustainability', and 'now'. I argue that as practitioners involved in SRI, and as serious people who think about the ethical implications of our actions, we ought (a) to support a broader and stronger understanding of sustainability, and take a long view of the issues at hand, but that (b) our policy discussions and political decisions need to take place and take effect quickly. The simple fact that the global economy is in turmoil should not prevent us from attempting to change the way business gets done; if anything, it should encourage SRI practitioners to push even harder to create a just and sustainable economy.

---

[1] See, for example, Bendik-Keymer (2006), especially Lecture Two: 'Moral Attention and Justice'; see also May (1996), especially chapter 5: 'Social Responsibility', and in particular, 99–100. For a somewhat more skeptical take on the question, see Dobson (2003).

What Is Social Justice?

This phrase carries, for many Americans, two strong connotations. For some, it is reminiscent of the Catholic Church's active role in the social movements of the late nineteenth and early twentieth centuries. Pope Leo XIII and Pope Pius XI both published encyclicals describing what they saw as the failures of both capitalism and communism to address the needs of the working classes (Leo XIII 1891, Pius IX 1931). The Catholic Church maintains official positions on social justice, detailed in the *Compendium of the Social Doctrine of the Church* and summarized in the Catechism: 'The equal dignity of human persons requires the effort to reduce excessive social and economic inequalities'.[2] For others, the phrase 'social justice' evokes the American civil rights movement of the 1950s and 1960s. Extending 'the equal protection of the laws' promised in the 14th Amendment to the Constitution to the victims of the 'Jim Crow' regimes of the American South, and thus fulfilling the Amendment's promise of political and civil equality, was certainly an important part of the focus of the movement. So too was economic equality – as Reverend King wrote from the Birmingham City Jail,

> when you see the vast majority of your twenty million Negro brothers smothering in an airtight cage of poverty in the midst of an affluent society . . . then you will understand why we find it difficult to wait. (King 1963)

With these two connotations in mind, use of the phrase 'social justice' tends today to be associated with broadly progressive political movements aimed at spreading the exercise of fundamental human rights to groups that have previously been excluded.

But among philosophers, 'social justice' carries a somewhat different meaning. For philosophers, the phrase implies a society in which the concept of justice is applied far beyond the merely procedural sense of 'justice under the law', to all the society's structures and institutions. In some respects, though, this pushes us to another difficult question: what kind of society would count as 'just'? What do we mean by 'justice'? This is a very old question, to be sure – Plato's *Republic* may be one of the earliest systematic treatments of the question in the Western canon, but it certainly was not the last. Most contemporary discussions of justice begin with the work of John Rawls – most notably in his 1971 masterwork, *A Theory of Justice* (Rawls 1971).

Rawls asks that we begin deliberations about our society by stepping behind a 'veil of ignorance', setting aside any considerations of who we actually are in favor of a neutral decision-making position. From this 'original position', in which we have discounted any information about ourselves which might bias our judgment, we can hand down 'objective' decisions about the shape which an ideal society would take. And if, Rawls argues, we have absolutely no clue as to which position we might be asked to fill in the ensuing society, rationality dictates that we choose a 'maximin strategy' – a strategy which maximizes the benefits afforded to those

---

[2] See Pontifical Council for Justice and Peace (2004). See also Benedict XVI (2006).

who have the minimum. Since we can't really *bet*, much less *know*, where we might end up in the ensuing society, we have every reason to choose that system of social rights and obligations which results in the best results for the least well off. In his later refinement of his theory, represented in his 1993 book *Political Liberalism*, Rawls argues from similar grounds that the ideally just society is 'a fair system of co-operation over time, from one generation to the next' (Rawls 1993: 14). In this refinement of his theory, Rawls added a temporal dimension to the 'veil of ignorance': we can't know where *or when* we might land in the society we're helping to design.

Since it is clear that we do not live in an ideally just society already, 'social justice' (in a Rawlsian sense) is served when we move in the direction of improving the lot of the least-advantaged member of society, where- or whenever he might be. Naturally, when we begin to discuss how we might improve our society, we disagree about just how any such 'improvement' might be most probably accomplished – politically speaking. Those on the left might argue that income and property redistribution (or at least more progressive taxation) are necessary for increasing economic justice; those on the right might argue that maximal liberty will create the greatest equality of opportunity (and the greatest opportunities for philanthropy). All seem to agree, though, that some subset of what are generally recognized as 'basic human rights' need more emphasis in order to draw our contemporary society in the direction of greater social justice, in order to leave a better-structured society to the next generation.

The vast majority of investors find it difficult to see how investments could be put to work in support of something as abstract as 'basic human rights', however. Those investors who are served by SRI-focused investment advisors, on the other hand, probably know that their ownership stake in problematic corporations gives them certain rights, including the right to raise important questions at those corporations' annual shareholder meetings. For example, in 2008 and 2009, some of my clients took part in a shareholder advocacy campaign targeting Enbridge Incorporated, a Canadian energy pipeline company. Enbridge participates with many other firms in the 'Northern Gateway Pipeline Project', designed to tap the oil available in the 'tar sands' reserves under Alberta. In December 2008, a shareholder resolution was co-filed by Ethical Funds of Canada, First Affirmative Financial Network, Trillium Asset Management, and Green Century Capital Management (among others), in which Enbridge was asked to disclose the material risks related to negotiations with those First Nations that have territorial claims to the area under development.[3] We took part in this particular resolution because of our commitment to human rights, including the right to self-determination: we wanted to make certain that Enbridge (a) undertake the appropriate consultations with the First Nations that might be impacted by their portion of the Gateway project, and (b) disclose to its shareholders the status of these consultations. The resolution secured the support of 32% of shareholders at Enbridge's annual meeting in May 2009 – and although this appears

---

[3]For the online full text of the resolution, see Enbridge (2009)

to be a defeat, any resolution gaining the support of more than a few percent of shareowners is seen as a significant victory.

Although we have environmental concerns regarding the exploitation of Alberta's tar sands, in filing this resolution we were very careful *not* to spend time on those issues – to the surprise of some of our clients, on whose behalf we participated. A significant proportion of those clients who are drawn to SRI strategies tell us that their most important issues are environmental, and for these 'green' clients, issues of social justice may seem like a distraction. At First Affirmative, we had a few questions, from our network advisors and their clients, about why we were addressing only the issues of indigenous rights in our shareholder proposal: 'Why not', some asked, 'also ask Enbridge to address our environmental concerns as well?'

We and our co-filers had three key reasons for limiting our efforts. First, sticking to a single set of issues allows us to focus our energy more effectively. Trying to tackle more than one issue would just dilute the resources available for such projects, and might make them less likely to succeed. Second, those previous shareholder efforts with Enbridge that focused on the environment were not particularly successful, but those that focused on human rights and other issues of social justice had clear results. In 2001, resolutions were filed by our colleagues at Real Assets and Meritas regarding Enbridge's operations in Columbia; these were withdrawn in 2002, when the company agreed to sign the 'Voluntary Principles on Security and Human Rights'. And third, the specific human rights issues at hand – regarding the self-determination rights of Canada's First Nations – are clear and well-defined by legislation and litigation, while the environmental issues are contentious at best.

To my knowledge, Enbridge has not taken any official action with regard to our proposal since the annual meeting; we intend to re-file this resolution until the company agrees to act. Other shareholder resolutions regarding human rights were filed at many of the world's largest corporations in 2008 and 2009, including Cisco Systems, ExxonMobil, Motorola, and Wal-Mart. Although most of these were less successful than the Enbridge resolution, all had an impact – and all allowed ordinary investors to use their power as shareowners in support of social justice.

What Is Sustainability?

In some respects, this is a simple idea – 'sustainability' is something's ability to sustain itself, of course, usually (at least implicitly) for an indefinite time period. In this context, however, that can only be the beginning of the story. There are more than a few things we might be discussing, after all, and it seems rare indeed for those who speak of investing for sustainability to explicitly identify what it is that they are hoping to sustain. What *is* a 'sustainable world'?

The most widely cited discussion of sustainability is that of the World Commission on Environment and Development, also known as the Brundtland Commission, which offers this definition: 'Sustainable development is a development that meets the needs of the present without compromising the ability of future generations to meet their own needs' (Brundtland et al. 1987).[4] Most contemporary economists, it seems, point to this sort of 'intergenerational equity' as a fundamental part of any discussion of sustainability, and most appear to agree that the general stock of capital is the best way to measure this, so that 'a development is called sustainable when it leaves the capital stock at least unchanged', if not increased (Figge 2005: 16).[5] Noting that there are substantial differences between various types of capital – between 'human-made capital', things like smelters and tractors, and 'natural capital', things like iron ore and farmland, for example – the key dispute in discussions of sustainability right now seems to revolve around the question of 'substitution':

While the idea of leaving capital stock at least unchanged is widely accepted, differences arise concerning the question of whether one form of capital (e.g. natural capital) may be substituted by another form of capital (e.g. human-made capital). (Figge 2005: 186)

While there are a variety of positions that have been staked out in this debate, they fall into two basic camps: 'weak sustainability' arguments hold that most forms of capital are substitutable, and 'strong sustainability' arguments hold that most must be held to be 'complements'.[6]

Weak sustainability is a narrow notion: wealth is wealth, and as long as the total amount of capital we leave to the next generation is augmented by our activity, we are treating the next generation equitably. No doubt future generations will have plans and projects that we cannot envision now, just as the denizens of the early twentieth century could not have imagined our early twentyfirst century reliance on silicon chips; if we use up some natural resources, but more than replace them with other forms of capital, our development is 'sustainable'. In this sense, the Onceler of Dr Seuss's *The Lorax* is operating in a sustainable way when he turns the last of the Truffula trees into Thneeds – 'which everyone, EVERYONE, *EVERYONE* needs!' – because the total stock of capital is increased (Seuss 1971).[7] Sure, the local ecosystem has been wrecked, and all that remains of the indigenous flora and fauna are 'grickle grass' and 'old crows', but the Onceler and his family got 'mighty rich', so the natural capital of the area was transformed into Thneeds, a factory, and

---

[4] 'Development' in this context means economic and social growth: increasing economic activity, to be sure, but also thereby reducing unemployment, poverty, and social inequalities as well. For an early discussion of this definition of 'development', see Seers (1969).

[5] Notice the resemblance between this formulation and the 'Lockean Proviso': the requirement that we leave 'as much and as good' available for others, if our appropriation of property is to be justifiable. See John Locke (1689/1924: 128).

[6] There are, of course, many different variations on these themes; R. Kerry Turner, for example, identifies four main forms of sustainability existing in a spectrum from weakest (total substitutability) to strongest (no substitutability at all). I will speak only of a 'very weak' and a 'fairly strong' version, trying to avoid attacking straw men. See Turner (1993).

[7] This quotation is close to the end of the book (p. 49, though the pages are unnumbered).

money, and the society's total capital was (apparently) increased.[8] For these reasons, weak sustainability is often derided as simply false, because, for example, as Frank Figge puts it,

[f]rom the standpoint of weak sustainability, fish stocks and fishing boats are substitutes. If this were true, diminishing fishing stocks could be substituted by an increase in fishing boats. (Figge 2005: 186)

For a short while, this substitution might work – in a sense. The rate at which tuna, for example, were removed from water might remain the same, if we increase the number of tuna boats to offset the increased difficulty each boat has in catching a tuna, but eventually the last tuna will be caught. Of what use will those boats be then? Weak sustainability is narrowly focused on measures of wealth, and its conditions appear to be satisfied if there is as much or more capital tomorrow as there was yesterday. Other measures of societal and environmental well-being are left out of the picture, unless they can be expressed in terms of 'stock of capital'.

Strong sustainability, on the other hand, is a much broader notion. It asks that we look not only at the *value* of our stock of capital, but also at the *context* for the accumulation or use of each type of capital. Think again of the fishing boats: it seems clear that the fleet is at least less valuable (if not completely valueless) once the last fish is caught – and thus that '[f]ishing boats and fish stocks are complementary', and the development of our fishing fleet must be limited by the fishes' population (Figge 2005: 186). This consideration then brings not-traditionally-economic issues into our economic calculations. Suddenly, in order to determine whether or not a course of action (say, increasing our fishing fleet) is sustainable in the strong sense, we need to look past the sum of the value of the fleet and the fish; we need to investigate the fish population, its rate of reproduction, the minimum size of a healthy population, the impact of ocean pollution on fish health . . .

In short, when we use strong sustainability, a vastly more complicated set of variables comes into play. In 1990, Herman Daly offered what are now known as the 'Daly Rules', for the sustainable use of natural capital:

Renewable resources (fish, forests, soils, groundwaters) must be used no faster than the rate at which they regenerate;Nonrenewable resources (mineral ores, fossil fuels, fossil groundwaters) must be used no faster than renewable substitutes for them can be put into place;Pollution and wastes must be emitted no faster than natural systems can absorb them, recycle them, or render them harmless. (Daly 1990: 1–6)

Others are seeking to extend these rules to other forms of capital, so that the same kind of analyses can be performed on them as well. As Donella Meadows puts it,

Surely there is a stock or endowment of health, skills, and knowledge that can be invested in, enhanced, and used to produce a steady stream of productivity, or that can be overused, eroded, allowed to depreciate. Surely there must be social capital in the form of functioning

---

[8]For more on the implications of *The Lorax* for environmental philosophy, see Klaassen and Klaassen (forthcoming).

civic organizations, cultures of personal and community responsibility, efficient markets and governments, tolerance and public trust. (Meadows 1998: 47)[9]

Strong sustainability, then, assumes that we can have a broad accounting of a variety of different kinds of capital, holds that some of these forms of capital are not substitutable for one another, and requires that we leave our stocks of all these different forms of capital intact (if not improved) for the next generation.

In the context of investments, though, we normally want to focus our attention on financial capital, and ask how it can be marshaled to support other forms of capital. For example, how can we use our financial capital to support ecosystem health? Making donations to environmental charities will certainly put some portion of that capital to work in support of environmental health, but investors willing to engage in shareholder advocacy efforts can leverage their assets even further. For example, in 2008 and 2009, some of my clients took part in a shareholder advocacy campaign targeting ConocoPhillips, the Houston, Texas-based integrated energy company. Like Enbridge, ConocoPhillips is involved in projects designed to extract oil from the 'tar sands' in Alberta. While our efforts with Enbridge centered on the human rights issues involved in negotiations with local First Nations tribes, this resolution asked ConocoPhillips to provide a full and accurate accounting of the financial and environmental impacts of their tar sands operations. Extracting usable oil from tar sands is energy intensive, uses vast amounts of fresh water, and appears to risk substantial pollution of the water and air – but ConocoPhillips, one of the key players in the development of Alberta's tar sands, has so far done only superficial preliminary studies of the long-term environmental impacts. More than 30% of shareholders voted in favor of the resolution we co-filed (with Green Century and Trillium), another significant victory.

This first decade of the twentyfirst century has been marked by dramatic stock market activity, a global recession, and renewed interest in corporate regulation by newly-energized governments. Some have tried to use this turmoil to justify *not* making any significant changes to the way businesses operate: 'We simply cannot worry about global climate change right now', they seem to say, 'because we are struggling right now just to keep the company afloat!' This kind of argument rests on what seems to me to be a false dichotomy: why should we believe that we must choose between protecting the environment in their regions of operation, on the one hand, and bankruptcy on the other? How can those be the only two alternatives? What's more, it seems there will *always* be *some* crisis to which the management of such a company could appeal as the reason that they cannot consider human rights, or environmental sustainability, 'at least not right now'. As Dr King wrote,

> For years now I have heard the word 'Wait!' ... This 'Wait' has almost always meant 'Never'. We must come to see, with one of our distinguished jurists [Thurgood Marshall], that 'justice too long delayed is justice denied'. (King 1963)

---

[9]For an interesting recent take on the concept of social capital, see Lewandowski and Streich (2007).

Too many companies are mired in short-term thinking, focused on the current crisis, this quarter's financial results, the next year's projections, and the probable impact of those factors on the company's stock price. Too few companies are willing to consider the impact their operations are having on the fabric of the society in which they operate, or on the natural environment around them. Investors, too, suffer from this kind of myopia, focusing too much of their attention on this quarter's portfolio performance – so their advisors must as well. But investors, in our role as shareholders, have the right to demand that the leadership of the companies they own look beyond the current crisis, and formulate long-term plans that bring consideration of social justice and environmental sustainability into clear focus. And investors pursuing SRI strategies are already engaged on these issues, making a difference in the corporate governance of the companies they own.

'Sustainability' is such a resonant concept right now in part because many of us have begun to believe that a global climate crisis is either underway, or looming – and that we can and must do something to shift our economic behavior sooner, rather than later, if we're going to survive the crisis. Current science appears to imply that severe climate impacts could be felt in 10–20 years, unless substantial steps are taken 'now'.[10]

What Do We Mean by 'Now'?

In speaking of both social justice and sustainability, I have made references to long spans of time: definitions of justice and sustainability refer to 'the next generation' and 'intergenerational equity'. A 'generation' is traditionally defined as 30 years, and financial folklore has it that Thomas Jefferson urged that the maturation of the longest US Treasury bond be set at 30 years so that one generation could not burden the next with its debt. But contemporary society is notoriously short-sighted, and 30 years seems an eternity.

This is particularly obvious in the world of investment advisors. The financial news cycle is very short: stock prices can move substantially within the course of a few minutes, and the markets can shift drastically in the course of a day. Companies report on their financial situation quarterly, and compare the most recent quarter's results with the same quarter of last year. When I worked as a phone representative for a mutual fund company, on more than one occasion I heard an investor say 'Oh, yes, I have a long-term time frame for this investment – I intend to hold this fund for at least a year!' (thinking perhaps of the current tax code, which specifies that the gains or losses on any security held for more than 1 year are to be counted as 'long-term' for tax purposes). Mutual funds can be evaluated daily, using services such as Morningstar, report their official returns quarterly, and are generally considered to have a 'long-term track record' when they pass their third anniversary. And financial planners tend to describe a 'long-term time horizon' as being 5–10 years, sometimes

---

[10]See, for example, Eilperin (2006); see also Arctic Climate Impact Assessment (2004).

more. Is it any surprise that we have trouble thinking about intergenerational equity, if we only rarely stretch our thinking out 10 years into the future?

Stewart Brand and Danny Hillis founded the Long Now Foundation in an attempt to draw attention to the *really* long-term – the Foundation's key project is 'the Clock of the Long Now', designed to last 10,000 years or more. Brand (2010) describes the project this way:

> Civilization is revving itself into a pathologically short attention span. The trend might be coming from the acceleration of technology, the short-horizon perspective of market-driven economics, the next-election perspective of democracies, or the distractions of personal multi-tasking. All are on the increase. Some sort of balancing corrective to the short-sightedness is needed – some mechanism or myth which encourages the long view and the taking of long-term responsibility, where 'long-term' is measured at least in centuries.

Thus 'the Clock'. Its mechanism is, in a sense, mythical: 10,000 years ago, human beings were just beginning the Agricultural Revolution, on the cusp of thinking beyond the next hunting expedition, to the next growing season. What will human beings be like 10,000 years from now? The unconventional thinkers at the Long Now Foundation are optimistic, fairly certain that we will not have completely destroyed our planet and ourselves. Just in case we have managed to cause a collapse of our present civilizations, though, the Clock will also house a 'Library', documenting currently-existing human languages and cultures in a fashion and format designed to be retrievable far into the future – a 'Rosetta Disk' utilizing micro-etching that requires only magnification to be readable.[11]

It may not be necessary to extend our everyday understanding of the word 'now' to the full 10,000 year timeframe of the Long Now Foundation – but surely it is valuable to occasionally allow our attention to focus on something beyond the next ten minutes, 10 days, even 10 years. A deep global economic crisis pulls us in both directions: on the one hand, it gives us a clear opportunity to address a much longer 'now' than we might otherwise; on the other, it forces us to focus a lot of attention on the *immediate* 'now', in that we need to prevent a further slide, from recession into full-blown depression. Governments around the world have made various efforts to stimulate their economies, to prevent further short-term economic harm, with various degrees of success. Most of those governments are looking at this crisis as an opportunity to make fundamental changes to the way the world's economy is structured. As Rahm Emanuel, President Barack Obama's Chief of staff said, shortly after the election:

> You never want a serious crisis to go to waste. ... Things that we had postponed for too long, that were long-term, are now immediate and must be dealt with. This crisis provides the opportunity for us to do things that you could not do before. (Seib 2008)

The crisis of the Great Depression led the US to create a structure of economic regulation which lasted nearly to the end of the century. Some of the suggested regulations floating around Washington DC right now could have similarly long-lasting impacts. The idea of the Long Now can help us to extend our planning out much

---

[11]For more on the Rosetta Disk, see http://www.rosettaproject.org.

farther than we might otherwise, and so to help with the kind of intergenerational thinking that both social justice and sustainable development require.

Conclusion: Politics and Policy

This volume is focused on the financial crisis plaguing world economies, which began early in the decade. If we look at 'real' returns, and make sure to account for the impact of inflation, the US stock markets are still far below their peaks of early 2000. This has certainly had a significant impact on our clients, and their plans for the future, since all of our financial planning tools are based on the notion that decades like this one are very unlikely. But there is another ongoing crisis, which does not receive the attention in the financial media that it deserves: the global climate crisis.

The clients who come to investment advisors specializing in SRI strategies usually have just one main reason that drives them to seek our advice, and environmental and social justice issues are probably at the top of, but are not the only items on, that list. One of the most interesting trends that we SRI practitioners are seeing currently is a convergence of all these specialized interests. It seems to me that we have reached the point where we need to act quickly to keep all Four Horsemen of the Apocalypse at bay ... though it may already be too late. Worldwide outbreaks of Famine, Pestilence, War, and Death are among the likely consequences of continued global climate change, and of the contemporary threats to social justice. If we allow ourselves to focus exclusively on the urgent needs of our current financial crisis, and do not spend the time and effort to engage with these other crises, we risk a financial and human disaster greater than the Great Depression. On the other hand, because of the coupled nature of environmental sustainability and social justice, I believe that any efforts we make to alleviate the climate crisis will alleviate threats to social justice, and vice versa.

Part of the appeal of the idea that we need to be careful not to decouple questions of social justice from our currently-urgent concerns for sustainability derives from the scariness of a couple of nightmare scenarios:

LIBERTARIAN NIGHTMARE: An avowed environmentalist is elected President of the United States, and by appealing to the global climate crisis manages to push through an extensive program of radical environmental regulations. These regulations are so stringent that many existing businesses cannot comply and are forced to shut down; many new businesses are prevented from starting up for similar reasons. The global economy crashes catastrophically, creating a decade-long Depression severe enough to make the 'Great Depression' look mild by comparison.

LIBERAL NIGHTMARE: A neo-fascist dictator takes power in the United States, taking opportunistic advantage of the American people's confusion and panic at the earliest signs of the global climate crisis. Part of the new regime's program of centralized political and economic control is radical environmental regulations, combined with the nationalization of certain key industries. The global economy crashes catastrophically, creating a decade-long Depression severe enough to make the 'Great Depression' look mild by comparison.

In both cases, the broader concerns of social justice are ignored. The tree-hugging President ignores them because of the immediate need for drastic action to prevent further climate degradation, and in the hopes that once the climate is back on an even keel we can all renew our commitment to social justice. The neo-fascist dictator ignores them because he never cared about social justice anyway.

But these nightmare scenarios are just that, nightmares. They only really make sense if we take a very narrow view and short time-slice of the climate crisis itself. Both scenarios only work if we're thinking of 'weak sustainability', looking only at the crashing systems of natural capital and seeking relief by making adjustments to the systems of human-made capital. And they rely on our modern tendency to treat the near-term result – a 'decade-long Depression' – as the end of the story.

I think that we must think instead of 'strong sustainability', and take the wider view of all the systems of capital at our disposal. Attempts to address a crashing system of natural capital must take into account *all* other forms of capital, and seek a solution which preserves natural, human, social, and human-made forms of capital as best we can. And if we are willing to adopt a longer 'now', to consider the implications of our decisions for, say, 'seven generations' – 210 years, far short of the 10,000 years suggested by the Long Now theorists, yet much longer than the single decade of the nightmares, or even the single generation of our longest investment time horizons – we may well find a new flexibility and willingness to take longer-term risks. I don't mean to suggest that we should not act immediately to stem the threat of a global climate crisis. It is clear that any actions we mean to take will require substantial preparation, and will almost certainly not show immediate results. But our world's leaders – environmental scientists, politicians and civil society leaders, even investment advisors – need to be willing to set in motion the long term projects that will allow us all to work together to create a just society in a sustainable environment.[12]

---

[12] Because I am an Investment Advisory Representative of First Affirmative Financial Network, LLC, an SEC-regulated Registered Investment Advisory firm, I must make the following legal disclaimers: I do not own any of the securities mentioned in this article. Nothing in this article should be interpreted as investment advice, or as an offer to buy or sell securities. Any performance figures contained herein are based on information sources believed to be reliable, and are not to be interpreted as a guarantee of future results. The views expressed are my own, and not those of First Affirmative Financial Network, LLC, or of anyone else associated with First Affirmative. Many thanks to Angela Klaassen, Christie Renner, Jeremy Bendik-Keymer, Gary Matthews, Andy Loving, Susan Taylor, the discussants at the Colorado Springs Philosophy Discussion Group, and the editors of this volume, for their extraordinarily helpful comments on earlier versions of this essay.

References

Arctic Climate Impact Assessment. 2004. Impacts of a Warming Arctic. Cambridge: Cambridge University Press.

Bendik-Keymer, Jeremy. 2006. The Ecological Life: Discovering Citizenship and a Sense of Humanity. Lanham, MD: Rowman & Littlefield.

Benedict XVI. 2006. Deus Caritas Est (God Is Love). http://www.vatican.va. Accessed January 2010.

Brand, S. 2010. The clock and library projects. Available at http://www.longnow.org/about Accessed May 2010.

Brundtland, Gro Harlem and the World Commission on Environment and Development. 1987. Our Common Future. Oxford: Oxford University Press.

Daly, Herman E. 1990. Toward some operational principles of sustainable development. Ecological Economics 2: 1–6.

Dobson, Andrew. 2003. Social justice and environmental sustainability: Ne'er the twain shall meet? In Just Sustainabilities: Development in an Unequal World, eds. Julian, Agyeman, Robert Ballard, and Bob Evans, 83–95. Cambridge, MA: MIT Press.

Eilperin, Juliet. 2006. Debate on climate shifts to issue of irreparable change. Washington Post, January 29, 2006: A1.

Enbridge 2009. 'Free prior and informed consent northern gateway project' Available at http://www.onlineethicalinvestor.org/eidb/wc.dll?eidbproc~reso~8611 Accessed January 2010.

Figge, Frank. 2005. Capital substitutability and weak sustainability revisited: The conditions for capital substitution in the presence of risk. Environmental Values 14: 185–201.

Green, Stephen. 2009. Promoting a Sustainable Financial System; Speech made to the Hermes Fund Managers and the Corporation of London Conference, 24 November 2009. http://www.hsbc.com/1/PA_1_1_S5/content/assets/newsroom/091124_skg_speech.pdf. Accessed January 2010.

King, Jr., Martin Luther. 1963. Letter from Birmingham Jail. Widely available, including online at http://www.stanford.edu/group/King/frequentdocs/birmingham.pdf. Accessed January 2010.

Klaassen, Johann A. and Mari-Gretta G. Klaassen. Forthcoming. Speaking for business, speaking for trees: Business and environment in the lorax. In PhiloSeussical Investigations: An Introduction to Philosophy through the World of Dr. Seuss, ed. Jacob M. Held. Lanham, MD: Rowman & Littlefield.

Leo XIII. 1891. Rerum Novarum (On Capital and Labor). http://www.vatican.va. Accessed January 2010.

Lewandowski, Joseph and Gregory Streich. 2007. Democratizing social capital: In pursuit of liberal egalitarianism. Journal of Social Philosophy 38: 588–604.

Locke, John. 1689/1924. Two Treatises of Government, ed. Mark Goldie. London: Everyman.

May, Larry. 1996. The Socially Responsive Self: Social Theory and Professional Ethics. Chicago, IL: University of Chicago Press.

Meadows, Donella. 1998. Indicators and Information Systems for Sustainable Development: A Report to the Balaton Group. Hartland Four Corners, VT: The Sustainability Institute.

Pius XI. 1931. Quadragesimo Anno (On the Reconstruction of the Social Order). http://www.vatican.va. Accessed January 2010.

Pontifical Council for Justice and Peace. 2004. Compendium of the Social Doctrine of the Church. Washington, DC: UCSSB Publishing. http://www.vatican.va. Accessed January 2010.

Rawls, John. 1971. A Theory of Justice. Cambridge, MA: Harvard University Press.

Rawls, John. 1993. Political Liberalism. New York, NY: Columbia University Press.

Seers, Dudley. 1969. The meaning of development. International Development Review 11: 2–6.

Seib, Gerald F. In Crisis, an Opportunity for Obama. Wall Street Journal, November 21, 2008: Page A2. http://online.wsj.com/article/SB122721278056345271.html. Accessed January 2010.

'Dr Seuss' (Theodor Seuss Geisel). 1971. The Lorax. New York, NY: Random House.

Turner, R. Kerry. 1993. Sustainability: Principles and practice. In Sustainable Environmental Economics and Management: Principles and Practice, ed. Turner R.K. London: Belhaven.

Chapter 12
Reality and Potential of Responsible Investment

Carlos Joly

> *Anyone who hasn't learned by now that there's almost no*
> *relationship between the Dow and the real economy deserves to*
> *lose his or her shirt in the Wall Street casino.*
> Robert Reich, former US Secretary of Labor, 16 Oct 2009

Introduction

The potential of Responsible Investment has to be seen in relation to its mission: to act in 'the best long term interest' of savers and investors, to preserve their capital over the long term and in a way that 'aligns with the broader objectives of society', as stated in the Preamble of The UN Principles of Responsible Investment (UNPRI).[1] This body places environmental and social issues at the center of the commitments its signatories pledge to uphold. Thus, it is fair to ask: have the pension funds and asset managers who have signed onto the UNPRI performed any better than other investors as regards upholding the best long term interests of their beneficiaries? In this chapter I want to compare the reality – how the RI community has actually behaved – relative to how it should have in the current crisis, and in the context of 'the broader objectives of society'. My aim is to propose a number of measures that would help bring the reality of RI closer to its potential. I start with a quick summary of what the crisis is about, in particular to underline how it has

---

C. Joly (✉)
Ecole Superieur de Commerce, Toulouse, France; BI Norwegian
School of Management, Oslo, Norway
e-mail: carlos.joly@gmail.com

[1] In early 2005, the United Nations Secretary-General invited a group of the world's largest institutional investors to join a process to develop the Principles for Responsible Investment (PRI). Individuals representing 20 institutional investors from 12 countries agreed to participate in the Investor Group. The Group accepted ownership of the Principles, and had the freedom to develop them as they saw fit. http://www.unpri.org/about/ The author of this paper was Co-Chair of the Expert Group that drafted the PRI.

W. Vandekerckhove et al. (eds.), *Responsible Investment in Times of Turmoil*,
Issues in Business Ethics 31, DOI 10.1007/978-90-481-9319-6_12,
© Springer Science+Business Media B.V. 2011

negatively affected the interests of savers as regards their income, employment, and preservation of their savings. And to remark how little RI has done to prevent this.

In 2008, governments prevented the complete implosion of the world financial system by injecting massive amounts of money into banks, insurers, and investment houses. In 2009, banks began transacting with each other again, although they are keeping capital to themselves, giving priority to trading their own book and preparing to pay out-sized bonuses to their traders and executives rather than making credit available to business. The real question now in 2010 is whether the economy will be able to do what it is supposed to do: create well paying jobs,[2] provide good investment opportunities for retirement plans[3] and generate enough profits to cover the government services a modern civilized society requires.[4] As 2010 gets started, it looks increasingly like the Great Recession will probably last into 2011 and beyond, adding millions more to the 212 million unemployed workers in the world today.[5]

Getting the financial system out of the emergency room was the easy part. Fixing the economy in such a way that it does not continue to destroy jobs and the environment we all depend on, that is the hard part. Two policies seem to be at odds with this: the first is the policy of seeking to ramp up consumption as a way of getting us out of the Great Recession. More consumption should result in more jobs. But more consumerism means more greenhouse gas (GHG) emissions. The second is the policy of more global trade as the way towards prosperity. More globalization also means more GHG emissions. Whether and how we find a way through these dilemmas will determine whether we indeed have *A Common Future* in the way proposed by the Brundtland Report. The discord resulting in The Copenhagen Accord at COP15 does not auger well. We need to reflect what role Responsible Investment can play in all this. We need to think about our methods and techniques, but we also need to go beyond the technical discussions. This chapter sets up an agenda for doing so.

The past 30 years have seen increasing environmental degradation and diminishing inter-and intra-generational economic justice, despite gains in eco-efficiency (Speth 2008, Worldwatch Institute 2010), that is, in less pollution per unit of

---

[2] Jobs loss in the US in this recession exceeds job losses of all post WW2 recessions. See Calculated Risk 2010. Worldwide unemployment reached 212 million people in 2009, the highest ever and an increase of 34 million unemployed people over 2007 (ILO 2010).

[3] Vs. the record $17.5 trillion plunge in US household net worth since the recession started at the end of 2007 through first quarter of 2009, and the loss by US pension funds of about 1/3 of their assets. 'Though the pensions' assets [of the 100 largest US pension funds] gained an average of 9.12% over the last 12 months, their funded status fell by a total of $68 billion and their funded ratio dropped from 93.8 to 75.0%.' (Milliman 2009).

[4] Government services have been devastated in 2009 and beyond, along with taxes: 'The first three quarters of 2009 were the worst on record for states in terms of the decline in overall state tax collections, as well as the change in personal income and sales tax collections. The Great Recession hit virtually every single source of tax revenue.' (Rockefeller Institute 2010)

[5] This paper was written at the end of 2009, with some additions in early 2010. 2009 saw the worse recession in the UK in 88 years. I subscribe to Joseph Stiglitz' and Paul Krugman's view that the inventory boost now taking place in Q1 2010 will be a passing blip in this sad story.

production. The course we are on is not rosy for most people. In the US, the lion's share of benefits and opportunities has been going to a smaller share of the population. Half of all income growth has gone to the top 1% in recent years, whereas the bottom 40% has remained stagnant (Saez 2008).[6] This distribution is even worse than in the 1930s. In contraposition, the large middle survives on very tight budgets and struggles to hold onto jobs they fear losing. Fully 30% of US homes are worth less than their mortgages. Thus, convergence towards greater inequality seems to be the trend in mature economies. What is RI to do in this context?

Is RI Responsible?

This chapter is written from the perspective of an investment professional and RI activist. It is not a detached piece of academic research. In fact, as Co-Chair of the Expert Group that drafted the UN Principles of Responsible Investment[7] I believed Responsible Investment had important potential for channelling society's savings in the direction of sustainable development rather than passively allowing economic injustice and environmental degradation. Now, 5 years later, I still believe in it, but its potential still looms larger than its implementation. Just look at the trillions of dollars of assets under management by the 675 mainstream signatories of the PRI. The accomplishments of RI so far fall much too short of the influence and resources of its participants. In a sense, this article is a call for self-examination on the part of self-proclaimed Responsible Investors and Socially Responsible Investors, and an appeal to policymakers and regulators to take more seriously their role in harnessing capital markets for the ends of sustainability. In times of turmoil, RI has not been

---

[6]In the most recent past, the very highest earners did very well indeed, capturing almost three-quarters of total income growth in the economic expansion of 2002 to 2006, while the remaining 99% of the U.S. population split among themselves the final 25% of the increase. (White House 2009). During expansions, most of the income growth is captured in the US by the top 1%, whereas in countries like France income is distributed more fairly. Thus, while average real incomes in the US grew by 30% from 1975 to 2005, whereas in France by 19%, if the top 1% is excluded, average US real incomes grew only by 16.5% during the period while average French real incomes grew by 19.7%. In other words, the 'better' macro economic performance of the US was appropriated by the top 1% of the population with the remaining 99% of US families receiving less than the French (Atkinson et al. 2009).

[7]The Group was supported by a 70-person multi-stakeholder group of experts from the investment industry, intergovernmental and governmental organizations, civil society and academia. The process, conducted between April 2005 and January 2006 involved a total of five days of face-to-face deliberations by the investors and four days by the experts, with hundreds of hours of follow-up activity. The Principles for Responsible Investment emerged as a result of these meetings. As a fund manager, in 1989 I launched Scandinavia's first environment fund, MiljøInvest, investing in pollution control tech stocks; in 1996, I launched one of the first global sustainable development Best in Class funds, Storebrand Scudder Environmental Value Fund; in 1994 co-founded the UNEP Finance Initiative and its Asset Management Working Group; in 2006 Co-chaired drafting the PRI; in 2009 helped launch the Natixis Impact Climate Change fund and now chair its Scientific Advisory Committee.

any more responsible than the investment business generally. I now believe that the voluntary, aspirational and self-regulatory approach espoused by the UN-sponsored PRI needs to be complemented by government regulatory standards backed by robust sanctions.[8]

RI has failed on two major counts: first, most RI managers have failed to foresee, have not tried to prevent, and have not reacted in time to the financial crisis of 2007–2008. As a result, RI pension funds and asset managers have lost money for their retirees, savers and plan participants in the same way as non-RI managers. The OECD estimates private pension fund losses at \$5 trillion in 2008, with many government and private pension funds losing up to 30% of their value and not much chance of gaining it back soon (Washington Times 2009). This is a major failure of fiduciary duty. In general, I see very little differentiation between the investment performance of mainstream RI funds and SRI funds from that of non-RI and non-SRI funds. Second, for the most part the asset allocation strategies and the investment portfolios of RI funds mirror those of non-RI funds. The portfolios of Best in Class sustainable development funds and SRI funds are surprisingly similar in composition to those of their traditional counterparts, and the investment decision making processes are also by and large the same. The exclusionary screens adopted by mainstream investors seek to exclude as little as possible, so as to have as little effect on tracking error as possible.[9] The sustainable development Best in Class positive selection actively-managed funds also generally seek to have fairly conservative tracking error relative to the market indices, rarely exceeding tracking error of three, as their results are compared quarter to quarter against their traditional counterparts and commercially they cannot afford to underperform. As a result, the trillions of dollars controlled by RI asset owners, managers and consultants are not deployed consistent with long term investment strategies that would conduct our economies in a direction consistent with sustainable development, environmental protection, and greater economic justice – which would imply radical departures from what the market feels comfortable with and the valuation it puts on the large cap listed shares that dominate most global portfolios.

Peel away the layers of intermediation, the trustees, retirement plans, banks distributors, unit link insurers, brokers and fund managers, and you find the money managed by RI fund managers, money that belongs to the great mass of salaried employees and retirees, ends up benefitting the intermediaries disproportionately relative to the end owners. Conventional wisdom in the industry tells people to invest steadily in stocks throughout up and down periods because 'in the long run stocks outperform cash and bonds'. Well, during the decade from 2000 to 2010 stock

---

[8]The UN Secretary-General pays homage to the UN PRI (see www.unpri.org) but neither the EC, the OECD, or the SEC have made moves to establish RI performance standards beyond the UK's and other country's measures requiring pension funds to declare whether they have an environmental, social or governance investment policy and if so to describe it.

[9]Tracking error measures the dispersion of a portfolio's active return, which is the difference between the portfolio and bench-mark returns.

returns in the US markets were negative.[10] After fees, ordinary savers lost money, while our industry's profits and our earnings have grown out of proportion to returns and to the economy.

That is not what Responsible Investment was created for. What, then, needs to take place for RI to live up to its promise?

Is RI Possible Without a Sustainable Reality to Invest in?

In the largest possible sense, we need to rethink two things: one, *what* we invest in; in practice this means whether all the investment sectors or objects in the Global Industry Classification System should form part of the RI investment universe or whether certain of them should be excluded outright because of their inherent unsustainability. Clearly this involves difficult decisions, and few investment boards or managers today have sufficient scientific or environmental competence to engage these judgments. But a way needs to be found for making these decisions. However, the deeper problem of what to invest in is not primarily what RI should exclude from its investment universe; but rather the fact that we do not have enough good investment objects on offer. We need a better investment universe. We invest in the corporate and economic realities that are given, and this is our most severe limitation, so we must add our voice and creativity to promoting the realities that should obtain, rather than passively accepting the realities that we are given. As I suggest below, this has to mean positive involvement in the legislative process in favor of measures that cause greening of the economy, and more investment in non-listed investment objects.

Two, we need to rethink the basis upon which we make decisions or *how* we conduct the investment process – the primacy of passive investment strategies, index-tracking strategies, and the whole box of tools based on the dubious hypothesis of efficient markets has got to give,[11] because this toolkit fosters crisis and prevents good judgment and common sense from acting against irrational market conditions or from getting out of the market when a bubble obviously obtains.

---

[10]Since December 1999, a typical 60/40 — equity/bond portfolio in the US would have recorded the lowest average annual returns since the 1940s at about 1.4%. Adjusted for inflation, it was the worst decade since the 1970s. Wall Street's S&P500 index is set to record its first negative decade — down 24.6% since 1999. It remains in the red to the tune of 9.8% even when dividends are reinvested. And if you happened to be an unhedged investor from overseas, you suffered a double whammy. The dollar lost some 23% against a basket of the most traded world currencies. (Dolan 2009)

[11]As an asset manager and investor, the efficient markets hypothesis never made sense to me, as it explains nothing about how prices are actually set in the stock market. Kristian Falnes (2010) of Skagen Fonds, probably the best performing active asset manager in Scandinavia, simply says: 'The market is always wrong'. Soros has a similar view, based on his theory of a dynamic reflexivity between perceptions and reality. The CEO of the Norwegian Government Pension Fund, Yngve Slyngstad, is also quite skeptical of passive investing.

Policy Recommendations

As observed, RI has serious shortcomings in actual practice. In this section I propose a series of policy and programmatic recommendations for consideration by asset owners, the large pension funds that steer the UN PRI. Clearly, in these few pages all I can do is skim the surface, but I believe the overview presented in Table 12.1 might be useful as a policy agenda for discussion and self-reflection in my industry.

In the next sections I go into some of these points and on one of them, climate change, indicate an approach I advocate for putting it into practice. In fact, a major RI investor I work with has launched a €100 million fund based on this approach.

Why RI Needs Government Regulation

The US government did not do as Sweden, Denmark and Norway did in their banking crises in the 1980s – the Scandinavians, true to their social democratic way of thinking, nationalized the banks, fired the boards, replaced senior management, and re-privatized later, maintaining proper controls over capital ratios, spreads and fees to the public, and the flow of loans to good clients. Most importantly, the banks do not run the Finance Ministries or staff the regulatory authorities; the Finance Ministries and supervisory authorities run the banks; the career paths of their public officials is not a revolving door to the private sector. In Scandinavia, banks do not unduly intervene in government elections and do not have undue influence through lobbyists.

So far, the US has wasted the current crisis and has not used it to enact structural reform. If Wall Street and the major money center banks are allowed to continue to have a stranglehold on the economy, to decide how much credit is created and distributed and for which purposes, and if their regulators are drawn from their own ranks, no amount of corporate social responsibility or RI will do any good. Corporate Social Responsibility (CSR) and RI will achieve their potential when they become complementary parts to a regulatory system that is designed to transition to a sustainable development economy rather than designed for business as usual. I've come to believe that without this RI will never go beyond well-intentioned aspiration and marginal efficacy. It is unrealistic to expect Citibank, Goldman Sachs, Deutsche Bank or HSBC to voluntarily rein in growth of their structured products, derivatives and securitization businesses, and instead redeploy their vast resources towards greening the economy.

The self-regulatory route has been tried and it works within a limited range of issues. It has made strides in advancement in women's pay and their place in middle management, in occupational safety and health in dangerous workplaces, and, in some countries, in improving ethnic diversity in the workplace. But it has done little to improve decent pay for the tens of millions who do menial work in the service industries and little if anything in terms of caps on executive pay or aligning bonuses with the interests of the various stakeholders of the company; and nothing when it comes to mass firings that improve short term profits even when at the expense of

Table 12.1 Problems and possible ways forward

Problem	Possible ways forward			
Unavailability of a sufficiently large number of truly sustainable investment objects	Support more effective government regulation to force a sustainability revolution by companies (performance standards, carbon taxes, review of licenses to operate, etc.)	Establish stringent packaging reduction standards for all consumer goods	Prioritize investment in companies that deliver product durability, repair, reuse and recycling	Prioritize investment in companies that create fulltime jobs and seek to avoid mass firings in times of turmoil
Excessive consumer debt creates economic unsustainability and too much consumerism creates environmental unsustainability, in contradiction with sustainable development and the goals of RI	Prioritize debt and equity for the greening and modernization of infrastructure and other re-engineering for greening the economy, invest in assets that promote experiential goods over consumption of stuff	Support regulations that establish minimum durability standards for consumer goods (it breaks, the manufacturer must fix it, analogous to the polluter pays principle)	Stimulate consumer marketing and education for green products and services, thus turning demand towards more sustainable consumption	

Table 12.1 (continued)

Problem	Possible ways forward	
Long distance trade in all manner of products creates carbon pollution that increases climate change risks	Support regulations for preferential purchasing standards for the kinds of goods that are or can be produced closer to home (for example, many agricultural and artisanal products)	
	Support carbon taxation of ocean shipping industry and airfreight	In RI rating and screening procedures, give strong weight to a carbon footprint criterion for transport of goods sourced and distributed
Systemic financial risks from excessive securitization and derivatives products	Support legislation to impose limits and controls on derivatives markets, introduce robust standards for product origination; split banks into transaction, deposit-taking and lending public utilities with deposit insurance, as distinct entities from the investment banks that will not be able to count on public money for bailouts (no more privatized profits and socialized losses)	
Too much lemming behavior in stock and bond markets, causing bubbles of increasing frequency and severity	Limits on passive investment strategies for large institutional investors	Require independent own credit rating by major players, and limit investment rules pegged to notation by the rating agencies

Table 12.1 (continued)

Problem	Possible ways forward	
Short term return expectations take priority over long term investment strategies and convictions	Institutional investors to lengthen investment performance measurement periods, to increase allocation to private equity and venture capital, to invest alongside corporates on industrial projects with well-defined sustainable development goals (special purpose vehicles), and to tie performance pay to multi year performance with claw back clauses	Restrictions on passive and near passive investment strategies, minimum requirements on diversification into small and mid cap, promotion of theme-driven investment strategies
Conflicts of interest. Investment decisions often benefit managers and intermediaries to the detriment of the financial and social needs of savers. The activism of RI engagement managers can be co-opted by the commercial interests of the corporate loan officers, investment bankers or insurance underwriters belonging to the same financial conglomerate.	Support rewrite of Fiduciary Duty laws to require attention to the economic and social conditions that underpin a prosperous and sustainable investment universe, with personal penalties for negligence and lack of due diligence; in short, introduce a sustainable development criterion in fiduciary law	Find ways of immunizing against the conflicts of interest within a commercial bank/investment bank/insurance company that is also a manager of mutual funds and institutional mandates.
Increasing inequality and economic injustice throughout society, in part driven by practices that favor finance over the real economy	Bring core corporate decisions into RI screening criteria: develop a criterion for the fair distribution of value creation between workers, execs, shareholders and lenders, attending to dividend policy, exec and board compensation, wages, share issues vs. borrowings, and payment of fair share of taxes.	

Table 12.1 (continued)

Problem	Possible ways forward	
Big banks have excessive political lobbying influence, which is used to maintain their oligopoly and plutocratic privileges	PRI to exclude banks that oppose structural reform aimed at avoiding repetition of financial crises or aimed at limiting excessive executive and trader pay; PRI to implement lobbying efforts to counteract bank lobbying against regulations that aim to curtail irresponsible banking; RI investors to exclude irresponsible banks from their investment portfolios.[12]	
Mainstream asset managers, including many RI, are generally not integrating climate change, arguably the biggest environmental challenge of the twentyfirst century, into strategic asset allocation, sub industry sector weighting, and stock and bond picking and weighting	Create thematic funds for listed stocks that integrate the economic, social and financial impacts of climate change at all levels of investment decision	Make major direct investments in carbon mitigation and climate adaptation projects in energy, transportation, housing, infrastructure, via special purpose vehicles, private equity, venture capital, or special purpose bonds

[12]Despite being saved by the government, the bailed out banks have since then consistently lobbied against banking regulation aimed at avoiding repeated crises, such as the Consumer Financial Protection Agency and the proposed tax on the super profits of bailed out banks.

strategic advantage. Eco-efficiency has not been able to outweigh the environmental damage that has accompanied economic expansion. Only in recessions have emissions and waste diminished in absolute terms. The concomitants of CSR – SRI or RI – cannot demonstrate having effected significant enough changes in corporate strategy and behavior to generally cause a change of course. They are a useful complement to regulation – a necessary instrument but far from sufficient – and the extent of their application and effectiveness is bounded by conflicts of interest along the investment supply chain. As mentioned earlier, engagement managers at mutual funds owned by banks or insurers dare not become too critical of companies that are big clients of their parents.

Another example of conflict of interest is the credit rating agencies. They are paid by the entities they rate, so their unreliability regarding corporate credits and structured products should come as no surprise. They do not factor climate risk into credit risk. Is it not yet material? Or is it simply their clients are not willing to pay them for it yet? Perhaps they will come around after the fact, as they often do. Furthermore, the sovereign ratings they have given in the past to countries like Brazil, Argentina or Turkey have more to do with their own political prejudices than with a country's real willingness and ability to pay. Leading up to Lula's first presidential win and in the period thereafter, S&P, Moodys and Fitch all lowered their Brazil ratings drastically based on nothing more than fear of Lula's labor union credentials. Interest rates soared causing a recession that would otherwise not have materialized. Argentina's terrible sovereign risk rating during 2008–2009 bore no relation to its willingness and ability to pay and to the country's upbeat economic performance since the debt restructuring of 2002, but rather reveals resentment to President Kirchners rejection of the IMF's policies that brought the country to default and served the interests of the large money center banks rather than of the country.

The regulatory route includes a variety of means, such as tighter standards, more stringent capital requirements, state co-ownership, transaction taxes and so forth for financial services. In the environmental field it means clean air and water standards, emissions ceilings, carbon taxes, real enforcement, and penalties that really bite. These measures are necessary, and where they have been put into practice robustly, they work. A Tobin-type tax on trading, as proposed by Mr. Turner, the head of the UK's financial authority, would help reduce churn behavior in listed market portfolios and help public coffers without sacrificing direct investment, project finance, private equity or venture capital.

We know, and it is no secret, that this financial and economic crisis was foreseeable, foreseen, foretold,[13] and that nobody in command wanted to listen and much less believe or act on it, even those that knew it was coming. In the infamous words of Chuck Prince III, CEO of Citigroup just before it collapsed and he got fired, 'you keep dancing while the music plays'. Why is this so? What makes people keep

---

[13] Nouriel Roubini was the most vocal, but at least a dozen other top economists gave strong and timely warnings, such as Kenneth Rogoff, Raghu Rajan, Nassim Taleb, Hyun Shin, William White, Gillian Tett, and Paul Krugman. Roubini references them in RGE Monitor, 1 May 2009.

acting in ways they know are likely end in disaster? The question applies to the looming climate crisis as well as to the extant financial crisis.

There are two kinds of explanation, at least. The psychoanalyst Slavoj Zisek says it is because of 'fetishist disavowal'.[14] Disavowal is involved in thinking: It won't happen, or It won't happen to me, or I can get away in time. What to do about this then? In my experience, people's behavior in business is driven by monetary incentives (pay, profits, fringe benefits) and nonmonetary incentives (social recognition, prestige, fame). In other spheres it may be driven by a sense of solidarity, or strong political, religious, esthetic or ethnic beliefs that are not self-directed. But in business, most people cannot conceive of a different way of making money or earning a living than how they are used to doing it; as in life most cannot bring themselves to change the way they live unless they have to or unless they think they will be much better off if they change. That's why, when the public good is at stake, the state has to push people via command and control regulation and penalties on the one hand and with incentives on the other.

Green Infrastructure Renewal as the Priority Over Wasteful Consumption

In the developed world we need to design and transition towards an economic order that makes more money from the growth of dematerialized goods and services and less from unnecessary stuff that creates more pollution and waste. We have to tilt the scale of monetary value-creation more in line with the social and environmental values we want to protect. What gets rewarded most has to change, so that capital can get the highest return from goods and services that do less environmental damage. In other words, the role of RI is to invest in the transition from today's industrial and consumption reality to what is required in a sustainable tomorrow. A simple example to illustrate: RI in the water sector means investing in the preservation and wholesale distribution of clean water at affordable rates to the public rather than buying shares in bottled water companies, which is the most inefficient and polluting way of distributing water. Wherever investment in bottled water for retail sale is more profitable than investing in wholesale distribution (potable water plants, distribution through pipes, metering, waste water treatment, etc.), RI should lobby to change this. Whenever equally financially attractive shares are available in wholesale water supply they should be favored over bottlers. Sustainable investment in water is not consistent with investment in bottled water companies.

---

[14]Slavoj Zizek: '...our everyday dealing is controlled by what in psychoanalysis we call the mechanism of fetishist disavowal. 'Je sais bien, mais quand même...' 'I know very well, but...' You know, we can know very well the possible catastrophic consequences, but somehow you trust the market, you think things will somehow work out, and so on and so on. It's absolutely crucial to analyze this, not only in economy, but generally.' (Zizek 2009)

RI's Role in the Transition to a Green Economy

The most important substantive move for RI is to prioritize finding profitable invest-ment opportunities in the green renewal of energy, transportation, real estate and infrastructure. Transforming the economy from a high carbon to a low carbon econ-omy will require enormous investment, will open up new career paths, will require new skills, and will generate new jobs and taxable income. The anti-recession stimu-lus plans in China, Europe and the US allocate up to 30% of spending to the greening of the economy. This is a very promising and good start. But it will need to be followed through by the private sector on a big scale.

The United Nations Framework Convention on Climate Change indicates that investment in the order of USD 300–400 billion per year will be required by 2030 to reduce emissions and deal with the impacts of climate change. This amounts from 1 to 2% of anticipated global investment for all purposes, or less than 1% of global GDP at that date. This level of commitment is doable, and the role of private sector investment is paramount; it will represent almost 90% of the future investment and financial flows (UNEP FI 2009). Particularly important is the observation that such investment has benefits not only for containing climate change and adapting to it, but also for job creation, economic growth and quality of life.

Investment firm Alliance Bernstein Advisors corroborates these figures in a recent study (ABA 2009). They state that a comprehensive set of efforts to sig-nificantly reduce emissions of carbon dioxide (CO_2) will cost an estimated US\$5 trillion in aggregate by 2030 just to reduce the CO_2 emissions from station-ary sources. Nonetheless, ABA believes the cost is manageable financially. Their model projects incremental spending related to mitigating climate change (including expenses related to carbon capture and storage) rising to approximately \$500 billion in 2030. This is certainly a large number, but represents less than 2% of forecasted global capital spending in the same year. As a further point of comparison, global military spending in 2006 exceeded \$1 trillion. Clearly, if the political will is there, the world can afford to mitigate emissions and adapt to climate change. Equally clearly, transitioning to a green economy opens up huge and profitable opportunities for private equity and venture capital.

In short, the greening of Private Equity and Venture Capital stands out as the next frontier in RI.

Modern Portfolio Management Technology Hampers Responsible Investment

Consider the incongruity of being mandated to produce positive long term invest-ment results for the preservation of capital but measuring the risk of obtaining this by volatility measurements that have nothing to do with macroeconomic risk, sovereign risk, even microeconomic risk. The yardstick is what happens in the stock mar-ket, not what happens in the rest of the world. 'Risk aversion' has come to mean aversion to departing too much from what everybody else is investing in or disinvesting and at about the same time they are doing it. In practice this means that the technology of index-relative investment ends up determining portfolio composition and investment strategy, which is putting the cart before the horse.

Indices like the MSCI or the FTSE, which most institutional investors use to fashion their portfolios, mirror the relative capitalization weights of companies as these weights are in the present moment. In other words, these indices reflect the structure of the economy and the beliefs of investors as is and not what is required in order to sustain wealth creation in the future. We know the world economy is not working within the limitations imposed by its natural resources and that stock and bond markets are generally not pricing this in. As mentioned already, this is particularly true of climate change. Investing for the future by looking at the traffic marks receding in the back mirror is not particularly anticipatory, or clever, or conducive to good long term investment performance, particularly at a time in history when one crisis leads to another. Investment managers operate in a technocratic straightjacket that works only when things are going well, only in bull markets, but is useless for spotting and getting through crisis and bubbles.

It is well known that the biggest gains in active investment are made when correctly anticipating the future valuation of equities. If a Responsible Investor is convinced that sustainable development is a precondition for the health of the economy in the future and that new environmental treaties and laws, changing consumer attitudes, and the inevitable impacts of climate change will have material effects on the competitiveness of countries and the profitability of companies, then the prudent investment philosophy is to be anticipatory and have a suitable early adopter process in place, so as not to be caught with large holdings that suddenly get down-rated, loose value and conform to what is fast becoming a past reality. The investor who follows index-relative investing or passive investment strategies will be saddled with large chunks of assets that are overvalued from a sustainability point of view. The irony is that most Responsible Investors follow indexing strategies for their core portfolios.

In the US, the concept of fiduciary duty under ERISA has been denatured by successive Department of Labor rulings under Republican administrations. The test of prudent investment conduct is conventional conduct. Trustees and managers find protection in lemming behavior. The *reductio ad absurdum* of passive index investing is that if everybody followed its dictate there would be no investors to make prices and there would be no buying and selling of shares. It is a self-defeating doctrine.

Integration of environmental, social and governance criteria in portfolio composition is permitted by ERISA if and only if it is 'material' to stock price performance, and in practice materiality must be verified in the short term. This can be criticized on two grounds. First, why should the financial interest of the saving public trump their environmental, social and ethical interests? Particularly when there is no necessary conflict between competitive long term returns and ethical guidelines applied to investment. Second, investors, managers and regulators can recognize a longer term time dimension of materiality – that the process whereby ESG issues become material means that what may not be material today may well be strongly material tomorrow (witness the history of materiality of asbestos, tobacco, contaminated land, and, in the making, carbon emissions and climate change impacts). An investor needs to be an active investor, and act with informed conviction before the world verifies the hypothesis he or she is acting upon.

Thus, fiduciary duty law needs to be reinterpreted and understood to include the environmental and social interests of principals and not only their short-term financial interests. A legal ruling of negligence against pension trustees or fund managers for failing to take some aspect of climate change into account would do wonders for RI. Being party in such a lawsuit should be on the UNPRI legislative agenda.

Conflicts of Interest Along the Investment Supply Chain – An Area for Engagement Activities by Pension Funds?

RI engagement activities look into the behavior of the supply chains in areas such as child labor issues, ethnic discrimination, corporate corruption, environmental purchasing standards and so forth. RI should also pay close attention to its own supply chain. RI mutual fund companies and pension funds have not been notably active against the bankrupting practices by the major money center banks they buy services from or hold shares in. Objections to lending to 50 times overleveraged hedge funds? Objections to TARP funds not being lent on to good customers but kept for acquisitions, bonuses, private planes, office décor? Objections to major money center banks transferring revenues to tax havens instead of paying their fair share of business taxes? Objections to boards approving huge bonuses despite the fact US money center banks are insolvent or would be were it not for being bailed out by the taxpayer? They had $1.8T losses vs. $1.4T capital going into 2009.

The Great Recession creates real opportunities for responsible actors, for the very large sovereign funds and pension funds, to promote 'a new paradigm for financial markets,' to borrow a phrase from George Soros. Clearly, if the pension funds at the core of the UN PRI were to act in concert they are in a position to be able to influence the behavior of the investment supply chain. And they have the standing to propose and put backbone into regulatory reforms. In the current crisis, not doing so is a major missed opportunity and calls into question whether Responsible Investment lives up to its worthwhile goals.

A Way to Integrate Climate Change in Portfolio Practice

In a recent Ceres survey (Ceres 2010), nearly three-quarters of asset managers said they do not expressly consider climate risks in their overall due diligence; half ignore climate risks, considering it non material. This is astonishing in light of all the scientific, economic, and financial research on climate risks and impacts (Enkvist et al. 2007, Hansen 2008, Stern 2006). Half of those who do consider it material nonetheless do nothing about it because their clients do not ask for it. In The World Bank blog a commentator suggests another answer: it may be because they don't know how. This may well be true, so let me present one approach to doing so that I've developed together with Natixis Asset Management, a French asset manager that ranks among the top 20 in assets worldwide (Joly 2009). NAM launched a fund based on this approach in November 2009. By year end it quickly raised € 100 million from French pension funds, proving the commercial viability and latent interest in a high alpha actively-managed climate fund with global exposure to listed equities managed without tracking error constraints to the traditional indexes.

This approach follows a straightforward investment process. Step One is the identification of salient and different types of climate impact to different sectors of the economy, based on themes/ sub themes developed on the basis of scientific research. It results in the selection of the sub industry sectors with most relevance for GHG emissions mitigation and adaptation to the consequences of climate change. We call this *Climate Impact Analysis*. Step Two is *Stock Selection* within the selected sub industry sector, on the basis of congruence with the sub themes and financial attractiveness in the short, medium or long term. This results in the Fund's investment universe of qualified companies. Step Three is the construction of the *Model Portfolio* based on an explicit set of portfolio composition guidelines such as relative country attractiveness, geographic diversification, capitalization size, liquidity, and potential for gain. Finally, step Four is the actual portfolio of 70 names with exposure in over 39 sectors in 36 countries, with a strong representation of emerging markets (Joly 2009).[15]

Concluding Remarks

'Responsible investing' should be responsible to the people who actually earned the money that is being invested – the vast working and middle class base of our economies. The mainstreaming of RI into the large investment houses sometimes seems to lose sight of this. I have pointed out that RI turns out to have been of no help in predicting the crisis and escaping from its effects. Worse, it does not seem to be addressing how to create alternatives to yet another crisis of the same or greater proportion.

I have suggested that modern portfolio theory (MPT), the efficient markets hypothesis, and index investing have failed. Reality has proved them wrong. In addition, these tools do not provide any viable way forward how to construct a portfolio that is not subject to the next financial crisis. RI is challenged to lead the way in theorizing new constructs to replace MPT. Sustainable development criteria might be a good place to start, agreeing upon the social and economic purposes of each asset

---

[15]The investment process and its results can be accessed at http://www.am.natixis.com/climatechange/eng/index.htm

category (commodities, equities, fixed income) and investing only in the products in each category that meet those purposes.

If we recognize excessive consumerism as an environmental problem and excessive consumer debt as a systemic financial risk, we should also pay close attention to the work of Joseph Stiglitz and Amartya Sen in developing, for the government of France, an alternative measure of national economic well being to GDP or GNP. As we know, the 'recovery' being touted in GNP runs concomitantly with growing unemployment and social suffering, and growing environmental degradation. We should perhaps recognize GNP growth as a measure of how proportionately worse things are getting rather than how much better. Here again is an intellectual challenge for RI and an opportunity for creativity in product innovation.

As I also suggested, a challenge still to be met by RI is analysis, sector by sector and company by company of those which equitably distribute surplus income and earnings, so that more employees and retirees can share in the value creation.

Finally, my point about Fiduciary Duty law is that it must be updated and redefined. In the US it is now geared to preservation of MPT behavior and the test of its satisfaction is whether an asset manager conforms to what everybody else is doing. This has become a recipe for crisis-making rather than for acting as an intelligent and prudent man would for the long term preservation of capital, the original criterion established in the case of Harvard vs. Amory in 1830.[16]

In conclusion, RI has much work to do to live up to its name and purpose. Theoretic work, to replace the obsolete MPT paradigm. And product development work, as there is a wide range of ways for different managers to go about doing RI. An old adage is appropriate here: when the going gets tough, the tough get going. It's time, now.

Acknowledgments I thank William Sokol of Weinberg, Roger & Rosenfeld for his comments and contribution to this chapter, and for enlightening discussions over the years about RI, even before it had a name.

References

ABA 2009. Abating climate change. What will be done and the consequences for investors. Alliance Bernstein Advisors.
Atkinson, Anthony, Thomas Picketty, and Emmanuel Saez, E. 2009. Top Incomes in the Run of History. NBER Working Paper, October 2009. Available at: www.nber.org/papers/w15408 Accessed 15 January 2010.
Calculated Risk Blog 2010. Available at: http://www.calculatedriskblog.com/2010_01_01_archive.html. Accessed 13 January 2010.

---

[16]The actual text: 'All that can be required of a trustee to invest is, that he shall conduct himself faithfully and exercise a sound discretion. He is to observe how men of prudence, discretion and intelligence manage their own affairs, not in regard to speculation, but in regard to the permanent disposition of their funds, considering the probable income, as well as the probable safety of the capital to be invested.'

Ceres 2010. Investment Managers Lagging in Response to Climate Change Risks and Opportunities. Available at: http://www.ceres.org/Page.aspx?pid=1175 Accessed May 2010.

Dolan, M. 2009. Dire decade heightens savers' anxiety' Reuters (30 December 2009) Available at: http://uk.reuters.com/assets/print?aid=UKLNE5BT00720091230 Accessed May 2010.

Enkvist, P., T. Nauclér, and J. Rosander. 2007. A cost curve for GHG reduction. McKinsey Quarterly 1:35–45.

Falnes, Kristian. 2010. Det verste ma gjør som investor. DN.no. Available at: http://www.dn.no/forsiden/borsMarked/article1817927.ece Accessed May 2010.

Hansen, James. 2008. Global Warming 20 years later: Tipping points near. Testimony to House Select Committee on Energy Independence and Global Warming. http://globalwarming.house.gov/ Accessed 2009.

International Labor Organization 2010. Press Release. Available at: http://www.ilo.org/global/lang%E2%80%93en/index.htm Accessed 26 January 2010.

Joly, Carlos. 2009. From Climate Change to Investment Strategy White Paper. Paris: Natixis Asset Management

Milliman 2009. Milliman 100 Pension Funding Index October 2009. Available at: http://www.milliman.com/expertise/employee-benefits/products-tools/pension-funding-study/index.php Accessed 8 January 2010.

Rockefeller Institute 2010. State Revenue Report No. 78. Available at: http://www.rockinst.\penalty-\@Morg/government_finance/state_revenue_reports.aspx Accessed May 2010.

Saez, Emmanuel. 2008. Striking it richer: The evolution of top incomes in the United States (updated with 2007 estimates). Pathways Magazine (Spring 2009). Available at: http://www.stanford.edu/group/scspi/media_magazines.html Accessed 25 January 2010.

Speth, James Gustave. 2008. The Bridge at the End of the World. New Haven, CT: Yale University Press.

Stern, Nicholas. 2006 The Stern Review: The Economics of Climate Change. London: HM Treasury.

UN Principles of Responsible Investment. 2009. http://www.unpri.org/about/. Accessed 20 October 2009.

US Government, House of Representatives. 2009. http://globalwarming.house.gov/ Accessed 2009.

Washington Times. 2009. Pensions Hurt Worldwide, Washington Times, 25 May 2009.

White House 2009. Available at: http://www.whitehouse.gov/Omb/Blog/ Accessed 25 May 2009.

Worldwatch Institute. 2010. State of the World Report 2010. Washington, DC: The Worldwatch Institute.

Zisek, Slavoj. 2009. On capitalism, healthcare, financial crisis, Democracy Now! Available at: http://www.worldbulletin.net/news_detail.php?id=48773 Accessed May 2010.

Chapter 13
Why Responsible Investing?

Henrik Syse

Introduction

This article is not about me. Nonetheless, a brief personal introduction will put my argument in context:

From 2005 until 2008 I worked for Norges Bank Investment Management (NBIM), for most of this time as their Head of Corporate Governance; indeed, the first one to have that title, since this was a new department within the bank. The term Corporate Governance was used to denote the bank's work on active ownership, meaning involvement through voting and engagement with companies in the bank's equity portfolio.[1]

NBIM is not just any money manager. It is a part of the Norwegian Central Bank, and it functions as the manager of one of the world's largest sovereign wealth funds, the 'Norwegian Government Pension Fund – Global'; known also as (and previously called) the 'Petroleum Fund', since the fund consist of the Norwegian state's petroleum-related income.[2]

The fund is explicitly set up as a vehicle for securing financial value. It is not a development or environment fund. But it also has an ethical dimension, and this is reflected in two ways: firstly, the fund should not be invested in a way that goes against the most basic moral values held by the Norwegian public, or in a way that is in clear contravention of internationally recognized norms; secondly, the fund must preserve values over the long term, on behalf of future generations, and thus has an obligation not to let short-term possibilities for financial gain come in the way

H. Syse (✉)
Peace Research Institute Oslo (PRIO), Oslo, Norway
e-mail: HENRIK@prio.no

[1] The views presented in this article are purely my own and should not in any way be taken to represent the views or opinions of NBIM or the Norwegian Government Pension Fund – Global.

[2] The fund is customarily referred to as the second-biggest worldwide in the category of Sovereign Wealth Funds, with assets under management totaling more than US$ 500 bn. as of November 2010. For articles covering sovereign wealth funds, including the Norwegian fund, see http://www.ft.com/indepth/sovereignfunds.

W. Vandekerckhove et al. (eds.), *Responsible Investment in Times of Turmoil*,
Issues in Business Ethics 31, DOI 10.1007/978-90-481-9319-6_13,
© Springer Science+Business Media B.V. 2011

of long-term sustainability. For the first of these purposes, the Finance Ministry (the fund's principal) has an independent Ethics Council ('Council on Ethics'), which recommends companies for exclusion if they are seen to violate the basic ethical standards set out in the fund's guidelines. NBIM, on the other hand, fulfills the second of these purposes through its 'Corporate Governance' (or, as it is now called, 'Ownership Strategies') group, which works actively on engaging with companies in the fund's equity portfolio on issues related to environmental policies, social and ethical challenges, and corporate governance, in order to secure long-term sustainability.[3]

My aim here is not to discuss the Council on ethics, NBIM, or the Norwegian Petroleum Fund per se, but rather the peculiar form of middle position such a fund finds itself in when it comes to responsible investment (RI).

To put it in very simple terms, one could imagine two kinds of funds at each end of an RI spectrum:

1. A purely financially driven fund, which has as its only motivation to secure returns for its owners, without any considerations of an ethical nature.
2. A purely ethics-driven fund, which makes investments based on ethical and social criteria, regardless of whether these are likely to make money for the end owner of the invested funds or not. (In *comparing* different ethical/social investment opportunities, though, such a fund could make decisions based on which opportunity would give the best projected returns, but this would not be the primary concern.)

Anyone familiar with the world of investing will know that these archetypes are rarely found in pure form. Most fund managers within category 1 will admit that *some* factors most naturally (albeit sometimes indirectly) labeled 'ethical' will play a role in their investment decisions, such as the dangers of negative publicity, risks of litigation in cases of unethical or illegal behavior within portfolio companies, and of course the danger of fraud. Also, most investors in category two will have some kind of financial incentive when investing their money; they do not simply want the money to disappear, but rather want to preserve their assets through their investment activity. Otherwise, it is not really investment in any reasonable sense of the term, but simply spending (which, of course, is legitimate enough, but hardly our topic here). An attempt at combining an ethics-driven agenda with returns, going beyond the framework of the Norwegian Petroleum Fund, can be found in the idea of 'impact investing' (Bugg-Levine 2009).

The point I wish to make is that many mainstream funds and their fund managers – especially pension funds and similar public funds with a large base of end owners and a long time horizon – fall somewhere between the two archetypes in an interesting way. They are actors charged with securing returns, and as such they have

---

[3]For the fund's ethical guidelines, see http://www.regjeringen.no/en/dep/fin/Selected-topics/the-government-pension-fund/responsible-investments/the-ethical-guidelines.html?id=434894.

no explicitly social agenda as their *raison d'être*. But simultaneously, they have several (more or less) clearly articulated ethical responsibilities that play an important role in their day-to-day work. These arguably include:

- a responsibility to live up to standards expected by one's end owners,
- a responsibility to abide by the highest standards set within the investment community,
- a responsibility to contribute to the development of a better and more transparent market place,
- a responsibility to address issues that are not necessarily detrimental to short-term returns, but which in the longer run can pose severe risks to the legitimacy, functionality, and profitability of the market place – these include environmental, social, and governance-related (ESG) issues. (For a good overview of the way in which investors can address these sorts of issues through investor activism, see Sullivan and Mackenzie 2006).

The adoption of the UN Principles for Responsible Investment (UN PRI)[4] is a clear sign of the increasing acceptance of these responsibilities by mainstream funds, including funds that traditionally would not have been categorized as socially responsible investment (SRI) funds.

It is against this background that I want to ask the following question: What is, and what should be, the motivation for engaging in responsible investment for such an investor, i.e., an investor with long-term financial returns as its goal? Should one engage in RI in order to make more money, or (certainly a related issue) to minimize risk, or to comply with rules and expectations, or to make the markets (or some segments within it) better and more legitimate, or to make the world (or some part of it) a better place?

The obvious, mainstream answer to the question is that these belong together. By skillfully and prudently integrating ethical concerns, and creating a portfolio strategy that takes such concerns seriously (either through stock picking or active ownership – or both), we do reduce risk and produce better returns. Thus, the primary motivation is to secure returns, and the other concerns are instrumental.

I think, however, that there are three weaknesses to the mainstream view, by which I mean the view that even RI must in the end conform purely to a business and profit logic, and that all other concerns are in the end instrumental to that logic. I will discuss these, and thereafter conclude by linking these concerns with the outlooks for responsible investment after the financial crisis.

Single or Multiple Motivations?

First, human beings do not have only one motivation at a time. I admit that some motivations may be 'primary', a phrase I used above. By this I mean that this

---

[4] See www.unpri.org.

motivation (or, we could also say, 'intention' or 'aim')[5] is what puts something on one's agenda in the first place. To take an everyday example:[6] If my primary motivation in going to a restaurant is to eat good food, I will seek out restaurants that serve good food, and then let other concerns (getting a nice table, a place where I can meet my friends, etc.) be subservient to that. If, on the other hand, my primary motivation is to hang out with friends and have a good conversation with them, other criteria than food will be essential to my choice, or at least to the narrowing down of my choice. After, in the latter scenario, having found three restaurants with good seating arrangements, where it's convenient to meet, I may choose the one out of these three restaurants which is reputed to have the best food. *Then* the food would be a motivation for my choice, indeed, but only a secondary motivation.

In other cases, though, I may not really be clear about what are primary and what are secondary considerations. My different aims in going out to dinner may be mutually reinforcing, and they are all necessary, although neither is sufficient in itself. (I would not go out alone, and I would not eat in a place with bad food.) So if someone asks me why I am *really* doing it, I would be hard pressed to give one, unequivocal answer.

In the case of mainstream investment funds – by which I mean funds without an explicit ethical goal (i.e., not a development fund or an environmental fund, etc.) – we seem to be dealing with an entity that has a clearly stated primary motivation: namely, creating returns as part of one's fiduciary duty towards one's end owners. But even if that is the case, certain ethical considerations can play a real role in making decisions about where to invest or how to engage with companies in one's portfolio – a role that often seems to go beyond the merely instrumental. This can happen in several ways: (a) as a fulfillment of fiduciary duty, in the sense that the end owner(s) has (or have) expressed clearly that there are some non-financial values they do wish preserved in and through their investment activity; (b) as an acceptance that unethical behavior creates financial risk in the long run; or (c) as a result of laws or outside expectations, such as the rules laid down by national commissions that

---

[5] By 'motivation' I mean what drives a person to do something. By 'intention' and 'aim' I mean the end result aimed at, although 'intention' can also be used in a sense closer to the state of mind of the actor, which often underlies the expression 'acting with a good (or a bad) intention'. Michael Bratman defines 'intention' as 'conduct-controlling' attitudes, or – as he puts it – 'pro-attitudes', i.e., attitudes that say something about what I want, judge desirable, care about, etc. (Bratman 1987: 6, 15). This comes close to the way in which I use 'motivation' here.

[6] As one of the book's editors has perceptively pointed out during the review process, such examples can be misleading, since they most clearly apply to intuitions related to the sort of situation described – in this case, the choice of restaurant. And obviously, choosing a restaurant does not equate with, nor truly resemble, investing. My point, however, is to tease out a general point about the thoughts and actions of human beings, namely, the relationship between primary and secondary motivations, and as such I believe the example works well. It may even be more useful to utilize an example from another walk of life than one related to the topic mainly under consideration, in order to avoid an issue-specific discussion of some particular point within (in our case) responsible investment.

oversee financial dealings, documents such as the Global Compact or the United Nations Principles of Responsible Investment, or even expectations and rules within one's own investment company.

The important point to note, however, is that the ethical goals we are dealing with here (which could be avoidance of child or slave labor, clean water policies, or transparent and honest reporting) all have such an independent value – being what most would consider fair or just actions in themselves – that the person or persons working on them will inevitably come to see them as important in their own terms. They are admittedly on your table and need to be addressed because they are also financial concerns, directly or indirectly. But they are hardly mere means to an end; most sane human beings would say that they are laudable goals as such. To use my own experience from the corporate-governance work of the Norwegian fund as an example: We would raise issues touching on children's welfare and safety with a range of companies. The dialogues would be initiated from a need to manage risk and secure the legitimacy and proper governance of the companies under scrutiny, thus safeguarding the fund's long-term financial returns. But if you work hard to ensure that children are not mistreated, it is rather obvious that this comes across as so important that it also becomes a goal in itself. The conscience of those working on the case, and even of the investor and the target company (to the extent we can speak about a corporation's or company's conscience; identity may be a better term), will most likely be troubled by dealing with such a matter half-heartedly or without a proper attempt at achieving success, once the process has been started and it has been put firmly on the agenda.

Put into other words: It is hardly sound or reasonable to think of the world of investment as ideally consisting of people with one motivation and one idea in their heads only, period: to make money. It also lacks nuance to think of ethics merely as instrumental, and therefore not as a proper motivating aim in itself. To think in terms of primary and secondary motivations is more useful.

Division of Labor

This leads me to my second point. Imagine a CEO who is really single-minded; not at all living up to the more pluralistic ideal I have just pointed to. He (in the name of political correctness, I prefer to use the male pronoun here, given the unpleasantness of the person) has noticed that several employees with young children keep working shorter hours and express dissatisfaction at the location of the local kindergartens, which are all far away from the company's offices. He decides to start a kindergarten at the office site. This will be a good service to the employees, making them happier and more content. And it will mean that they can come earlier and leave later, without having to leave their young children in the kindergartens for a longer time than they would prefer to, and without having the same time pressure vis-à-vis the kindergarten's closing hour. In short, we are faced with a win-win proposition.

The question is, however: What kind of person should he hire to run the kindergarten? Should he pick someone as eager to save money and perform efficiently as he is himself? Or should he pick someone who is really good at looking after children? The latter pick would also have to stay within his or her budget, of course. But apart from that, it seems rather obvious that the best person to pick, who would fulfill the aim of making employees happy, would be someone whose primary motivation would be different from that of the CEO, namely, someone who would be keen to give the children the best care possible.

This reminds us of an important fact: that different roles demand different qualities in the persons playing them. And thus, to go back to the world of investing, a person in charge of RI should admittedly be someone who knows the ins and outs of investing, with the necessary prudence and care, but he or she should also be someone for whom the actual contents of social responsibility or ESG is a specialty, and someone who really cares about such issues. ESG issues are complex and demand different kinds of measuring and KPIs (Key Performance Indicators) than purely financially oriented investment activities. Even if RI or ESG strategies are used for the sake of securing higher or safer returns, hence making monetary gain the primary motivation – or rather, one could say, *for that exact reason*! – those working on such strategies must have real competence within the social (or more broadly ESG) areas addressed if the work is to be done properly. This, again, means that a work force with few competencies outside of hard-core finance, and so to speak illiteracy in the fields of environmental, social, or governance-related affairs, will be badly placed to integrate such concerns in the investment agenda – and do it well.

Hence, if the mainstream view says that financial value should always be the ultimate and decisive factor in making investment decisions, this view of a division of labor and competencies point in a slightly different direction. Still, ethics would admittedly be instrumental, institutionally speaking, to an overarching goal of producing financial returns. (This is in line with the distinction between primary and secondary motivations that was used above.) I say 'institutionally speaking', because we are talking about institutions whose goal it is to produce financial returns. They would change their meaning and mission if this were not the case. But at the same time, they may set themselves intermediary goals of great importance, for which you need top-notch people intent on reaching those intermediary goals in a competent and professional way, because that will serve the larger goal. Many of these intermediary goals will, moreover, be shaped and molded through interaction with wider societal ideas and expectations (such as prevailing views about the environment, corruption, labor rights, child labor, women's rights, etc.). My point is that such matters cannot be addressed by people who see them as purely coincidental to a larger goal, with no need for in-depth, topic-specific competence. And the more important and weighty the 'intermediary' goal, the more competence and strength are arguably needed.

Relative or Absolute Returns?

The final, rather weak part of what I called the mainstream view is the belief that investment activity primarily consists in securing relative returns, i.e., results that beat the market. According to such a view, the investment enterprise is competitive, and RI constitutes just another strategy for beating the competition. Admittedly, in most cases, the best business strategies of a company or an investor are not something that the company (or the investor) will want to share, for the exact reason that beating the competitors to the best ideas is the surest way of gaining a foothold in the market and staying ahead of the pack.

But when it comes to ESG improvements in an equity portfolio the improvements will often gain all participants in the market, since the gains are, at their best, market wide (i.e., not just affecting one single stock), at least in the longer run. This is especially true of social and environmental issues, but could also be true of governance changes that come to affect the standards and expectations within an entire market. This also means that improvements in these areas, that *others* can help make, will be to *my* advantage. This surely creates a free-rider problem. And these are, to complicate the matter further, issues where creating change often takes time, and where we cannot immediately measure the quantitative gains. The financial plusses are often seen only in the long run.

Why should, then, an investor spend time on such issues – large-scale environmental and social issues, and system-wide governance improvements, most clearly among them – if they are not to the immediate benefit of one's own portfolio? Here, what is often called the universal-owner argument provides an important answer. A universal owner is the kind of shareholder who holds ownership positions in such a wide variety of companies and markets that she becomes exposed to the general functionality and sustainability of those markets. Several authors have focused on the challenges large investors have as universal owners. (Gjessing and Syse 2007, Syse 2008, Monks 2001, Thamotheram and Wildsmith 2006).

Social conditions, governance mechanisms, absence of corruption, eco-diversity, clean drinking water, absence of large refugee streams: all of these are crucial factors affecting the functionality and profitability of markets in the longer run, and for a 'universal owner', especially one with a long time-horizon (which is typically true of public wealth funds and pension funds), they will have to factored in, not as political issues, but as long-term financial and risk-related issues.

As already indicated, one can always lie back and expect others to address these market-wide, systemic questions related to ESG. The free rider will, after all, benefit as much as the activists. Yet, there is a danger related to this particular field if there is not a broad supply of attention, work, and critical thinking. Good ESG and RI policies are after all complex; this is a field in need of fresh ideas and new research. And in spite of being in vogue as a discussion topic, we are still a long way away from making sustained attention to ESG truly mainstream.

Hence, no investor seriously believing that unsustainable ESG practices in the markets are dangerous, can sit back and simply expect that others will take care of it. The fight to create a better marketplace, which retains functionality and opportunities for profitability in the long run, has to be everyone's task. Arguably, this is not true only of what we can reasonably call large universal investors, since sub-standard ESG practices will also have detrimental effects locally, and since a functioning and legitimate market is a prerequisite for most sorts of equity trading. The latter point is, however, one I will not discuss in any detail here.

But with what motivation should one do it? To earn money? Yes, surely, but at the same time with a longer time-horizon and a wider view of social responsibility than the classic 'the business of business is business' maxim. Just as an effective shoemaker must truly care about making good shoes and long-term customer satisfaction, even if her primary motivation is earning money, it makes sense for many kinds of investors actually to care about social responsibility and ESG issues, because lack of attention to such issues heightens the risk of serious market abuse, lack of long-term sustainability, and loss of legitimacy. And just as we all need to make an effort in order to change deeply-held prejudices within a community, so a broad range of serious investors must do their bit to move the environmental, social, and governance-related concerns from a niche associated with naïve 'do-gooding' and over to mainstream investment practices.

Conclusion: ESG After the Financial Crisis

The financial turmoil of 2008 and 2009, with continued repercussions in the markets for years to come, in my view strengthens the arguments just made for a serious integration of ESG issues into investment practices rather than as an incidental, purely instrumental concern. By 'serious integration' I mean that it becomes something earnestly engaged in by competent actors intent on bettering the behavior of the markets as such.

The reasons, on a philosophical level, can be divided in two. First, the financial crisis has revealed myopia – nearsightedness – in parts of the financial industry, in the sense of an almost extreme attention to short-term financial gains on financial products, but far less attention to the larger social dimension of investments, including the responsibility vis-à-vis shareholders, the transparency of products sold, and the long-term trust in the markets. The proposals for securing more of a place for the long-term considerations go in different directions, with emphasis alternately on legal rules and self-regulation. But independently of the actual mechanisms that come to be built up to avoid the sorts of excesses that contributed to the financial crisis,[7] we can agree that short-term calculations must not be allowed to overshadow the legitimate rights of end owners and the long-term interests of the public at large, whose money is being invested. This also has consequences for incentive systems

---

[7] And I am not here claiming that short-termism or greed in financial companies alone produced the financial crisis; clearly, systemic factors, not least related to trade and debt imbalances, contributed heavily to the gravity of the crisis.

within the investment world, but most importantly for our purposes, it means that the financial and investment industry cannot look upon itself as existing in a social vacuum, where the consequences visited upon society at large are not integral to an evaluation of their success and legitimacy.

Second, the financial crisis has shown us that wider ethical and social concerns are not necessarily addressed in the everyday workings of a financial system, if they are not consciously and systematically looked after. In an ideal world, all relevant factors will be factored into investment decisions; i.e., if ESG issues are indeed important for the long-term functioning of corporations and markets they *will* become part of investment decisions. But with the financial crisis, that thesis has been dealt a serious blow. ESG issues are often less tangible and quantifiable than hard-core financial issues, and they demand a different sort of vocabulary and competence. And, not least, they often take time to discuss – and to understand. Accepting this, and thus accepting that time and space(s) are needed for truly addressing ESG and investment responsibilities, is hopefully one of the real and lasting results of the financial crisis.

References

Bratman, Michael E. 1987. Intentions, Plans, and Practical Reason. Cambridge, MA: Harvard University Press.

Bugg-Levine, Antony. 2009. Impact investing: Harnessing capital markets to drive development at scale. Beyond Profit 1 May/June 2009: 17–21.

Gjessing, Ola Peter, and Henrik Syse. 2007. Norwegian petroleum wealth and universal ownership. Corporate Governance 15: 427–437.

Monks, Robert A. G. 2001. The New Global Investors. Oxford: Capstone.

Sullivan, Rory and Craig Mackenzie. 2006. Shareholder Activism on Social, Ethical and Environmental Issues. In Responsible Investment, eds. Rory Sullivan and Craig Mackenzie, 150–157. Sheffield: Greenleaf.

Syse, Henrik. 2008. Investments, universal ownership, and public health. In International Public Health Policy and Ethics, ed. Michael Boylan, 175–188. Dordrecht: Springer.

Thamotheram, Raj and Helen Wildsmith. 2006. Putting the Universal Owner Hypothesis into Action: Why Large Retirement Funds Should Want to Collectively Increase Overall Market Returns and What They Can Do about It. Delegate Handbook Corporate Governance & Responsible Investment. May 31, 2006, Stockholm. Available at: http://www.rotman.utoronto. ca/icpm/files/Putting%20the%20Universal%20Owner%20Hypothesis%20into%20Action_ Raj%20Thamotheram%20and%20Helen%20Wildsmith.pdf. Accessed April 2010.

Post Scripta – An Owl's View

Jos Leys, Bert Scholtens, Henry Schäfer, Wim Vandekerckhove, Kristian Alm, and Silvana Signori

This *post scripta* is philosophical in nature. It is composed by the Owl who flies by night and reviews what has happened and what has been written and done during the day. The eyes of the Owl are sharp: he is able to focus and spot a tiny mouse. As he is flying high, the Owl is also able to oversee what individuals during the day have accomplished while working comparatively secluded and unaware of each other. By virtue of his timing and position, the Owl is able to come up with questions and interpretations of his own. The Owl is old and therefore rather grumpy; he is not easily persuaded nor lightly enthused.

In his eyes, so far, responsible investment has been a social failure. A lot of human energy has been spilled on zero-sum-games, a lot of money has been invested in projects that were financially unsustainable, such as housing for Americans without assets nor income and outright consumption by the Athenian citizen as well as by Joc Sixpack. The nature and the functioning of financial markets is still misunderstood by the largest part of the population and the financial edifice is vulnerable to hostile violence by outside forces such as angry masses or populist politicians and regulators. In times when myriad economic and social phenomena are financialized, i.e. embodied in securities and continuously quoted on markets, financial turmoil reflects social and economic turmoil. But this is not easily grasped by the majority of the population or by politicians who blame malicious and unidentified 'speculators' (*Financial Times*, Monday 10 May 2010: 9).

The financial crisis that serves as a mental background to all the contributions in this book was caused by financially irresponsible behaviour. People who had no income or assets to speak of, were often allowed to lie and were granted a loan to buy a house that, eventually, they could not afford (*Financial Times*, Thursday 13 May 2010: 6). Some populations indebted themselves in a manner that defies financial orthodoxy and elementary social discipline. Financial institutions were overleveraged and unable to absorb even the minor shock that was caused by the bursting of the credit bubble regarding American housing: banking equity was wiped out across the globe. If anything, managers of financial enterprises were found massively unable to protect let alone to produce shareholder value. Successively, shareholder value in the other industries too, was proven illusionary: stock prices fell sharply as it dawned that cash flows were pictured too rosy and investments were overstretched.

W. Vandekerckhove et al. (eds.), *Responsible Investment in Times of Turmoil*,
Issues in Business Ethics 31, DOI 10.1007/978-90-481-9319-6,
© Springer Science+Business Media B.V. 2011

The financial architecture has been proven a shaky edifice and the behaviour of many of its occupants largely irresponsible if not outright predatory. *Financially irresponsible*, that is.

If the above has any truth and pertinence in it, it seems strange that none of the contributors interprets the ethics, the sustainability, or the responsibility of finance as pertaining to finance itself. This observation applies to the marketing endeavours of the retail funds analysed by Sandberg to the macro-governance analysis by Waddell. Instead, all refer to ethical or (un)sustainable practices with reference to other spheres and topics, such as ecological topics, safety issues, social justice issues and many others. This blunt observation may easily explain the fact zoomed in upon by Waddell, namely that 'responsible investors' are not linked with the institutions and bodies that occupy themselves, *ratio essendi*, with the sustainability of the financial edifice itself, such as the IMF and the BIS. The fact that RI does not refer to the financial dimension of finance but solely to real world issues is also evident in Del Bosco and Misani: private equity can be deployed for funding initiatives that balance, somehow, financial, social and environmental considerations and hopefully attract customers with the necessary purchasing power. Likewise, private equity may also be deployed to fund hallal projects or may develop as a way to carry kosher investments (*Financial Times*, Tuesday 2 March 2010: 2). In fact, private equity as a funding technique can be deployed for every enterprise of the befitting scale and scope and an expected return that matches the risks involved.

The Owl finds that, in general, the contributors do not express any concern or opinion regarding the ethics of financial practices except for the demand that finance is used to finance sustainable projects or to create a sustainable society. When it comes to the content of those projects and the contours of a sustainable society, even the Owl cannot but be impressed by the wide and heterogeneous range of purposes to be pursued by investors that take into account ESG-factors. Put otherwise: what these ESG-factors are and by which techniques they are to be impressed upon financial processes.

Some contributors and investors are concerned with social justice and future stages of technological development, others want to cut off some industries from the body economic by refusing them access to liquidity. Indeed, a considerable part in the RI-endeavour is to exclude the production of preservatives, pork meat, nuclear energy, arms production, gambling, alcoholic beverages, cars, fast food, and so on. Most, if not all, of these corporate purposes are perfectly legitimate for other citizens and participants in the economy – if not, they would not thrive as businesses. Indeed, when a societal consensus on illegitimacy is actually present, activities are already legally excluded from access to the financial system, such as terrorism and narcotics. Hence it is solely when societal consensus is lacking that RI pops up in all shapes and colours. In view of this diversity then, it is not that simple to introduce non-financial responsibilities in the fiduciary duties of intermediaries, as Eccles demands. Indeed, there is no limit to what might be 'responsible investment' in this sense. Quite evidently and gaining momentum, nationalist-protectionist motives too, might be subsumed under ESG-factors: 'let us throw liquidity at the local community rather than deploy it in foreign activities.'

Coherence and consistency too become difficult, as some RI-purposes are bound to conflict with one another, such as the demand for not-shedding jobs and being as eco-efficient as possible. The demand for 'responsibility' with financial intermediaries, to go beyond the rationality of finance itself or beyond 'rational man' as Eccles has it, is in view of this, nothing but an invitation to arbitrariness on the side of people who very recently destroyed investor value on a massive scale. To circumvent the issue of heterogeneity of material focuses by turning to the governance of investee projects, as Cadman does, only postpones the pivotal question: in view of what goals and purposes should projects be governed by whom?

But, indeed, the Owl has to acknowledge the success story of 'Responsible Investment' – it has become omnipresent and numbers are rocketing.

The world's leading financial paper carries advertisements for 'socially responsible' or 'sustainable' products by index providers that occupy an entire page. A more striking symbol of success in conquering the minds can hardly be imagined (*Financial Times*, Friday 23 April 2010: 14).

Of course, the trillion dollar success of RI in terms of quantity ('assets under management') is first and foremost due to the aforementioned heterogeneity. When definitions are lacking and coherence is not a requirement, all assets under management can be RI. Whereas the exclusion of preservative production is viewed as RI by some religious factions in society, the promotion of preservative production is viewed as RI by the people who hold that human overpopulation is unsustainable. Added up, both RIs total the investment universe. Hence, astronomic numbers can be attained, because second order investment (in derivative-structuring, for instance) also enters the 'assets under management'.

The diversity in goals and purposes is, secondly, further complicated by a diversity in actual implementations: some exclude, some overweigh, some underweigh, some engage. In view of both diversities, several contributing authors demand a definition (and outcome) authored and maintained by an Authority. The authority of Government and the Law are called upon to end the bewilderment, to avoid in-compatibilities between conceptions and to guarantee integrity of the (particular) ESG-concept at hand. It is not easy to see though, how the secular state could come up with any other definition than that 'Responsible Investing' is simply within the boundaries of what the law permits in the real economy and discharging one's financial duties in the process. Unless of course the state would be colonized by one particular political or religious faction in society.

Anyway, the diversity in actual implementations also contributes to the numeric success of RI. Simply to exclude a few corporations from one's investment universe suffices to qualify a billion-USD-portfolio or an entire balance sheet of a bank as 'RI', irrespective of what the portfolio does contain.

A third contributory factor to the success of RI is the marketing endeavour by asset managers and banks. Actually, the composition of RI-portfolios does not differ too much from main stream portfolios, the consequences of which are highlighted by Weber et al. But, as might be expected on the basis of behavioural finance and economics: a good cause is more likely to attract customers than no cause at all. Hence, customers are approached by appealing to the human instinct to wish for a better future (who does not? *Ein guter Mensch sein! Ja, wer wärs nicht gern?*) and not by explicitly involving them in the less glamorous and even dirty work that goes on in our economies as well. Sandberg unmasks the illusions inherent in such marketing endeavours which do not prevent them from being effective.

Hence quite commonly now, the development and marketing of new financial structures is enhanced by referring to RI. For instance, the latest RI-product-offering that hit the Belgian retail market is a mutual fund that aims at capital protection at maturity and at obtaining 75% of the possible positive return of a an actively managed RI-index. The active management of the subjacent index consists in varying the exposure to a basket of stocks that itself also is actively managed in view of SRI-criteria within a range from 0 to 150%. If the marketing endeavour for this particular structure is successful, European RI-assets-under-management will go up a notch. But the lucid question 'What is your money doing right now?' regarding this particular investment vehicle has a quite clear answer: 'Your money does not *do*; only people *do*. For a while, your money is tied up in betting against other investors and the bets are on two levels. In the meantime, you will not receive dividends from the subjacent RI-shares.'

Real world impacts of such constructs are nil, unless, of course, one of the investors overplays his hand and goes bankrupt. Likewise, the recent launch of a Christian stock index, the Stoxx Europe Christian Index, 'comprised of 533 companies that only derive revenues from sources approved according to the values and principles of the Christian religion' (*Financial Times*, Tuesday 27 April 2010: 1), will not have any real world impact, except perhaps for launching a debate on 'the values and principles of the Christian religion' (*Financial Times*, Saturday 8 May 2010: 6). As a matter of fact, to state that companies are in an index is committing a particular financial illiteracy: it is not companies that are in an index, it is securities and their prices that are arithmetic components of an index. For financially lucid citizens, it is clear that moving liquidity from one security to another has no real world dimension at all except for the winning and losing between the players and the bonuses of the intermediaries. Buying stocks and selling others in order to cause real world effects is nothing but shadows of shadows hitting at each other in Plato's cave.

Indeed, in line with Sandberg, one might ask whether the supposition that financial activity shapes the world that is inherent in many of the contributions, has any merit at all. Every activity is financed somehow, but no financial act ever brings any activity about. The contribution by Engelen and van Essen indicates clearly that happenings on the stock market merely reflect information about (expectations of) future cash flows. Yet, the authors use ambiguous language by applying morally charged terminology; they do not clearly state that there is no such a thing as 'a reputation penalty' by participants in financial markets. The observed stock price movements, however, cannot be denied. The authors could reapply the research model to very recent occurrences, such as the reflection of the Toyota product recalls in the evolution of its share price. But it is not solely the price of equity that suffered from souring expectations about real world impacts: Moody's cutting its debt rating on Toyota. So, bondholders take a hit too and pro-active investors who shorted the bonds have obtained a nice return. The financial phenomenon observed here is simply the conveying of expectations by investors who back up their informed opinion with betting money on it.

This is basically not different from the channelling of funds into stocks not quoted on the market. Here too, investors convey their expectations by putting an amount of liquidity at risk. Here too, private equity does not cause projects to come about or to behave in a certain manner. Investment bankers can and do not 'create' private equity and then offer it to projects. Private equity is construed when real world projects are submitted for funding and not by offering money to entrepreneurs who then may do as they please. In the appraisal of submitted projects, expectations about possible cash flows are determining. The appraisal of cash flows and their degree of risk will determine whether the investment banker places the bet. And of course, in the exercise of formulating expectations about those cash flows, all possible ESG-factors enter the accounting and are weighed as to their materiality. This has always been the case and will always be the case: the financial sustainability or suitability of a construct always depends on real world happenings and on our expectations about them. But then again, 'responsible' expectations are not homogeneous and opinions on what might work and what might not work in the real world tend to differ widely according to religion, political persuasion, and so on. It leads, however, to the question whether RI-private equity can reasonably be conceived of as an 'asset class' and how it can be discerned form non-RI-private equity.

Earlier on, the Owl pointed to the curious fact that SRI is not as much about finance as it is about real world issues. For example, there is no such a thing as a Christian fund per se versus a non-Christian fund per se, an ESG-index versus a non-ESG-index and RI funds do not differ from non-RI-funds qua fund. The remarkable exception of course, is Islamic finance. The ambition of Islamic religion to rule all spheres of life, duly pointed at by Jauferally, sets it apart from less totalitarian RIs. Contrary to ecological RI, Islamic finance entails definitions of financial structures that are allowed and financial structures that are outlawed. Derivatives, for instance, are not allowed for 'speculation' but solely for hedging. Yet, what is the sense of this in view of the plain fact that hedging is nothing but the implementation of the speculation that assets might go sour and a transaction that usually entails the payment of interest besides? Nonetheless, Islamic finance is reported to be mainstreaming, i.e. relaxing its more stern views. This evolution is estimated to open up a market in Islamic (and hence RI) derivatives and structured finance of several billion USD per annum (*Financial Times*, Wednesday 5 May 2010: 24). At the same time, it is also reported that Islamic legal uncertainties regarding particular issues pertaining to debt and contracts, might have disruptive impact on financial constructs or their prices (*Financial Times*, Wednesday 21 April 2010: 12).

The question then arises whether shari'ah compliant derivatives should be cleared by shari'ah compliant clearing houses or in a process separate from the non-compliant ones. The question also arises whether interest on Islamic debt and derivatives should reflect the possible legal uncertainties – as financial orthodoxy prescribes.

These observations taken together lead the Owl to ask whether the RI-movement is not a factor that threatens the financial ecosystem by being indifferent to its intrinsic beauties and qualities, by trying to occupy and dominate it, or by trying to subject it to the agenda of political and religious programs, however noble and laudable they may be.

Earlier, the Owl already noticed that most RI-discourses are silent on the financial dimension of financial activity. This curious feature is best illustrated by Sievänen: she wrestles with the ambiguity that she understands RI-policy as a tool for directing the liquidity of the pension fund in the pursuit of some real-world objectives whereas with some of her interlocutors, it seems to dawn that responsibility might also be applied reflectively. They start applying the responsibility- or sustainability-discourses in a reflective manner, pertaining to their own activity, meaning that they understand it as sensible risk management and good governance.

The more adequate discharging of the fiduciary responsibility rather than the transgression of it constitutes RI, then. Particularly interesting is that, since Sievänen wrote her contribution, it was reported in the press that Belgian pension funds financially underperform due to lack of scale (leakage) and made very unfortunate investment bets on stocks versus bonds during the financial turmoil. This should confront them with the question whether they should not envisage mergers before taking on the task of changing of society for the better by adopting RI-discourse and practices. In view of this, some will claim that society is well served by pension managers who aim at improving the world, but some will insist that beneficiaries are best served by pension fund managers who succeed in keeping their legitimate pension expectations intact. In this sense, what Eccles castigates is a rather reassuring phenomenon: intermediaries who are firmly committed to the purpose at hand and to none other.

Before the break of dawn, the Owl returns to his nest. As usual, he is not in a very sunny mood. He witnessed a marvellous ecosystem of world-encompassing finance brought about by the inventiveness of man. The very sustainability of that ecosystem is seriously threatened by the occurrence of financially untenable practices among which first and foremost the piling up of debt by people who cannot or do not want to repay those debts. In the process, the managerial class in the financial industry massively destroyed shareholder value and shattered illusionary expectations about future pensions.

Meanwhile, voices are raised to entrust those intermediaries with shaping our future on top of the fiduciary duty they so clearly failed to discharge properly. Marketeers in the financial industry act as if they are prepared and willing to do this for you if you hand over your moneys to them.

Concurrently, factions in society try to occupy as large a part of the financial ecosystem as possible, perhaps inspired by the delusion that finance shapes the world rather than the other way around.

Anyway, if the mountains of debt would cause the financial system to implode further, or if the financial ecosystem would drown in excessive liquidity, or if it would be destroyed from outside, RI would no longer be possible. Simply because there would no longer be processes of investment, no intermediation of liquidity and conveying information through financial activity. Without currencies, without financial markets, without finance, man would have to recur once again either to barter or to violence to alleviate the burden of a short and brutish live. Of these, most would concur that barter is to be preferred as the most peaceful of the alternatives. Perhaps then, next time around, the Owl would view all kinds of aspirations, demands and strategies regarding 'sustainable' or 'socially responsible' or 'ethical' *barter*.

Index

229